GAMRIE

An Exploration in Cultural Ecology

A Study of Maritime Adaptations
in a Scottish Fishing Village

Ed Knipe

Virginia Commonwealth University
Richmond, Virginia

UNIVERSITY
PRESS OF
AMERICA

LANHAM • NEW YORK • LONDON

All University Press of America books are produced on acid-free
paper which exceeds the minimum standards set by the National
Historical Publications and Records Commission.

To William C. Lawton

Teacher and Friend
Who made me aware of technology

ACKNOWLEDGEMENTS

In the research and writing of this monograph I was aided by a number of people. First and foremost, I should like to thank the people of Gamrie who knowingly and unknowingly gave me the necessary information to write this monograph. In keeping with my policy not to identify informants, their names cannot be mentioned, but they will know who they are after reading this document.

A special acknowledgement goes to Rex Taylor from the MRC Medical Sociology Unit at the University of Aberdeen. As both a friend and a colleague, Rex was, in many ways, responsible for me doing this study. Not only did he introduced me to the village, but he was always available at critical points in the research, giving advise and encouragement. And while the advise was not always taken, the encouragement was. He is a rare friend. In addition, both Rex and Raymond Ilsey, C.B.E, director of the Institute of Medical Sociology, made the resources of the Institute available to me.

In writing the monograph a number of people donated their time and knowledge. Dr. Forrest McDonald read the first draft and made many useful comments. Marcy McDonald labored long at checking spelling and punctuation in the first drafts, a task sometimes ungratefully accepted, but nonetheless greatly appreciated. She also drew the village map on page 25. Dr. Mary Odell read through the theoretical material and suggested a number of changes that I incorporated in the final draft. An early draft was also read by a number of villagers and one non-villager fisherman-writer. All of these people, in their own way, made contributions for which I am indebted.

The real yeoman's task of final proofreading and editing was done by George Cruger. His attempt to de-jargonize this document, straighten my syntax, and correct my spelling required many hours of labor. To a large extent, the readability of this monograph belongs to George.

I am also indebted to the unnamed reviewer for University Press of America who encouraged me to examine the original ethnography of Gamrie as an ethnology and in particular, a test of cultural ecology.

The initial word processing of the monograph was done through the office of Dean Ilske v.p. Smith, College of Humanities and Sciences, Virginia Commonwealth Univerity. To Gene Dunaway, who oversaw this task and eventually taught me how to use a word processor I am most appreciative.

One last acknowledgement is necessary. There was one

friend who was always available while in the field, who asked nothing, and was always encouraging and supportive. Had it not been for this friend in need, this study would have been more difficult to complete, and surely would have been different. A genuine scotch, in the true sense of the word, I toast you my friend, Glen Morangie.

GAMRIE:

AN EXPLORATION IN CULTURAL ECOLOGY:

A STUDY OF MARITIME ADAPTATIONS IN A SCOTTISH FISHING VILLAGE

TABLE OF CONTENTS

CHARTS, TABLES, AND ILLUSTRATIONS

CHARTS

TABLES

View of Gamrie from St. John's

I: THE ECOLOGICAL APPROACH

This monograph is a study of both social change and continuity in a small fishing village located along the Moray Firth in the North-East of Scotland. It reports data collected during four field seasons over an eight year period from 1974 through 1981. My interest in this particular village came not from any special concern with fishing communities, but rather more global questions about the relationship between those instrumental aspects of culture, broadly included under the designation technology, and the bio-physical environment, and especially how this relationship molds or influences expressive elements of culture, namely beliefs, values, and ideologies. To best understand this relationship between culture and environment I assume that it is necessary for one to examine it under conditions of change because it is under such conditions that one is able to observe a wide variety of adaptive strategies, both successful and unsuccessful, employed by people when coping with the environments within which they live. This approach to understanding human behavior, from the perspective of environmental adaptation, is called "cultural ecology."

Cultural Ecology

It is not my purpose here to review in great detail the history and variations upon the cultural ecological approach in anthropology. This has been done elsewhere (Anderson, 1973; Geertz, 1963; Harris, 1968, 1979). However, a brief review of three approaches to cultural ecology would be helpful in understanding the model which I propose and which was used to guide my observations and collection of data.

The genesis of the ecological approach is frequently assumed to be the seminal work of Julian Steward (1955). Steward views cultural ecology as a method, "for recognizing the ways in which cultural change is induced by adaptation to environment (5)." Arguing against the assumption that culture creates culture, Steward suggests that human populations must adjust to local environments, and the degree to which such environmental adjustments are free to vary is one of the questions answered using the cultural ecological method. In this adaptive process, there are two features that determine the characteristic of any cultural configuration. One is what Steward calls "core" features, those behaviors most directly related to subsistence activities. These core features are assumed to have more importance in the determination of cultural characteristics than "secondary" features, which are cultural-historical "accidents." Thus, for Steward, "Cultural ecology pays primary attention to those features which empirical analysis shows to be most closely involved in the utilization of environment in culturally prescribed ways (37)."

1

Corresponding to the assumption about the relative importance of core and secondary features, Steward suggests a methodology or procedure for "doing" cultural ecology. First, one should examine the interrelationship of exploitative or productive technology and environment. How, in other words, are environments transformed from a "natural" to a "cultural" state? In societies with simple technologies such transformations are usually direct. Such societies must be effective in coping with the natural behaviors of plants and animals, as well as the immediacies of weather, terrain, and other geo-physical conditions on a day-to-day basis. In industrial societies such technologies include not only the tools for transforming natural resources, but also trade networks, economic structures, money and credit systems, and any other non-material "tools" which aid in the production, distribution, and consumption of these transformed materials.

The second procedure is to examine the behavioral patterns of people in the exploitative process. Here one looks at the division of labor, or perhaps more specifically, the organization of work. In technologically simple societies one would expect to find the organization of work to be a more direct response to the behavior of animal and plant species upon which the society depends. Steward suggests that the social processes, such as cooperation, competition, and conflict, are adaptive strategies determined by variations in environmental factors, and one goal of cultural ecology is to ascertain the limitations or conditions under which such relationships exist.

The third procedure is to look at all other aspects of culture--the secondary features--in relation to the above core elements. Secondary features are free to vary and can be explained only as outcomes of historical accident. However, it is only when one fully understands the basic adaptive strategies that one can understand these secondary features of a culture. Included under this procedure would be an examination of: "demography, settlement patterns, kinship structures, land tenure, land use, and other key cultural features (42)," all of which are to be considered as a whole. Implicit in Steward's discussion of this third procedure is that secondary features may have outcomes which influence or are related to subsistence patterns. That one dresses in a particular costume for a religious ceremony may be a secondary feature; that the religious ceremony functions to redistribute goods created through the exploitative process makes it a part of the core culture.

The determination of what is core and what is secondary is an empirical question. One must collect sufficient data before such distinctions can be made. The most critical kind of data that one can collect is data on change. What is to be included

2

in core and secondary culture can be determined by observing what happens to cultural features under conditions of change. If a feature changes when exploitation and adaptation change, then it would be admitted to the cultural core. If it does not change, or if it changes without a corresponding change in exploitation, then it must be a secondary feature. Therefore, change is a key or central process in the determination of core and secondary elements.

Steward's assertion that core elements are the most important consideration in assigning causation to culture change was not embraced universally by the anthropological community, even among those who advocated an ecological approach. In particular, Geertz (1963) maintains that the ecological approach is more a sensitizing device than a master science which:

> trains attention on the pervasive properties
> of systems qua systems (system structure,
> system equilibrium, system change) rather
> than on the point-to-point relationship
> between paired variables of the "culture"
> and "nature" variety (10).

Geertz' own analysis of Indonesia began with an ecological approach, but he found that what he described as "agricultural involution" could only be understood if one went "beyond the analysis of ecological and economic processes to the investigation into the nation's political, social, and cultural dynamics (154)." Thus, Geertz sees cultural ecology as a reminder of the holistic commitment of anthropology, but not as a rigid prescription for the analysis of cultural phenomena.

The most recent statement on the ecological approach comes from Marvin Harris (1979). Enamored with the "sciencing" of anthropology, Harris insists that his "Cultural Materialism" offers a theory capable of generating empirically testable hypotheses. Harris' model of socio-cultural systems includes four components-- etic behavioral infrastructure, structure, super-structure, and the mental and emic superstructure. Under etic behavioral infrastructure are the categories, "mode of production" and "mode of reproduction." The mode of production is the working relationship between technology and nature; the mode of reproduction includes practices concerned with population size and characteristics. Included in the etic behavioral structure component would be behaviors associated with domestic economy and political economy, e.g., the organization of the division of labor and the organization of power. The etic behavioral superstructure is the expressive aspects of culture such as art, music, sports, and any other non-instrumental activity. The fourth category, mental and emic superstructure, would include such phenomena as myths,

3

symbols, ideologies, and any other beliefs characterizing a culture.

Methodologically important to Harris' model is the etic/emic distinction.* Without great elaboration, this distinction is basically the difference between what people do or how they behave, and what they think or believe. Etic phenomena are those derived from observing behaviors and the relationships between and consequences of those behaviors. Emic phenomena are what people think. Harris is an eticist. If there is to be a science of culture, it must depend upon that which can be measured, and what can be measured is behavior and its outcomes. The etic perspective does not deny the possibility that people's explanation of their behavior will not correspond to the behavior itself; it only maintains that saying or thinking is not necessarily a reliable predictor of behavior. In Harris' model the behavioral components are the most important. And of the four, infrastructure determines both structure and superstructure. The "principle of infrastructural determinism" states:

> The etic behavioral modes of production and reproduction probabilistically determine the etic behavioral domestic and political economy, which in turn probabilistically determine the behavioral and mental emic superstructures (55-56).

For Harris, change is also an important consideration. He suggests that changes occur when they offer adaptive advantages to a culture. Such advantages can be measure by cost benefits. If costs are reduced by a change, then change will take place. If there are no benefits from a change, then traditional practices will persist.

There is a close similarity between Harris' infrastructure and Steward's core features. In both models what distinguishes one culture from another is subsistence patterns, and in both it is these subsistence patterns that determine all other patterns. Only Geertz presents ecology as less than a deterministic model.

While the above "ecological sandwich" does not review all the variations and permutations of the ecological approach, one does note that there are a number of agreements on what variables are to be considered in an ecological analysis. The three variables are: environment, technology, and social organization. Environment refers to the behavior and characteristics of bioforms that occupy an ecological niche. Technology is the process

_____

*For a more complete distinction between emic and etic, see: Harris, 1968.

by which part or all of the bioforms in that ecological niche are transformed from their "natural" state to units that are used by people. Technology includes inventories of "tools" as physical objects, as well as the procedures for using those tools. Social organization refers to the rules, regulations, and procedures that bind people together into functioning groups, as well as the means by which people are socialized into such groupings. Taken together, these three variables constitute a system characterized by some degree of equilibrium or consistency between the variables.

Study Model

The purpose of this study is to use these three variables-- environment, technology, and social organization--as a way of organizing data to determine which changes in the organization of a fishing village can be attributed directly to ecological causation and which changes cannot. It is not the purpose of this study to develop a "grand theory" of change, but rather to better understand how this particular village, with its present-day characteristics, is the end product of a series of adaptations, some of which are related to changes in environment and in fishing technology. For this reason it is necessary to understand how each of the variables in the ecological model is defined.

In this study, environment refers to the sea as well as the characteristics and behaviors of fish. Technology is the means by which the sea and the fish are exploited by humans. This would include such considerations as boat design, power sources, and methods of fishing. Social organization is the way human activities are coordinated to operate boats and carry out fishing methods; in short, the organization of the boat and the means by which people are socialized to become fishermen. Graphically, the model I took into the field as a guide for collecting and ordering data was as follows:

Model I
Initial Model Used to Organize and Collect Field Data

Attribute   Environment ◄──► Technology ──► Social Organization

Variables   The Sea   Methods of Fishing   Boat Organization
            Weather   Boat Designs   Recruitment of
            Fish and their   Fishermen
            behavior

I would suggest that in order to assess the power of the ecological model, it is necessary to examine the relationship between the three attributes under conditions of change. It is only under conditions of change that one is able to note the temporal priority of the variables in the model. Therefore, it is important that one select a research setting where one or all of the variables have changed and where there are sufficient data available to measure such change. Given this consideration, how does one go about measuring or describing the relationship between environment, technology, and social organization? A number of research strategies are possible. I shall describe two, one based upon my previous research among coal miners and the one used in this study. In the study of coal miners (Lewis and Knipe, 1969), different groups of coal miners were compared to each other. The miners worked in mines characterized by different mining technologies that reflected the history of mining in the United States. That study found significant differences between miners and their families in beliefs, values, and ideologies that were related to differences in mining technology. The environment was constant. Coal seams do not change. What did change historically was the technology of mining. We not only demonstrated the consequences of different mining technologies on people's behaviors and beliefs, but we were also able to infer what the consequences of changes in technology had been in the past.

The research strategy in the mining study came largely from the setting itself. Were that research to be carried out today, the same comparisons could not be made because mines having the earliest technologies no longer exist. Much anthropological research is of this nature. One finds that different strategies must be employed for different settings. There is no one anthropological method.

In this study, the comparative strategy could not be employed. By 1974 there were no Scottish fishermen using fishing techniques from the eighteenth and nineteenth centuries. However, there was a fishing village with a history that could be analyzed with reference to changes in fishing technology. Historical reconstructions are not new to anthropology. Analysis of written data in literate societies can be valuable in reviewing changes in the past. And the use of older informants as sources of oral histories (ethnohistory) in both literate and non-literate societies can push our knowledge of the past back a hundred years or more.

Whether one uses written or oral histories, or a combination of the two, some consideration must be given to the unit of analysis. In the coal mining study, the units of analysis were the section, a group of men who worked together underground, and the families of these men. In this study, the unit of analysis is the community, "an area of social living marked by some degree of social coherence. The bases of community are locality and community sentiment (MacIver and Page, 1961:9)." The criteria used to select this community were threefold. First, the

6

community must have experienced a period of technological change. Second, the community should be relatively isolated and have a distinct set of either geographical or cultural boundaries. Third, it must be a single occupation community; that is, the residents of the community must derive their livelihoods from a single work source.

The village of Gardenstown, known locally as "Gamrie" (Game-Re), meets these three criteria. It is located in what I call the "silent corner" of Scotland, a remote area of Scotland largely ignored by historians. Unlike the Highlands to the north which are historically rich, this part of the North-East corner of Scotland had little impact on social, governmental, and military history. Nor does it figure prominently in industrial history, as do, for example, the southwest and the borders* of Scotland.

The village is located in a rather remote, inaccessible part of this silent corner, three-quarters of a mile off a secondary coastal road. It is not a place one goes through in getting from one place to another. Rather, the road into the village is the same road one uses in leaving. The closest communities of any size are located eight miles to the east and twelve miles to the west. It has been a fishing village from its beginnings in 1720, and descendants of those who first settled the village still live there today. Thus, the village of Gamrie has both occupational and genealogical depth coupled with geographical and cultural isolation, factors that make it an ideal research setting within which to study the impact of changing fishing technology upon community organization.

Because the community is the unit of analysis, the variables included under "social organization" in the initial model must be expanded to encompass a wider range of behaviors. Factors such as population size and demographic processes, kinship and marriage patterns, political organization, religion, and any other behaviors and practices that define and maintain village boundaries will be analyzed. Where possible there will be data on these variables going back in time and paralleling changes in fishing technology. Beyond the village itself, I will report historical data on what happened regionally, nationally, and internationally that had an impact on village practices.

The reporting of these data may at times appear to be irrelevant because they make no direct contribution to the ecological model. However, the ethnographer has obligations which make such reporting mandatory. One obligation is documentation. Given the precarious nature of small communities and the fact that many of these communities are rapidly changing

---

*borders: Those counties or area along the Scotland-England border.

7

or disappearing altogether, their way of life should be carefully recorded, both as a historical document and as a data base for future ethnographers. Another obligation is to science. By carefully selecting what one reports, any model can be "proved." One does not just report those data that "fit" the model, rather one is obligated to report all data, in spite of the fact that it may appear irrelevant or even contradictory. As will be noted, the initial model I took into the field is not the same model as when I left the field and attempted to make sense out of the data. This modified model would not have been possible had I only looked for and reported data that fit the initial model.

Plan of the Book

In keeping with the purpose of this study--the analysis of the impact of changing fishing technology on the organization of a fishing village--the next six chapters will explore various aspects of the ecological model.

In Chapter II each of the field seasons is reviewed to illustrate how the ethnographer goes about collecting data and the sometime fortuitous and serendipitous routes field work often takes. Chapter III is a basic ethnography of the village, including both historical developments and present-day characteristics. Chapter IV is the core chapter in terms of the initial ecological model. In that chapter I review the changing relationships between environment, technology, and social organization in reference to fishing. Taken together with the ethnohistory of the village, the initial model is expanded and modified. In chapters V, VI, and VII the emphasis shifts to the village itself and how some changes in family and kinship, religion and churches, and boundary maintenance and integration behaviors over the past 200 years are linked to changes in fishing while others are responses to exogenous or extra-village developments in Scotland and industrialized society itself. In the final chapter a completed model of the village is presented and discussed. There the limitations of applying ecological models to industrial society are presented.

II: FIELD WORK AND DATA COLLECTION

Anthropologists do field work. Unlike other social sciences where one might study social phenomena from afar, the anthropologist is obligated to collect data from people living and acting in geographical space. The "field," as it is called, can be anywhere. It could be a village in South America, a community in Melanesia, a street corner in Washington, D.C., or a neighborhood bar in San Francisco. No matter where it is, a decision had to be made by the field worker to study those particular people in that particular place. A number of factors may influence who and where one studies. Theoretical considerations might influence one to choose a setting where crucial hypotheses might be tested. The availability of funding could make a topic or a population attractive as a subject of research. And one cannot discount personal influences from teachers or colleagues. In this section, I shall review how I came to select the village of Gamrie and the kinds of data that were collected during the four field seasons.

Site Selection: Interest and Friendship

As already mentioned, my interest is in the relationship between technology and social organization. To best examine this relationship I thought that one should study single occupational areas or communities. In addition, I was looking for an occupation that was similar to the coal miners I had studied before. These factors led me to consider fishermen and fishing communities as a possible subject for analysis. But having a generalized interest does not account for the selection of a specific village in Scotland. This can only be explained by a series of fortuitous events.

In 1969 I met a British anthropologist who had been doing research among coal miners in northern England. An acquaintanceship grew into a friendship, and in 1973 I decided to visit him in Aberdeen, Scotland. As part of the pre-visit correspondence I had asked him about the possibility of studying fishing communities in Scotland. When I arrived, I found that he had arranged a short Highlands and North-East coast tour. The first stop on the tour was Inverness, where we spent a morning talking to the director of research for the Highlands and Islands Development Board, a regional planning agency. The director reviewed the studies that had been and were currently being done by sociologists and anthropologists in the region. To my surprise, I found that the region was the object of research by a large number of social scientists and that there might be some problem finding a suitable research site. Further, not having an automobile restricted the possibility of visiting possible locations.

9

Needless to say, I was somewhat discouraged by this situation. To make matters worse, the weather was bad even though it was July. The Scottish summers can be cold and rainy. In the few days I had been in Scotland the sky had been overcast, there was intermittent rain, and I never seemed to be warm enough. We left Inverness by train and traveled north and east to Elgin. In Elgin we caught a bus that took us down the east coast. Almost as soon as we caught sight of the Moray Firth, the weather began to clear. There was actually sunshine in Scotland! Traveling along the coast we passed by and through a number of small fishing villages--Portgorden, Buckie, Findochty, Portnockie, Cullen, and finally into Macduff. Each of these villages seemed attractive. In some, the houses were made of locally quarried rock that had been left natural. Others had been painted a bright color with mortar joints carefully painted in a contrasting or highlighting color. To the north of these villages the Moray Firth was a wide expanse of bright blue. On the landward side there were lush fields of green and yellow, many of which were dotted with Herefords, Black Angus, and sheep. I must admit, I was impressed.

Soon after arriving in Macduff we went to the house of my friend's "aunt." She is actually his father's cousin. The widow of a successful Aberdeenshire farmer, she lived on what had previously been the local laird's* estate, which is located only a short distance from Gamrie. Also living on the estate was a geographer who taught at the academy in Fraserburgh. He had been involved in some local archaeological excavations and was also a contributor to a small mimeographed volume published in 1968 about the village. His knowledge of local history and his descriptions of the village made me think that this might be the village to study. After a walking tour around the estate, he suggested that we go into the village and visit the local pub. It was Friday night and there were bound to be fishermen there. At last, I was going to meet real Scottish fishermen.

The pub is located in the only hotel in the village. The hotel is at the end of Main Street. As we walked down Main Street, I noted very little activity. The shops were closed, and except for the sounds of sea gulls, it was quiet. We pushed our way through a low narrow door and turned left into the lounge. In contrast to the quiet, almost deserted street, the lounge was loud and crowded. The room was heavy with smoke, men were standing shoulder to shoulder talking to each other in what sounded like an unintelligible language. The plaster between the open beams in the ceiling, which once had been white, was stained brown from years of smoke; between one set of beams someone had taped a Playboy centerfold. We pushed our way through to the serving bar, and our host bought us a

*Laird: Scottish equivalent of an English lord; a landowner.

10

"round"--a whiskey and a pint of beer. We were introduced to a number of people in rapid order. Everybody seemed very friendly and in spite of the fact that I could only understand about half of what was being said, the conversation was lively and animated. A few minutes after the first drink, someone took the glass out of my hand only to return it with more whiskey. In a short while it was taken again and the same process repeated. It wasn't long before I felt I could understand what they were saying, and I was more convinced than ever that this was the place to study. I had expected to find dour Calvinists but instead found open, giving fishermen willing to talk to outsiders.

The morning of the next day was spent nursing a hangover and wishing we had exercised some restraint the night before. We spent most of the day touring the area, both on foot and by motor vehicle. We were told that the village was prosperous, but had not always been so; that it was unique in that most of the fishermen fished for herring in contrast to other fishermen along the coast who fished for white fish*. We were also told that they traveled to the west coast to go fishing as opposed to sailing out from nearby harbors. We were informed of the various religious groupings in the village, and the more I heard, the more attractive the village became.

It is one thing to have an enjoyable evening in a Scottish pub. It is quite another to go back the next night and have an equally enjoyable experience. After our day of touring, we went back, and again the fishermen were gregarious and vociferous. Again my glass never seemed to empty. By the end of the evening I knew this was the place, and the next step was to make arrangements to return the following year. I presented my plan to our geographer host who said he would look into the possibility of my being able to move in with a fisherman and his family.

In the spring of 1974 I received word that a fisherman had been located who was willing to take me in for the summer months. Thus, what had begun as two enjoyable days in a village was to become an eight year research commitment.

First Field Season: 1974

The arrangements made for me by my geographer friend turned out to be ideal. I had a self contained second-story flat. The fisherman and his wife lived on the ground floor and their son had a room on the third floor. The house was located on Main Street, convenient to all the shops in the village. During the week, both the fisherman and his son were gone fishing. On

*White fish: Any fish found in the sea except herring.

the weekends the son was usually away visiting his fiancee, who lived in another fishing village ten miles down the coast.

Gamrie is largely a women's village during the week because most of the fishermen are away. Women often gather at each other's houses for a "fly cup," a cup of tea accompanied by a food snack and a lot of conversation. Being on Main Street, where there was more foot traffic, meant that the tea pot was kept boiling a large part of the day. Often when a number of women were convened downstairs, I would be invited down, introduced, and given the opportunity to listen to the conversation. Most of the women who came by were of the same age cohort and had traveled together for the "gutting." When herring were plentiful and there was a European market for cured herring, there was also a need for labor to gut and pack the herring. It was usual for unmarried women from the village to contract their labor with one of the curers. The herring migrated around the coast of Britain and the fishermen, along with the "gutting lassies," moved from one curing station to another. The women usually went as a group from the village, and for many it was a holiday with their friends as well as a way to earn a little extra money. Much of the conversation I heard centered on the gutting days. I was told in great detail how herring were gutted and the proper way to pack them in the barrel. I was shown the fingers of those who had been cut while gutting and the scars that resulted from their hands being in the salted water for days and weeks on end. I heard stories of both good and bad curers: those who provided adequate accommodations and those who didn't; those who paid well and those from whom one was fortunate to get any pay at all. I suspected that many of these conversations were for my benefit. However, the information I was able to obtain about women and changes in women's roles far outweighed the suspicion that this was not the topic of conversation every time women got together. Other topics, only tangentially related to gutting, came from these conversations. They spoke about sickness and health; they spoke about families and kinship and women who stayed where they were gutting to marry a local fishermen. They recalled growing up in the village and how they were treated by their parents. In fact, they spoke about everything except sex. The gender of the field worker often limits the kinds of information collected from informants. Being a male in this situation precluded gathering information on sexual behavior.

In retrospect, I think the first season would have been far less fruitful had I lived alone. Not only did I become identified with a family, but I became part of a number of social networks. During the week I was introduced to friends of the wife. On the weekends, I was exposed to both the fisherman's and his son's contacts. One problem faced by many field workers is establishing an identity. Often one's identity is not established until one has a sponsor, someone local who is willing to represent you. Fortunately, living with this family gave me a base from which to operate and lessened many of the problems often faced during the early phases of community research.

It soon became apparent that the chance to observe on a number of boats was difficult to arrange. Part of the problem was related to the work cycle of fishermen and skippers. Being at sea during the week meant they were usually very busy on the weekends. Negotiations to get out on a boat had to be done when they were home and it was often impossible to contact them on the weekend. Another problem was the question of responsibility. Taking someone out on a boat meant that someone or everyone had to be responsible for that person's safety. It also meant that the cook would have to feed one more person and additional food would have to be taken. The decision to take someone out for a week, it became clear, was not unilateraly made by a skipper but involved discussion with the crew. In spite of these problems, I was able to get out on two boats. The first was a small overnight boat which sailed from Fraserburgh. The family with whom I lived knew the skipper and they negotiated my being taken along for an evening's fishing. The other boat was larger. It also sailed from Fraserburgh, but it stayed out a week. Arrangements for that trip were made through a friend whose son-in-law was mate on the boat. It was on this boat that I was a full participant in one negative aspect of fishing, namely seasickness. In spite of this, the trip proved to be a valuable experience. Not only was I able to observe the technology of fishing, but I was better able to understand what fishermen on land told me about fishing.

Field workers often find that data come from unlikely sources. For example, I became acquainted with the local doctor through my anthropologist friend's aunt. My initial reason for wanting to meet him was to obtain information on health and illness in the village. In our conversations he mentioned a listing he had made of his patients that was organized by birth date. This listing was used to construct a population pyramid of the village, something that could not have been done with available census information. If I had not had this listing and had I wanted the age and sex characteristics of the village, it would have been necessary for me to do a house-to-house survey, a task that would have taken most of the summer.

The field diary is the most valuable book the field worker owns. In it are written observations, feelings, ideas, and reconstructed conversations. I made it a practice to carry a small spiral bound notebook with me at all times. On walks around the village I would talk to people, and after our conversation I would jot down key phrases and words that would be used later as a basis for more extended entries in the field diary. In some situations I would take out the notebook and write while in the presence of an informant; in other situations entries were made after the conversation was terminated. Whether I wrote in front of an informant or not depended upon a number of factors. One consideration was how well I knew the informant. If it was a casual encounter while out walking and it was a person I did not know, an entry was made later. If it was a person I knew, I would write while talking to that person. Another consideration was the kind of information received. Impersonal information about things or places could be written out in front of an informant. Personal information was usually entered later. When some people got to know me they would suggest that I write down what they had said. With others, no mention was made of the notebook. Whether or not one writes in front of an informant is a decision that has to be reached through the field worker's knowledge of the situation. There are no formal rules.

Another question, related to note-taking and information gathering, is what one tells informants about what one is doing. It is common to see visitors in the village during the summer months. They usually stay one or two weeks in houses rented from villagers or outsiders who have purchased some of the older houses in the Seatown or the nearby village of Crovie. Staying beyond two or three weeks, especially if one is seen taking photographs and asking questions, was, I am sure, rather puzzling to many villagers. The fact that I am a university professor and I was socially friendly with the doctor and the woman who lived in the laird's old estate made me even more of an enigma. But the villagers are shy and polite and would never ask me directly what I was doing. Rather, I would be asked, "Are you here for long?" or, "Is your holiday about up?" Even people who knew that I was interested in the village and its history would not ask me what I planned to do with the information. This point was impressed upon me during the 1981 season when a woman I had known for eight years, who had entertained my daughter and her friends when they came to visit, with whom I had corresponded between field seasons, and whose husband I consider to be a close friend, rather reluctantly asked my traveling companion, "Is Ed writing a book on Gamrie?" The family with whom I lived and who even came to the U.S. to visit me, never asked what I was doing. Even if I had been asked, I am not sure how I would have answered. Because the original idea of going out on a number of boats had to be scrapped, the bits of information I was able to collect directed me to consider more seriously the village as the unit of analysis. In a community study it is not always possible to state specific research objectives. Rather one collects everything possible and then pursues more focused problems from what the

14

data suggest. Therefore, my answer to the question of what I was doing depended upon when the question was asked. At one time I might be interested in kinship; at another time it might be boat ownership or religion or inheritance or public morality. Even if I had been able to clearly state specific topics that I was investigating, whom would I tell? The village is acephalic. There is no head man or chief. There are no sanctioning bodies that could review my plans. I did not have to ask anyone for permission to study the village. My relationships with inform-ants had to be individually negotiated.

The changing and often nonspecific nature of community research is not without its negative consequences on the researcher. There is one problem that is almost universally encountered when field workers are cut off from familiar surroundings. This is culture shock. The field worker is a stranger in a strange land. He or she is faced with the task of making sense out of symbols, rituals, and behaviors that are alien. And there is always the feeling that what one is doing has no scientific merit. There were times during this season when I would stay in my flat for days because the weather did not permit me to go out. On those days, the afternoons would often be turned into extended naps or feelings of frustration about not having anything to write in the field diary. I would look forward to the pub's opening so that I could at least be around people. The cure for culture shock is time. The more familiar one becomes with one's surroundings, the less one experiences those feelings of frustration and alienation. By the end of summer I did feel more comfortable in the village and most of the symptoms of culture shock had disappeared.

In reviewing this first season, it was clear that most of my time was spent developing a network of informants on a variety of topics. It also became clear that more questions had been asked than answered, and that in order for me to answer these questions it would be necessary to return to the village. This I did in 1975.

Second Field Season: 1975

Census data revealed that the village had increased in population until 1910, when it then began a steady decline. In order to ascertain why, I felt it was necessary to analyze the "demographic processes," birth, death, and migration. Fortunately, there were public records on births, deaths, and marriage readily available back to 1900. However, these records could not be photocopied, nor were writing instruments allowed into the record area. This dilemma was solved by a careful reading of the rules and regulations pertaining to the use of official documents. Apparently they had either been written before the popularity of the tape recorder or the writers had not anticipated anyone's using one to record these data. Having no other alternative, I voice-recorded all the births, deaths, and marriages of persons in the village. The tape recorder can be both a blessing and a curse. The blessing was that it enabled me to collect these data; the curse was that it took almost two years to transcribe it into a form that I could use. Nevertheless, it was worth it. From these data it was possible to reconstruct genealogies of families and to note the changing ages of marriage, death rates, and a variety of other measures of population change.

I have already mentioned that where one goes to do field work can be influenced by one's teachers. Prior to going into the field in 1975, I was able to make arrangements for two of my students to participate in the University of Leiden's Summer Field School. Dutch students from the Instituut voor Culturele Antropologie use the east coast of Scotland as a training area for field methods, and my students were able to attach themselves to this group. They selected the village of Whitehills as their research site. This fishing village has a number of character-istics in common with Gamrie and their observations proved to be valuable supplements to my own.

Rites of passage which mark changes in an individual's status are universal. However, many cultures place different emphases on different transitions. In Gamrie the most elaborate and the most expensive rite of passage is the wedding. Weddings require extensive planning months in advance. Considerations of who should be invited reflect kinship obligations as well as network affiliations of those involved in the ceremony. The son in the family with whom I stayed was married during the summer of 1975. Being in the household enabled me to observe much of the prenuptial planning and, through interviewing, to reconstruct planning that had taken place before the field season. Being a guest at the wedding and the post wedding celebration allowed me both to observe the ritual and to talk to a wide range of people who were friends and relatives of the bride and groom.

The contacts made at the wedding led me to spend a week in Shetland. During the 1920s and 1930s economic conditions in fishing were not good. A number of people from the village migrated to Shetland, where conditions were somewhat better. As a result, many of the villagers have a Shetland connection. The trip to Shetland gave me an opportunity to gather data on migration as well as to make on-site observations of where many village females had spent time at the gutting. Additional infor-mation on migration was obtained through chance meetings with ex-villagers who now lived in nearby places such as Frazerburgh, Banff, Macduff, and Peterhead. Also, interviews with non-villagers gave me further insights into how people in the village are perceived as fishermen and skippers, as well as the outsider's views of the religion and morality of the villagers. The outsider's view often became the basis for later discussions with villagers. It soon became clear that the village was not a closed corporate entity. Rather, it was part of a network which tied it to both the immediate region and to more distant parts of Scotland. This meant that the village, to be understood, had to be viewed as part of a larger matrix held together through ties based upon kinship and on economic and political considerations.

By the end of the season, I had collected more information on shipboard interaction through interviews with fishermen. I had also collected data related to the questions brought home from the 1974 season. It was obvious that the more I knew, the more I became aware of what I did not know. However, I was now able to be more specific in identifying what kinds of information I needed to correct my ignorance. This only made it more imperative that I return.

Third Field Season: 1978

The first part of the 1978 season was spent talking to people about what had happened since I had been there last. Even though I had corresponded with people from the village, the letters often left out important details. Therefore, a few weeks were necessary to re-establishing contacts. This aspect of field work is rarely mentioned in the literature. Though I was spent eight weeks in the field, only about six were used to gather new material. This initial period was largely spent having meals or extended "fly cups" with friends both inside and outside the village. Almost invariably there would be a trip to the churchyard to see the graves of those who had died during my absence. Some villagers showed a genuine concern for my welfare. They lent me their automobiles; they took me to visit their friends and relatives; they did everything possible to make me feel at home. But sometimes hospitality reduces the amount of time one can devote to data collection, and the field worker often feels torn between obligations toward friends and obligations toward work. This is a hazard, albeit a pleasant one of field work.

During this season I was given access to the feu records for the village. A feu is a fee paid to a laird for the use of land. Traditionally, a house was owned by a person, but the land belonged to the laird. Each year a feu was paid to the laird for the use of the land. The feu records noted each parcel of land in the village and who was responsible for pay-ment of the yearly fee. The purpose of reviewing these records was to determine inheritance and ownership patterns. Unfortu-nately, the records were so poorly kept that a detailed analysis of land tenure could not be made. However, they could be used to infer some general trends in ownership.

I have already mentioned some problems related to collecting public information. In places where official records are kept which could be used to reconstruct cultural patterns, one sometimes finds that these records are not officially available. This was the case when I inquired into the possibility of getting crew lists for boats in the Gamrie fleet. I was told that while such records exist I could not officially see them. However, after obtaining a letter of introduction from an official at the University of Aberdeen I was permitted to use the records with the proviso that I did not acknowledge the agency from which they were obtained. The records contained a wealth of information. For each boat there was a list of the crew, the papers each held, their position on the boat, and the age, birthplace, present residence, and nearest kin of each crew member. With these data, coupled with information obtained from informants, it was possible to construct a profile of the Gamrie fleet's demographic characteristics. Further, when merged with the reconstructed genealogies, it was possible to explore the role of kinship in recruitment.

A major goal of field work is to uncover the rules that govern the everyday life of a people. For this reason, the field worker must wait for events to happen. At the end of the season a young fisherman was drowned in a non-fishing-related boating accident. I had known this fisherman from my first field season, and he had been a valuable informant on a number of topics. I also knew members of his family, some of whom I counted as friends as well as informants. During the past field seasons, I had observed funerals and burials from afar and I had collected information from informants on death and dying. This, however, was my first opportunity to observe this aspect of village life directly. It also made clear another pitfall of field work, personal involvement. While the field worker attempts to be objective, it is difficult to avoid personal involvement. In this case, I felt a personal loss, and this resulted in my not doing something I might otherwise have done. Throughout the field seasons I had taken many photographs. I would have liked to photograph the funeral and burial, but because of my personal involvement I would have felt very self-conscious about photographing this one. Thus, an opportunity was lost. At the same time I was able to gain information from the friends and family of this young man because of my having this personal involvement with them. Field work is often a series of such trade-offs, which might best be exemplified by the 1981 field season.

Fourth Field Season: 1981

During the previous field seasons I lived with the fishing

family on Main Street. In 1981, I returned to the village with a traveling companion. Because of this, I felt it appropriate to secure housing that would insure us some privacy as well as avoid any embarassment to my landlord. Since finding one place for the entire summer was not possible, we lived in three locations--the Seatown, the New Ground and in a council house. Both the Seatown and the New Ground are in the older sections of the village, but the council house is up the brae*. Living up the brae provided me with an opportunity to make observations in what seemed like another village. While I had visited people living in the council houses, living there and observing daily activities impressed upon me the differences in life styles among villagers. Because my traveling companion soon became defined as a "wife," I found that my relationships with others sometimes changed. We, as a couple, were invited places I would not have been invited. People would stop into see us when they might have been reluctant to see me. My evenings in the pub were reduced to one or two as compared with five or six when I was living on Main Street. In short, my change in status and residence resulted in my becoming a part of new social networks and with this, an opportunity to collect data on new topics, for example sex, or expand on old topics such as child rearing and medical problems.

Ideally, the field worker should collect data from all segments of the community being studied. However, the very process of field work may make this difficult. For example, in studying a factory one should collect data from both labor and management. But having spoken to one first may make it difficult to speak to the other later. My experience in the village indicated that once I had developed rapport with an informant I was able to utilize his or her social networks to gather additional information. But there was one social network that I had not yet explored in any depth--the religion network. It was clear from the very first field season that religion played an important role in the village. In the past field seasons I had collected some information on religion, including attending a Brethren evening service in 1975. The networks in which I was involved were largely made up of persons who were not active participants in local religious bodies. Many of these people had, at one point in their lives, been participants in one of the local religious groups, but because of a variety of experiences were now negative in their attitudes toward religion. Since a large percentage of the village does participate in religious activities there was an obvious gap in my data. To correct this, I spent most of this season gathering information on religion from informants who were actively involved in the various community religious groups. In addition to talking to lay participants, I also more formally interviewed spokesmen from both the Kirk and

*Brae: Scottish word for hill or incline.

19

the Brethren concerning attendance, ritual, and belief.

During this season, I also collected additional data on house ownership. The regional government publishes a volume on rateable values of properties each year. Rateable values are an estimate of property values which are the basis for property tax. Information on ownership is of particular value in reference to council housing. Council housing consists of residences that have been built by the local council and are rented to residents. Recently they have been made available for purchase, and therefore information on who has bought and who still rents can be used as an indicator of community commitment as well as differential income.

Ever since going into the field I had heard of the pre-nuptial practice called the "blackening." This practice is a form of "mock abduction" of the bride and groom to be. Friends of the bride and groom would lure them to a place and then procede to cover them with a concoction that blackened their clothes and faces. Afterwards the couple and the blackening party would drive noisly around the village on the back of a truck. Not all prospective brides and grooms go through this ritual, and I had not been witness to this event even though there had been a number of weddings in the village during the past field seasons. The main problem in observing this event is that it is kept secret for fear the bride and groom will evade the blackening party. So usually only a select group of people know when and where it will take place. During this season I did get to see this event from beginning to end because I knew the parents of the groom. Without advance knowledge it would have been possible to observe only the public drive around the village.

When is Field Work Over?

Ultimately the field worker must stop collecting data and write up the findings. The question of when one has enough data is sometimes difficult to answer. As we have seen, each year I came back from the field with new questions along with answers to old questions. But one has to put boundaries around any study subject. The boundaries to this ethnography are the years 1974 through 1981. What one finds in the following pages reflects the information I was able to collect during that period. The reader may find that they would like to see more information presented on some subject or less on another. I purposely cast a wide net over the village, knowing that some things might elude that net. Perhaps the next generation of field researchers will be able to catch the data that got away.

During the summer of 1982 I returned to the village for one month. A first draft of this manuscript had been completed and had been sent to a resident of the village, a fisherman in another village, and my friend at the university. The purpose of that trip was to confer with these people about the manuscript and to correct any errors in fact or in judgement that were contained therein. All together, three people from the village read all or part of the manuscript. Their comments and corrections were very useful. There were a small number of substantive errors, and they were able to detect a few statements that could have proven embarassing or might have provoked anger among village readers. The errors were corrected and the statements were altered.

One last question related to field work has yet to be answered. This is the question of whether or not I "went native" in the sense that I was able to see the world through these villagers' eyes. I must admit that I have fond memories of the time spent in the village, and I shall go back to visit the friends I made over the years. But no matter how many times I go back, or how long I stay, I shall continue to be an outsider, still curious, still puzzled, still not quite sure that I fully understand these people. Their world and mine are separate. I have had a rare opportunity to look into their world, and it is I who have benefited from that experience.

21

Main Street, ca. 1925

22

III: GAMRIE: A CHANGING VILLAGE

Geophysical Conditions

The village of Gamrie lies on the Moray Firth nine miles west of Macduff and 13 miles east of Fraserburgh. It is approximately 40 miles north of the city of Aberdeen. It is situated between two geological features. To the east of the village is a sandy beach one-quarter mile in length and no more than 100 yards wide. Immediately behind the beach is a steep incline of old red limestone formed during the Upper Paleozoic. To the west of the village is another steep incline made of Pre-Cambrian metamorphic rock.

The village is located in an area having geophysical characteristics conducive to early fishing technology. First, it is equidistant between two headlands, Mohr Head and Crovie Head, which form a natural harbor. Second, there is both sandy beach and rocky shoreline. The sandy beach can be used for landing small fishing craft. The rocky shoreline can be used for drying fish and is also a natural habitat for small crustaceans used to bait fishing hooks. The third feature is the presence of water for human consumption. There are two small streams to the east of the village, as well as a number of natural springs.

The village was officially founded in 1720 by a local laird who sought to encourage the catching of white fish. Crovie, a small village one-half mile east of Gamrie, was founded about the same time. The original settlement area of Gamrie--Seatown--is situated parallel to the shore line at the bottom of the brae. The incline leading to this area drops 500 feet in a little over one mile. Because of this, the road into the village must make a number of sharp bends. This slope is so steep that a visitor's first view of this part of the village is of chimney tops.

At the "braeheed"* one turns west onto the Main Street, a cul-de-sac about 200 yards long and so narrow that two automobiles have difficulty passing each other. From the end of Main Street there are a number of paths leading to houses in the Seatown. If one turns east just above the braeheed, the road leads to the New Ground, an area of reclaimed land, and the harbor area. A recently built sea wall provides a narrow one-vehicle road that one can take along the Seatown to a parking area on the edge of the "Sands," the beach area west of the village.

The harbor is the heart of a fishing community. Originally

---

*Braeheed: Literally, the hill head. This hill head is in reference to the harbor, not the top of the hill above the village itself.

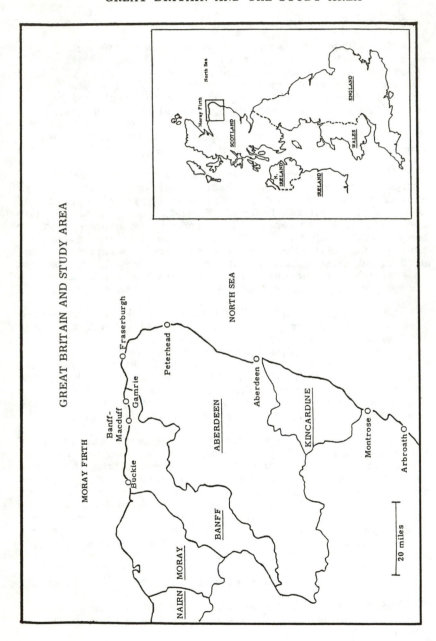

GREAT BRITAIN AND STUDY AREA

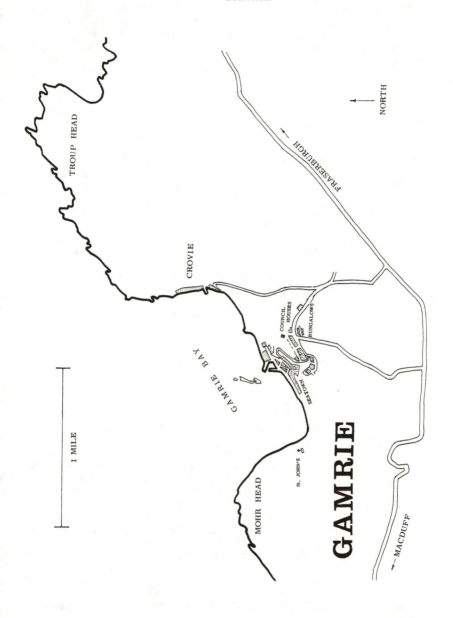

donated to the village by the laird, the harbor provided shelter for the small sail boats that were originally used by village fishermen. In 1913, construction to enlarge the harbor facilities was begun to accommodate the newer larger fishing vessels. A series of misfortunes resulted in the contractor going into receivership; and the modernization of the harbor was never completed. Thus, the harbor one views today is basically the original harbor.

The area around the village has been used for agricultural purposes for upwards of a thousand years. Written records indicating land transfers go back to the 1200s. Much of the surrounding lands were not naturally arable, and it was not until the 1800s, upon the introduction of the swing plow, the iron toothed harrows, and the wheeled cart, that agricultural production increased much beyond the subsistence level. Potatoes and turnips, the basic starch foods of the region today, were not introduced until the 1700s. Today the chief crops grown are oats, barley, turnips, and potatoes. In addition, cattle, sheep, pigs, and poultry are raised. The motor-powered tractor, introduced after World War II, made it possible to clear land previously covered with whin so that oats and grass could be planted for cattle and sheep feed. These changes in technology have resulted in the disappearance of the farm "toons," small, relatively self-contained communities where workers were "fued"--bound by work contracts for periods of six months or a year. The "chaumer" system, under which workers lived in a part of the steading and were fed in the farm house, has largely been replaced by substantial self-contained housing built on individual farms or public housing erected by the county council.

Within the village itself, the first automobile was owned by a villager in 1912. In 1918 the first indoor toilet and bath was built. Electricity was available to villagers after World War II.

A branch railway line between Macduff and Aberdeen was built in the early 1870s but was closed to passenger travel in 1951. The only public transportation available in the village today is bus. On Monday through Saturday, the first bus into the villages arrives at 9 a.m. It carries parcels and the morning newspapers. There is a morning bus to Fraserburgh,* and there are two buses to Banff each day. The bus schedule has been cut back during the last ten years because most villagers have automobiles. However, the morning bus is used by pupils who live in the village to get to the local primary school located up the brae.

January 31, 1953 was a significant date for the village.

*This service was discontinued in 1982.

Hurricane-force winds coupled with high tides caused widespread destruction and loss of life in Britain and Europe. In Gamrie, two houses on the west side of the village were destroyed, the earth below Main Street and to the west of the harbor was undermined, the New Ground was flooded, and wooden sheds and garages were destroyed. Power and telephone lines were blown down. Boats from the village that were berthed on the west coast were driven ashore, and there was considerable damage to the fleet. The inland populations were also hard hit by the storm. Stacks of straw were blown away. Roofs were blown off and some livestock was lost. The winds were so strong that 45 gravestones in the Gamrie churchyard were blown down. The only consolation was that no lives were lost in the area.

The greatest damage was to Crovie. According to Cameron:

> The footpath to Crovie along the foot of the cliffs was washed away and the cliffs now come right to the edge of the water. Sheds, garages and the sea wall at the west end of Crovie were also destroyed, and wheeled traffic can no longer come to the foot of the road leading to the village. From the west end of Crovie village to the burn of Crovie, the sea wall was completely undermined and parts washed away, while some of the houses were completely destroyed and others heavily damaged. (1961:208)

As a result of the heavy damage to Crovie, most of the residents sold their houses as holiday homes to outsiders, and moved to Gamrie. Crovie had been a fishing village with strong connections through marriage and fishing to Gamrie. Today there are only a few of original fisherfolk live there.

In the following sections I shall review, in more detail, various historical and contemporary characteristics of Gamrie.

Population Characteristics

Population characteristics are both reflections and determinants of other cultural practices. Formally, any population can be described as a result of three processes--birth, death, and migration. The explanation of changes in any of these processes is, however, social or cultural in origin.*

---

*This is not to deny genetic and biological considerations in explaining changes in birth and death rates. However, the impact these factors have on a population will depend upon technologies that are cultural, not biological.

27

The formation of breeding units--families--and decisions concerning numbers of offspring these units have is largely a reflection of cultural expectations. Who dies and at what age they die vary with such factors as social class, accessibility to medical technology, the ability of technology to provide food, and other social factors. The movement of populations from one place to another is an expression of individual and collective decisions in response to a host of social conditions. In this section, the population characteristics of Gamrie will be described. In later sections, this information will be used to better understand the interplay between population dynamics and cultural practices.

Chart 1 shows the total population of Gamrie from 1745 to 1974. Starting with just a few people in 1720, the population increased to 300 in 25 years. In the next 100 years it grew very little, but then began an increase which peaked at the turn of the twentieth century. Since that time the population has declined so that in 1974 there were 837 people living in the village. The only interruption in this depopulation is seen in the figures for 1961. This slight increase is explained by the 1953 storm when people living in Crovie moved to Gamrie.

The depopulation of Gamrie in the twentieth century can be explained by variations in the birth, death, and migration rates. In reviewing the birth records from 1900 to 1974 one notes that 1460 children were born in the village. For that same period, 743 persons died. If one considers only these two factors then the population in 1974 should have been 2120 (Population 1901=1403 +1460 children born - 743 persons died = 2120). Instead, the population decreased by 566 (1403 - 837 = 566). Thus, the changes in population were not due to declining births and increasing deaths, but rather to out-migration. In that 73-year period from 1901 to 1974, I estimate that 1283 people moved away from the village (estimated population size reflecting births and deaths=2120 - 837, actual population=1283).

Of particular note on this chart is the observation that the out-migration, and hence the decline in population, began after 1911. This time period is significant in that it corresponds to a major change in fishing, especially in boat design and power. I shall return to this point in a later section.

Age and Sex Characteristics

All cultures make distinctions between males and females, the young and the mature. While the expectations for what males and females and the young and mature should do vary from one culture to another, the number of people in these categories can effect the ability of people to fulfill these expectations. For example, if one is expected to marry a person the same age as oneself and there are no available persons in

28

Chart I
Gamrie Population: 1745-1974

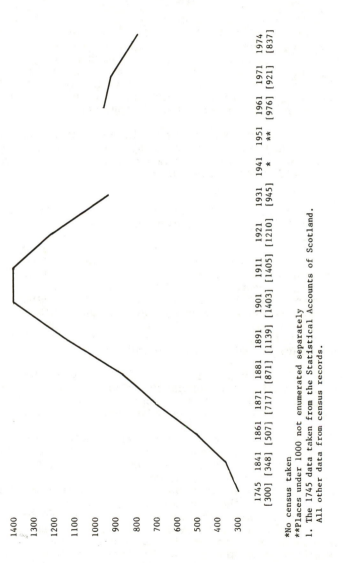

1745	1841	1861	1871	1881	1891	1901	1911	1921	1931	1941	1951	1961	1971	1974
[300]	[348]	[507]	[717]	[871]	[1139]	[1403]	[1405]	[1210]	[945]	*	**	[976]	[921]	[837]

*No census taken.
**Places under 1000 not enumerated separately
1. The 1745 data taken from the Statistical Accounts of Scotland. All other data from census records.

29

this age category, one may not be able to fulfill that expectation. Or if the young are expected to care for the aged and there are not enough young to do this, there might be changes in this expectation. The rules of culture change over time. One contributing factor to those changes is the age and sex composition of a population.

The demographics of sex are not equal. Usually males out-number females at birth, but the number of males and females in most populations tends to equalize because of higher male mortality. Thus, in populations having no specific practices regulating the sex of children, i.e., male or female infanticide, the number of males and females is nearly equal. That is, of course, unless migration is sex specific, with more males or females moving into or out of a population.

The relationship between the number of males and females in a population is expressed by the sex ratio--the number of males per 100 females. Data available for calculation of the sex ratio in Gamrie are available back to 1841. Table 1 shows these figures.

What is most obvious from these data is that at no time period in the last 143 years have there been more males than females in Gamrie. In general, there were fewer males per 100 females in the 1800s than the 1900s. A number of inferences might be drawn from this observation. First, there were probably more unmarried females in the village during the nineteenth century than the twentieth century. Second, this imbalance probably reflects sex-specific migration. More males moved away from the village in the nineteenth century than in the twentieth century. But sex ratios do not tell us what part of the male population migrated. For that information, it is necessary to look at both age and sex.

A population pyramid is a summary of the age and sex characteristics of a population. Chart 2 shows the age and sex distribution for the Gamrie population in 1974. This chart was constructed from data obtained through the local doctor.

The number of males in the newborn to five year old category is larger than the number of females. However, this difference begins to disappear as the population gets older. In the 16 to 20 year old category there are slightly more females than males. Then there is a dramatic shift after the age of 20. Here one notes the effects of migration. But this migration does not seem to be sex specific. Both males and females are beginning to leave the village at about 20 years old, the trend being toward greater female out-migration. This decrease continues until the age of 50 where one notes an increase in numbers of persons above that age. Thus we note that rather

30

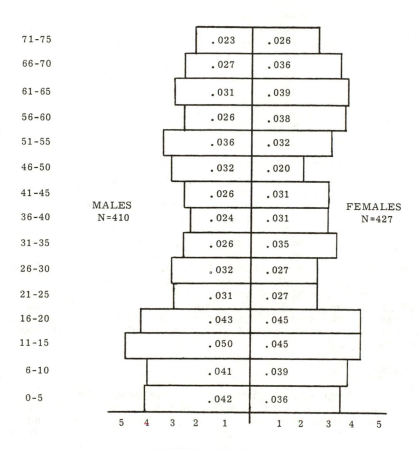

Chart II:
Gamrie Population Pyramid: 1974

	MALES	FEMALES
71-75	.023	.026
66-70	.027	.036
61-65	.031	.039
56-60	.026	.038
51-55	.036	.032
46-50	.032	.020
41-45	.026	.031
36-40	.024	.031
31-35	.026	.035
26-30	.032	.027
21-25	.031	.027
16-20	.043	.045
11-15	.050	.045
6-10	.041	.039
0-5	.042	.036

MALES
N=410

FEMALES
N=427

5 4 3 2 1   1 2 3 4 5

PERCENT OF TOTAL POPULATION

Table 1
Sex Ratios For Gamrie: 1831-1974

Year	Sex Ratio
1831	76
1841	70
1871	76
1881	76
1891	94
1901	87
1911	90
1921	86
1931	77
1951	89
1961	86
1971	90
1974	96

than a pyramid shape the age distribution is more like an hour glass. The bottom of the hour glass is comprised of people 20 years old or younger. The top part consists of those over the age of 51. It is a village populated by the young and the old.

In general, the most striking feature of Gamrie population is the dramatic decline in village size over the last 60 years. The rate of this decrease has slowed somewhat since the 1930s but the village continues to lose population. Whether this trend will continue or if the village has reached a state of stability is difficult to predict. This will depend upon those in the under 20 age category and their choice to stay or leave the village. And this decision will depend upon opportunities both within and outside the village.

Housing

The village can be divided into three residential sections-- the Seatown, the Council Houses, and the Bungalows. (see: Map 2.) The Seatown, the earliest settlement area, is located along Gamrie Bay and around the harbor area. The houses were built of locally quarried red or blue stone. The red stone, or red "steen," as it is called locally, was quarried from deposits of Old Red Limestone found to the west of the village. The blue steen, a blue-grey slate, came from quarries nearby. Although some of the earlier houses may have been built using the dry stone method, later ones used mortar. The walls are thick, between one and two feet; the windows are small and the doorways narrow. They are of similar design, being rectangular in shape, the gable end facing north with doorways on either the east or the west side. This design provides maximum

32

protection against cold northern winds. Roofs are covered with slate, tile, or asbestos. The houses are built close together, often with the gable ends joined in a party wall. Between the houses are narrow passageways, called "closes," many of which have stairs and hand rails to facilitate walking under such adverse conditions such as rain, snow, or ice. When looking down on the Seatown from the top of the brae, one is reminded of cattle standing close to each other when the weather is bad. The houses in the Seatown are huddled together for mutual protection against what can be cruel weather. Along Main Street the position of houses and shops changes. Rather than the gable end of the house facing the sea the houses have been built with the broad side of the house facing north or south.

Whichever way the house faces, the interior designs are similar. There are usually two stories. The downstairs has two rooms, one serves as a kitchen, the other as a living-bed room. In most of the older houses there is a "butt-in-ben," a bed that had been build into a wall with storage space below. The upper story was usually a loft that was used as a space to either mend nets or bait the long-line hooks. Government grants are available to build modern kitchens and indoor toilets and baths. There are only a few houses in Seatown where one can see the original exterior construction. Most have been harled* and painted.

The Council Houses are located up the brae. Sometime between World War I and World War II this area had a few dwellings constructed with the same materials and designs of houses in the Seatown. In addition, there was the village hall, two church buildings, and a manse for the minister. During the interim between world wars, sixteen houses, referred to locally as "prefabs," were constructed by the county council. After World War II, nineteen more were built. The expansion of village housing was restricted because of an inadequate water supply. But with the building of a new water system it was possible to build thirty-one new houses by 1950. These council houses are built of concrete block, brick, and some stone. The house designs are of two types, the town house and the flat. In the town house design the living room, dining room, and kitchen are on the ground floor, and a bath and bedrooms are on the second floor. The flat design has one to three bedrooms, a bath, the kitchen, and living-dining areas on one level. In neither of these design types does one find a loft suitable for net mending. The Council Houses were built in units that could accommodate two to four families. The town-house design is associated with two individual family dwellings, the flat design with four family dwellings. What loft space that does exist is

*Harling is a process where stone chips are thrown against a wet mortared surface. "Pebble dash" is the American word for this process.

used for storage of household items.

As compared to the Seatown, where most houses are owned by occupants, the Council Houses were rented to villagers. Recently council housing has been made available for purchase. Usually when they are purchased, the owner will make some alterations such as building on a garage or adding brick facing to distinguish them from council-owned buildings.

The Council Houses offer some advantages over houses in the Seatown, notably extra space, in the house itself and in the surrounding ground. The Council Houses have both front and back yards. Only a few houses in the Seatown have anything but a small patch of land in the rear of the house. The major disadvantage to living "up the brae" is that one is further from local shops.

The most recent addition to housing types in the village is the bungalow. Large, two-storied structures, bungalows are quite unlike the Seatown and Council houses. The first of these houses was built in the 1960s along the Macduff road out of the village. A few others were built directly above the council housing area. In 1974 a new street was added to the village, higher up the brae than any other residential street. The new bungalows on this street were built out of concrete block that has been harled. They boast large and elaborate entryways, and single-paned picture windows. The ground around the house is much larger than that of the council houses, and it is usually walled. It is in this type of housing that many, but not all, successful boat skippers and owners live. And it is with the construction of these houses that one notes, for the first time in the village's history, housing that symbolizes differences in the earnings of villagers.

Housing and Population

Corresponding to population increase up to the early part of the twentieth century was an increase in the number of houses in the village. The earliest available data on the number of houses are for 1831 (Table 2), when there were 72 houses inhabited by 343 people, or 4.8 persons per house. It appears from the records that housing construction did not keep up with the population increase of the late 1800s. By 1891, the number of persons per house had increased to 6.3. The decade beginning in 1891 must have been characterized by a building frenzy, for 131 houses were built, with the result that the number of persons per house dropped to 4.5. Beginning in 1911 there has been a decline in the number of persons per house, with 1981 having the lowest ratio since records have been kept.

In reviewing the above data, one might note what appear to

be inconsistencies with information previously presented. It was was stated that 66 council houses were built between World War I and 1950. Yet Table 2 shows only 13 new houses in the village from 1901 to 1961. This can be explained by the fact that as people moved out of the Seatown, many houses were expanded. What had previously been two or more individual houses became one house. Party walls were broken through adjoining houses to make one larger single-family house. In some of the Seatown houses two families shared a common entryway or a common set of stairs to the upstairs room or loft. When one family moved out the other bought its side. Thus, though it might appear that the number of houses in the Seatown had decreased over the years, in fact the number of buildings has stayed the same, while the number of families in those buildings has decreased.

Table 2
Population Size, Number
Of Houses, And Number Of Occupants
Per House: 1831-1981

Year	Number of Houses	Population	Occupants Per House
1831	72	343	4.76
1841	96	348	3.63
1851	--	---	----
1861	110*	507	4.61
1871	124	717	5.78
1881	148	871	5.89
1891	180	1141	6.33
1901	311	1403	4.51
1911	318**	1405	4.42
1921	318**	1210	3.81
1931	318**	945	2.96
1941	---	---	----
1951	318**	1063	3.34
1961	325	986	3.03
1971	325	921	2.83
1981	338	837**	2.48

*Population is for the electoral division and may be larger than actual village size.
**These figures have been estimated.

House Ownership and Values

In 1981, there were 338 houses in the village. Of these, 120 were council houses, 23 were bungalows, and 187 were older

Seatown type houses. The bungalows and the older houses were all individually owned. Of the 128 council houses which have been made available for individual purchase, only 29 have been bought by villagers. Thus, 71 percent of the houses in the village are individually owned. But not all the houses are owned by people from the village. Some 20 to 25 houses in the Seatown have been purchased by non-residents for use as summer homes. The purchase of houses in the Seatown by outsiders has become rather commonplace. Every summer I was in the field, at least two of these houses were on the market. As the older residents die or move away and their children or heirs have no use for an additional house, they are sold.

It is possible to derive a crude measure of property values through an examination of the tax rolls. These records show the amount of property tax paid on each dwelling in the village. The tax is approximately one percent of the fair-market price for the house. For houses in the Seatown and the older sections of the village, the average tax paid in 1981 was £ 127.88. The average rate for council houses, either privately or council owned, was £ 184. The tax on bungalows was £ 424. It is obvious from these data that the higher up the brae a house is, the greater its value will be.

House Names

The practice of naming one's house is widespread in Britain and Gamrie is no different in this respect. About 18 percent of the houses in the village are named. Almost all named houses are found in either the Seatown or the Bungalows. Of the total named houses in the village, 25 percent are officially recognized by the Post Office as an address. The names used can be class-ified into three categories--boat names, place names, and "other." The boat names are either the name of a boat owned by the present or previous occupant. Place names include both local place references or other places in Britain. Included in this category I would also put names which reflect the positional location of a house. Usually such names have the suffix, "view," such as Bayview, Seaview, and so on. In the "other" category are names of people or flowers or non-specific references. Whether a house is named and what name is chosen is arbitrary. House names are sometimes used to identify occupants when otherwise there might be confusion about who the referent is. Some named houses have historical significance for individuals in the village. Knowledge of the house names in the village also serve to mark the distinction between the villager and the outsider. There is nothing in the house name itself that would indicate where it is located. Only a familiarity with the village, gained over a lengthy residency, enables one to use house names as place references.

House Furnishings

While the outside of many houses in the village present a rather drab image of grey stone or stucco, the inside of a fisherman's home is often a showcase of color and brilliance. Thomson (Anson, 1965) noted in 1849:

> That there is much comfort intermixed with a good deal of poverty in the larger Scottish fishing villages is evinced from the interior of the dwelling. In many a cottage, the "but end," as it is called, has everything of the best; there the eye is gratified by the most inviting of beds for the stranger, the mahogany chairs and the chest of drawers, and all the other corresponding articles of furniture, betokening the rewards of thrift and industry. In the other or more common end, there is everything useful and necessary for the daily affairs of domestic life, whilst an array of Staffordshire ware stands on a bench opposite the fire-place, exhibiting the taste and fancy of the goodwife in a plentitude of variety, dazzling to the eye of the visitor and flattering to the vanity of the amiable possessor (21).

Anson (1965) reports that when fishing changed from local waters to offshore at the turn of the century and fishermen were away from home for extended periods of time, they often returned with:

> . . . money to burn, and much of it was spent on improving their houses. Invariably they brought back presents for their wives and children. So the mantlepieces were laden with stoneware figures, brilliantly coloured--sailors with their sweethearts, shepherdesses, and almost certain, Burns and Highland Mary, possibly Queen Victoria and her lamented husband the Prince Consort, together with one or two china dogs. . . .Most likely the "end room" now contained a glass-fronted cupboard displaying the best tea set, only used on special occasions. The walls began to display framed paintings of fishing vessels, bought at Lowestoft or Yarmouth; also family photographs. Framed memorial cards of deceased relatives were another popular form of decoration (21-22).

Little has changed from Anson's earlier observations. The glass-fronted cabinet still stands in the sitting room. Its contents reflect both the history and the purchasing power of the owner. Tea sets--brought back by relatives who have visited foreign lands, purchased on a holiday "down South," or bequeathed by a deceased mother or grandmother--are laid out for the visitor to see. These artifacts all have histories. They are seldom used, but when they are, the histories are recounted. On the mantlepiece can be found a ceramic team of Clydesdales or a gold-leaf clock or even a Royal Doulton figurine, depending upon the wealth of the owner. The imagery on the walls ranges from Tahitian females and tearful wide-eyed boys to oil paintings of boats or the village. In addition, there are likely to be family photographs and, depending upon the religiosity of the owner, framed biblical quotations. The wallpaper is usually a bright geometric design, and floors are covered with wall-to-wall carpeting of similar design and color. The furniture is overstuffed and covered with fabrics that add to the cornucopia of color. In the bungalows of the more wealthy skippers one finds an abundant use of glass for doors and room dividers. Sometimes the glass has been etched with seascapes containing the boat owned by that skipper. In almost every home one finds the ubiquitous horseshoe, either incorporated into the fire stand or brightly silvered and placed on the mantlepiece or in the glass-fronted cabinet.

New since the observations of Thomson and Anson is modern electronics. Along one wall of the living room there is a large color television and often a video tape recorder or a stereo. Even an electric organ is not uncommon. Dirt-floored kitchens with coal-burning stoves have been replaced by wood or formica cabinets, electric stoves, refrigerators, and dish washers. Washing machines and dryers for clothes are found in many homes and every household possesses an electric tea kettle.

One thing has not changed much from the past. Most houses in Gamrie are heated by coal burned in a fireplace. Fires are kept going most of the year. Even when daytime temperatures are high enough not to warrant a fire, one finds either a coal fire or a resistance electric heater on at night to break the chill. The fireplace performs two functions. One, it heats the room in which the fireplace is located, normally the sitting room. Two, it also heats water that is used for domestic purpose or for central heating. Most houses have two sources of hot water; an open fireplace and an electric "emersion" heater. Because coal is used to heat the house, one of the continuous tasks of the housewife during the winter months is to keep the fire going and the fireplace cleared of ashes. Bedrooms in houses without central heating are not heated, but most families have electric mattress covers. In contrast to council housing and houses in the Seatown, the bungalows have oil-fired central heating.

While the living room presents a message to those inside, the window of that living room presents an image to the passerby. Almost without exception, there is some decorative item in the living-room window, be it the small window in a Seatown house or the large picture window in a bungalow. It might be a vase with fresh or artificial flowers, or it might be a small statue. In addition to the items presented on the window sill, the window itself conveys a symbolic meaning. Windows may have curtains, though venetian blinds are more common. At night, the curtains are drawn and the venetian blinds closed. On waking in the morning, one of the first things done is to open the curtains or blinds. This signals to the outside that the household is awake and prepared to accept visitors. Thus, the daily cycle of household activities becomes visible to others. The only exception to this rule is when someone in the household or a close relative or a fellow crew member has died. Windows are normally covered from the time of death to the funeral and, in some cases, for some days after the funeral. When the windows are uncovered after a death it is appropriate to visit the house.

Shops, Services, and Local Employment

An examination of the feu records for the village reveals a great deal about the residence of shop owners over the past 260 years. During the 1700s, seven persons were listed as merchants, but of that number only one had a name that identifies him as being from Gamrie. Other businesses listed during the 1700s were blacksmith, tailor, shoemaker, shipbuilder, and vinter. As with merchants, most names of persons in these occupations were non-local. This pattern of non-local ownership continued through the 1800s. However, there was a slight difference in businesses listed because of changes in fishing. In addition to merchants, bakers, and shoemakers, there were also coopers and fish-curers. It is not until the twentieth century that one notes more property owned by persons with local names and a dramatic increase in the numbers of those whose occupations are listed as fishermen. Although the feu records were not detailed enough to make possible a systematic analysis of land transfers, they were suggestive of a general pattern. Ownership of real properties during the eighteenth and nineteenth centuries was by absentees and non-local merchants who rented these properties to fishermen and their families.

The feu records also indicate a change in the numbers and kinds of occupations in the village. No longer are there blacksmiths or tailors, and the number of businesses operating

39

in the village has declined. In 1910, when the village was at its largest, there were four general stores, two butchers, three bakers, four shoemakers, three tailors, two restaurants, two banks, two pubs, one hotel, a boat building yard, and nine fish houses. By 1974, there were four merchants, two with their own bake houses, one butcher, one ironmonger's shop, a chemist's shop, a shoe shop, a hotel with one pub, and one bank that was open only in the mornings. Seven years later one of the bake houses had closed, one of the merchants up the brae had retired, and the chemist's shop operated only part-time. The decline in the number and kinds of services available to villagers suggests a change in the village itself. No longer is the village a small, self-contained, closed corporate unit able to provide a full range of services. Villagers are now dependent upon outsiders for almost all their needs, increasingly purchasing their groceries at shops in Fraserburgh and Banff that are part of national chains. Automobiles, furniture, appliances, and most other household goods are purchased outside the village. Service and repair men are called from outside the village. What is purchased within the village tends to be small items that are needed immediately or items forgotten on the weekly or twice-weekly trip to collect one's "messages."*

This decline in local businesses has meant a reduction in the number of people employed within the village. In 1981, there were approximately 45 people, male and female, full and part-time, working in the village. In addition to the owners of local shops and businesses who are included in the total local work force, people are employed by the remaining bake house, the grocers, the butcher's shop, the chemist's shop, a local coal merchant, and a local transport business. A few retired fishermen and young men are employed during the local salmon fishing season in the summer months. In the fall of the year part-time employment is available harvesting potatoes. There are also a few self-employed local handymen who do painting and house repair, a father-son boatbuilding business, and a few locals who fish out of the harbor. The only full-time government employee is the local postmistress. Because of these limitations in local employment, people who wish to live in the village but need an income must commute to work. There are a few women who work in the fish processing plants in Fraserburgh. A few small manufacturing factories in the area employ a limited number of people, and a few females work as secretaries, receptionists, and clerks in Macduff, Banff, and Fraserburgh.

Attempts by villagers to start local business have largely been failures. When I first went into the field there was a

---

*To get one's "messages" is the term used to indicate going shopping. The origin of this term probably comes from writing a list or message to one's self as a reminder of what to buy.

small shop which sold souvenirs and small items to tourists. By the second year in the field this shop had closed. A small restaurant that served ice cream, tea, and cakes opened and closed during another field season.* There was a small knit-wear shop operating in the village part-time during the summer of 1981. Businesses that have been successful in the village are those with markets outside the village or those with some special needed service. Thus, the two grocers on Main Street have vans that service the surrounding rural population; the grocer up the brae has the only gasoline pump in the village. The transport company and the coal merchant have customers who are non-villagers. The butcher and the local grocers provide some of the local boats with their weekly stores.

Education

Education in the parish and in the village was controlled by the Church from the late 1600s to 1872. In 1875, Bracoden Public School was opened to serve the village, the adjoining village of Crovie, and the country children at the east end of the parish. It was intended for males and females between the ages of five and thirteen years of age. In 1910 an Infant School was built in the Seatown for the younger children, and Bracoden Public School became Bracoden Junior Secondary School. The Junior Secondary had both academic and non-academic courses in its curriculum up until the early 1950s. For those wishing to go on to the university, it was necessary to transfer to the Academy in nearby Banff. In August, 1955, the school had eleven full-time, two part-time, and three visiting teachers and a role of 199 pupils (Cameron, 213). In 1966, the secondary department closed. At the same time the Infant School closed and the younger pupils then went to what had been the Junior Secondary School, now renamed Bracoden Primary School. The secondary school students were taken by bus to either Macduff or Banff. In 1970, a new comprehensive school was opened in Banff and it absorbed students from the village, a number of other villages, and the surrounding farming population, as well as the towns of Banff and Macduff. Consequently the number of pupils in the local school declined, so by 1978 there were only 105 students and five teachers.

Most of the village males leave school as soon as they are 16 years old. Until a few years ago, they could leave when they were 15. On leaving school, most go into fishing. After a few years experience, they can take courses in Fraserburgh or Aberdeen to prepare them for various maritime certifications.

---

*During the summer of 1982 another "tea shop" opened on Main St. It is owned by the wife of a Gamrie skipper who is from outside the village. This shop has a kitchen and serves a full range of suppers.

Only a small number of students from the village opt for the academic curriculum in Banff. Even fewer go on to the university. From 1974 to 1981, I knew of only two village students who went on to the university in Aberdeen. One was graduated in 1974; the other in 1978 or 1979. Of those who have ever graduated from a university, only two live in the village at the present time.

There is a certain skepticism about higher education in the village. Part of this skepticism is practical. If one intends to be a fisherman, technical education is valuable. A university education is not necessary, and if one has aspirations to be a skipper, the four years at a university would be better spent getting the necessary sea time that is a prerequisite to taking courses leading to certification. Another dimension of this skepticism is logistic and religious. Some of the religious groups in the village have residence rules that make it difficult to attend a university. For such villagers it would be necessary to live at home and commute to the university. I shall say more about this in a later section. One further deterrent could be normative. There is a general expectation in the village that people inhibit any public display of differences. Enrollment in a pre-university curriculum would constitute such a display and might meet with negative sanctions. The result is that most children from the village, no matter what their capabilities, elect the non-academic tract in education.

Churches and Halls

The oldest standing church building in the parish is the Church of St. John the Evangelist. Presumed to have been built in 1004 by the Thane of Buchan to commemorate the defeat of invading Danes some years before, it was abandoned in 1827 as a place of worship because of its decaying physical condition. Located high on Mohr (see: Map 2.) the remains of this church and the surrounding graveyard are clearly visible from the village.

In 1981 there were five places of worship in the village, plus the parish church, which is located about one and a half miles away. The village church, the "Kirk," was formed in 1932 by the union of the congregations of the former "quoad sacra" Church of Gardenstown and the former United Free Church (originally the United Presbyterians) (Cameron, 1961). The Kirk building, constructed at the end of the nineteenth century, is located on a promenade overlooking the harbor part way up the brae. Most of the members of the Kirk are from the village. However, some villagers attend the inland parish church.

In addition to the Kirk, there are four "Halls" used by various divisions of the Plymouth or Christian Brethren. A

42

description and analysis of Brethren beliefs and practices is found in Chapter VI. The Open Brethren meet in the "Bog," that section of the village located where the village road forks east to the harbor area. This hall, originally a storage building, was purchased in 1947 and was greatly extended in 1958. The Close Brethren meet in two locations. One is the old parish church, located mid-way between the Seatown and the council houses, close to the present Kirk. Originally built in 1875, it has been remodeled and used by the Close Brethren since the early 1950s. The other Close Brethren hall was built in 1955. It is located further up the brae nearer the council houses. Up until 1981 there was a small Close Brethern hall in the Seatown. However, it was closed because of declining attendance.* The third division, the Exclusives, are housed in the old Primary, or Infants School that was closed in 1966.

Religious services have their large attendance on Sunday although there are meetings at other times during the week. For example, the Kirk has a meeting on Wednesday evening and on Saturday. The Brethren meet on Friday and Saturday evenings. On Sunday, the Kirk has both a morning and an evening service. And occasionally on a Sunday afternoon during the summer, members of the Kirk will meet at the harbor for hymn singing and prayers. The Brethren meet three times on Sunday. Their morning and afternoon meetings, are for members while the Sunday evening service is open to the public. The estimated attendance at the Sunday services in 1981 was:

Kirk	150-160
Open Brethren	30- 40
Close Brethren	160-180
Exclusive Brethren	30- 40
Total	370-420

Thus, approximately one-half the village attends the local Kirk or Brethren meetings on Sunday. Of those who do attend, the majority participate in Brethren activities. However, it is the Kirk that is usually thought of as the official religious body in the village. Community activities that include a religious representative will be attended by the Kirk minister, not a leader of any of the Brethren groups. Such activities include meetings in the public hall or local school activities of a ceremonial nature.

Politics and Governance

From the founding of the village in 1720 until the twentieth century the political life of Gamrie was ruled by a triumvirate:

---

*This reopened in 1982 due to reasons explained in Chapter VI.

the laird, the minister, and the dominie.* In parishes such as Gamrie the laird had power over his tenants in all matters of property. Persons wishing to build had to ask for permission from the laird and thereafter pay yearly feu duties on the building site. The laird was expected to make improvements on the land such as building roads, dredging harbors, and providing water. After the Reformation, the minister, along with the Kirk session, was responsible for the moral welfare of the people within the parish. Persons accused of moral transgressions could be called before the Kirk session. If found guilty, they could be required to pay fines, do public penance, and were even subject to public corporeal punishment. The dominie, like the minister, was appointed by the laird. He was responsible for educating the children of the parish. This feudal system led to wide variations in the treatment of parishioners, depending upon the character of the triumvirate. The early statistical accounts for the parish of Gamrie all agreed that the local triumvirate was judicious in their exercise of power and people were attracted to the village.

In 1899, a County Council system of governance was established in Scotland. The Council was composed of elected representatives from parishes or districts on the basis of proportionate size of the electing unit. Councilmen were elected for three-year terms. The County Councils had the same powers as the town councils, which governed cities such as Aberdeen, Edinburgh, Glasgow, and Dundee. Such powers included the regulation of public utilities and responsibility for road maintenance, police and fire protection, public health, and education. Under the County Council system, the parish of Gamrie had one elected representative.

The County Council system remained relatively intact until World War II, when some of its authority was assumed by the government for the war effort. After World War II, the passage of the National Health Services Act removed the council's control of health-care service and responsibility for gas and electricity was taken over by the state. In 1974, the county council system was abolished and in its place was substituted a series of regional and district planning offices staffed by administrators within the civil service system. In response to this change, there was an attempt to form a local committee that could act as a representative for the village and some of the surrounding country area. A meeting was called for a Friday night in the public hall. Notices for the meeting were posted in all the shop windows in the village. Of the 35 to 40 people who attended the meeting, only 16 or 17 were local. Of the locals, only two persons were fishermen. The others were local farmers, the laird, the doctor, the head teacher at the school, and shop

*Dominie: school teacher

44

owners. The discussion at the meeting centered on the advantages and disadvantages of such an association, how it might be organized, and what it would do. It was obvious from the subtle comments made by people around me that those in attendance were the people from the village who were most active in village affairs and that what they were saying at this meeting had been heard many times before at other meetings. In spite of the fact that these were the local "leaders," the association was never formed. The result is that the village has no collective group representing its interests to various administrative bodies. What actions are taken by villagers in reference to governmental services are taken by individuals with individual complaints or requests.

In spite of this difficulty in organizing villagers, there are a number of relatively permanent organizations in the village.

Village Organizations

One of the oldest standing committees in the village is associated with the public hall. Originally built in 1888 as a volunteer drill hall, it was bought after World War I by six local businessmen (H.B., et. al 1968). In order to guarantee the future of the hall they wrote a charter that established the composition of a Hall Committee. This committee was to include the local Councillor, the local School Headmaster, the local doctor, and two local bank managers. Additional members of the committee would be elected at the annual meeting. Although some of the positions originally stipulated no longer exist--the councillor and the bank managers--the committee still functions with a core membership that is basically non-local. The elected members tend to be farmers rather than fishermen. The committee's responsibilities include maintenance and improvements to the building and scheduling of activities. Funds to maintain the building come from an annual flower show at which donated goods are sold. The activities held in the hall have varied over the years. For example, after World War II, some of the Brethren groups met in the hall. The activities also vary according to time of year. At Christmastime, the Kirk gives a party for local children. At present, the hall is used for recreational activities such as bowls or badminton, and as a meeting place for the Youth Club and special interest classes such as "Keep Fit." Almost all the activities that take place in the hall are organized by non-fishermen. This includes people from the country and persons who have moved into the village from outside.

The WRI, Women's Rural Institute, does attract some women who live in the village, but are from rural backgrounds. The main activity of the WRI is a monthly meeting which features a speaker. The R.N.L.I., the Royal National Lifeboat Institution, is another women's group in the village. Its membership consists largely of fishermen's wives. Their main activity is collecting money for the building and maintaining of lifeboats used to rescue crews from distressed boats and ships. This they do by giving "teas" and selling items manufactured for the Institution. The Harbour Committee has responsibility for collecting harbor fees and generally supervising the harbor. It is an all-male committee composed of active and retired fishermen, as well as non-fishermen. It has historically been responsible for soliciting donations to improve the harbor and recently has been active in sponsoring a local gala.

Within the village there are a small number of people one could classify as social activists. They spend a great deal of time trying to encourage participation in groups that already exist as well as initiating new groups or activities. Their common complaint is that villagers are difficult to organize. For example, during the summer of 1978 there was an attempt to organize a "playscheme" for children in the village. Four local women were able to get space at the local school; they made arrangements to show films, for the children to play indoor games, and for arts and crafts activities. The playscheme was widely publicized in the village, but in spite of formal announcements and informal communication networks, it had difficulties from the beginning. According to the organizers, the problems were not with the children but with the parents. They expected parents to provide volunteer help as supervisors, but the parents did not. This reaction is typical. Whenever someone local assumes the role of leader, it is difficult to find others who will accept that role and then participate as subordinates.

There have been situations when people get organized without direct leadership or direction. For example, in 1978 I observed the launching of a locally built boat. Two village men, a father and son, had built a small motor-powered boat for a West Coast prawn and lobster fishermen. The launching was scheduled for 3 p.m. at flood tide on a cold and windy Saturday. A little after 2 p.m. people began to gather at the harbor and up the brae at the end of Main Street where one could command a good view of the launching site. By 3 p.m. approximately 200 people were watching the harbor. By this time, high winds, combined with the flood tide, had resulted in waves breaking over the harbor wall and spraying the bystanders with water. Each time this happened there were feeble attempts to avoid the sea water and laughter at those who found themself soaked. In spite of the weather, the onlookers were in a festive mood. A quiet came over the audience when the boat builder appeared with the new owner, and the owner's wife and family. But just as the formal launching was to begin, a local male dog walked by and, with total disregard for the seriousness of the event, urinated on the boat, then promptly walked off in the direction

46

of the Sands. The crowd broke into laughter once again. The boat had been faced, bow first, into the harbor. After a few words from the owner, his wife broke a bottle of champagne against the stern. Two long ropes were fastened at the stern and played out along the two quays that meet at the launching site. Without a word being spoken, 24 village men, 12 on each side, took up the rope. The boat builder went to the bow of the boat and began directing those on the ropes. Some men also pushed against the bow, and with some difficulty, the boat was launched. The crowd applauded and then dispersed.

Another example of this type of spontaneous cooperation was related to me by a local fishermen. A young fisherman from the village who was experiencing some emotional difficulties was reported missing on a Sunday. The police were called to organize a search party. In response to the call for a search, about 200 village males volunteered, including those whose religious beliefs forbid them from working on Sunday. The young fisherman was found and went fishing that Sunday night.

This type of short-lived grouping is characteristic of the village. People will respond to individual catastrophies and problems, but when the catastrophe is over and the problem solved the group disbands. Organizations with charters that demand long-term commitments and formal leadership have not been successful. This observation makes sense when one considers the structure of the village. Lacking a formal leader with the authority to mobilize the village into some action means that each person is free to participate or not participate in a given activity.

The Gala

The gala is an institution found throughout Britain. It is a community event held normally during the summer months and it may have a variety of themes--political, historical, social, recreational, or economic. Along the Moray Firth one sees advertisements for galas beginning the first week of July through the end of August. The gala usually has a number of activities that appeal to different age groups. There are children's events, such as rides on animals or mechanical devices, and adult activities, such as games of chance or skill where one can win a variety of prizes. There may be displays and there is usually a "sale of works."* Food items are usually available, including grilled items such as hamburgers or kippers, baked goods, and the ubiquitous cup of tea. Galas are truly community activities. People in the community volunteer their

---

*A "sale of works" is a general term referring to the sale of goods. This may include items locally produced such as home bakery items, berry preserves, knitwear, and flowers.

time and donate the items that are to be sold. Proceeds go toward some local charity or project.

The first gala I attended in Gamrie was during the summer of 1975. According to informants, this was the first gala in many years. In 1975 the Scottish National Party was trying to increase its fishing constituency. As part of this plan the local SNP organized a gala in the village harbor. The organizers were mostly country people. They had donkey rides for the children, boat rides for children and adults, and games of chance for adults. A Gamrie Queen was chosen from among the daughters of village fishermen.

Since 1975 there have been a number of galas. The most recent was organized by the harbor committee in 1981. The organization of a gala after so many years is symbolic of a change in community sentiment. A gala will attract many people from outside the village, including people from the surrounding country population, people on holiday, and fishermen and their families from other villages and towns. Although it is only lasts one day (unlike other galas that have events over a week-long period), it nevertheless marks a break in a long period of isolation from the outside.

The gala is held on Saturday, and a few days before the harbor area begins to display the symbols of the gala. Pieces of plastic fertilizer and feed bags are cut into pennant shapes and fastened to lines stretched between poles. Early in the morning of the gala day, booths are erected for the various activities. Usually a boat is made available for short trips just outside the harbor. The gala usually begins in the early afternoon, and by 4 p.m. the harbor area is crowded with people. People begin to leave between five and six o'clock, and by seven it is over. The last event of the day is some sort a fireworks display.

Health and Illness

The National Health Service (NHS) came into being after World War II. Prior to that, health care was the individual's responsibility or, in the case of indigence, a service provided through the district government. According to older villagers, pre-NHS medical care was expensive and was sought only when there was an emergency. If illnesses were longer or more serious than expected, the doctor was called. If the pain from a tooth-ache was unbearable, one went to the dentist to have it removed. Older villagers tell of persons who died because medical services were not available, and most agree that the National Health Service corrected a grievous wrong.

Under the National Health Service system, the village is part of a health district that has one general practitioner and one nurse for over a thousand patients. The area covered by this district includes the village and the rural population on the east end of the parish.

The village shares many health care problems with other rural areas of Scotland. Generally, rural practices are not considered prestigious by physicians. One reason for this is that in a rural practice one cannot be a specialist. The physician is called upon for all manner of diseases and illnesses. Another reason is that in rural areas one is expected to make house calls at all hours of the day and night. As a result, rural practices are sometimes difficult to staff and very often it is the less qualified physicians who are willing to take them (Williams, et.al.,1980). Under the National Health Service, physicians may be removed if patients are adamant enough with their complaints. But people in rural areas are more likely to tolerate what they perceive as less adequate medical care for fear that if the physician is removed it would be difficult to find a replacement.

A number of criteria are used by villagers in evaluating the quality of health care they receive. One expectation they have is that the doctor should come to the house of a sick person whenever he is called, at any time of day or any day of the week. In case of an emergency, the physician should respond immediately. If a person is sick and in bed at home, the physician should visit at least once a day and spend some time with the patient. Further, the physician is expected to prescribe medication as part of the treatment for sickness. Any physician who fails to fulfill these expectations is viewed as a bad doctor.

In addition to being responsible for the health needs of villagers, the local doctor is automatically a member of the Public Hall committee. In a sense, he is one of the few community members who has official power, albeit restricted to a small part of village life. Further, the doctor is a representative of the "outside" and is socially separated from the village by occupation, education, and class. Not being local, he is not subject to the same kinds of sanctions and controls that influence the behavior of other villagers. That the doctor is viewed by villagers as being "above" them is reflected in voiced references to him. Most villagers use first names when talking to or about other villagers. And the use of first name familiarity tends to disregard age, sex, and income differences. The only people in the village referred to by more formal designations are the doctor, the minister, the head teacher, and the country laird. The elevated social position of the doctor, along with the assumption that physicians are difficult to replace, makes it difficult to mobilize villagers to organize an

49

official complaint, regardless of how poor they believe the medical services to be.*

Given the expectations of a rural practice, it is difficult for a physician to spend a great deal of time with each patient. To aid the doctor there is also a local nurse who lives in the surgery. She has a number of different duties. For example, she changes bandages and dressings for patients who have been injured or are recovering from an operation. After a mother and her new baby return from the hospital, she visits each day to help the mother and to instruct her in proper infant care. She also monitors the health of the child. Those unable to care for themselves can ask the nurse to come by a few times each week to give them a bath or a massage. Without the services of the nurse, a rural practice would be much more difficult than it is.

The closest all-purpose hospital to the village is in Aberdeen. Patients are referred to this hospital in cases of emergency, for surgery, and for any diagnostic services the local doctor is not able to perform. In addition to these services, the hospital has an international reputation for its maternity care. Village women who might have difficult births are sent to this hospital. While excellent health facilities are available in Aberdeen, it is a one-hour drive from the village. This means that arrangements must to made to get back and forth to visit specialists. In case of emergency, ambulance service is available.

For emergencies at sea there are a number of methods for getting an injured or sick person to the hospital. Depending upon the location of the boat and the seriousness of the problem, three options are available: the boat can return to port, and the person is transported to the hospital; the boat can go to the nearest oil platform, from which he is air-lifted to the hospital; or the victim can be air lifted directly from the boat.

There is one other hospital in the area. Located in Banff, it has rather limited diagnostic facilities and is used basically for nursing care. Uncomplicated births are carried out there, and surgery patients who only need routine nursing services, but are not well enough to stay at home, use this hospital. There is a widespread belief in the village that a person who is seriously ill and not expected to live will be sent to Banff from Aberdeen. There is some truth to this belief, as the hospital does not have the staff or the equipment necessary to treat persons who are terminally ill.

*For an exception to this see: Inside:Outside in Chapter VII.

50

Dental Care

The National Health Service provides free dental care to children, students, and women who have recently had children. Others must pay. In the past, a dentist came to the village periodically and attended to dental problems. At present, villagers go either to Fraserburgh or Banff.

There is little emphasis upon dental health among villagers. Visits to the dentist are usually in response to a toothache or bleeding gums, and the usual cure for such problems is to pull the offending tooth or teeth. As a result, a large percentage of villagers over the age of 18 have false teeth.

Symptomology

Physicians respond to symptoms reported by patients. In order to determine what symptoms villagers reported, the Cornell Medical Index (Brodman, et. al., 1949) was given to a local physician and he was asked to indicate reported symptoms by sex of the patient. The Cornell Medical Index contains a listing of 195 symptoms that can be classified into 17 subscales or categories. The subscales have between six and 18 items.

The response by the physician reveals an interesting pattern of symptomology. Looking only at those categories in which half or more of the items were reported by villagers, one notes that males and females report many of the same symptoms but not necessarily in the same order of frequency. Table 3 shows the percentages of reported symptoms for males and females.

TABLE 3
Medical Symptoms Reported for Males and Females

Symptom Category	Males % of items checked	Females % of items checked
Anxiety	56	56
Cardiovascular	62	69
Digestive	87	65
Genitourinary	0	55
Eye-ear	55	0
Fatigability	57	57
Nervousness	50	61
Neuro-muscular	56	0
Sensitivity	50	83
Skin	86	0
Tension	0	100

Remembering that these are symptoms the physician reports hearing in the surgery and in home visits, one notes that both males and females report a high incidence of symptoms in the areas of digestive, cardiovascular, fatigability, anxiety, nervousness, and sensitivity. Included in the list of symptoms for these categories would be bad teeth, bleeding gums, upset stomach, ulcers, high blood pressure, cramps in legs, cold hands and feet, exhaustion, worrying, nervousness, difficulty falling asleep, and fear of being alone. Males reported more symptoms in the skin category, such as rashes, itching, and boils. They also reported more headaches and hot and cold spells in the neuro-muscular category. In the eye-ear category they complained of watery and inflamed eyes, running ears, and difficulty hearing.

Women reported more symptoms in two areas--tension and genitourinary. They reported being frightened for no reason, being awakened by frightening dreams, being constantly keyed up, breaking out in a cold sweat, and shaking and trembling. Under the genitourinary category, women complained of painful menstruation, being tense and jumpy during menstruation, and experiencing hot flashes and sweats.

Disregarding the specific complaints and the categories, one notes that most of the symptoms reported are stress related.* Villagers, both male and female, appear to manifest medical complaints that reflect uncertainty. This uncertainty, I submit, is a response to fishing as an activity. In fishing, incomes vary from week to week and are subject to fluctuations beyond the control of the fishermen. Fishing as a hunting activity, even a hunting activity aided by modern technology, is both uncertain and risky. The work cycle in fishing may require long hours without sleep, and the cramped quarters on most fishing boats preclude any exercise. Women know of the dangers related to fishing. And they worry about their husbands' safety and life. At home, they have been given responsibility for almost all the house related tasks, such as paying bills, maintenance, child care, and cleaning. When these tasks are done, they spend time talking to friends and kin. Vast quantities of coffee and tea are consumed and, to quote one local physician:

---

*Comparable data on symptoms expressed by the farm population present a very different picture. First, there was no category where over 60 percent of the symptoms were reported. For country males there were three categories--skin, respiratory, and musculoskeletal--where over 50 percent of the symptoms were reported. For farm females, skin and musculoskeletal were the only two categories. These findings suggest that the farm population report less symptoms in general, and those they report are a reflection of problems that are physiological as opposed to stress related.

52

> The conversation turns to health, or rather
> sickness and the worry would creep into
> their mind--a sickening fear for herself, her
> bairns,* or her man.

Disease

In addition to treating stress related conditions, the local physician does treat villagers for physical diseases. There is a very high rate of diabetes, pernicious anemia, and coloboma, a congential fissure of the eye. Village males are prone to arteriosclerotic heart disease and malignancies of the digestive organs, genitals, and urinary organs. Fishermen are likely to have more automobile accidents than non-fishermen, largely because they drive only on the weekends. Fishermen also have a high incidence of respiratory conditions such as the common cold, influenza, and pneumonia. Village women suffer from thyroid conditions such as goiter, iron deficiency anemia, nephritis, and various diseases of the ovaries.

Before the reader reaches the conclusion that the village has been immobilized by illness and disease, it should be pointed out that not everybody has the above conditions. It is just that the physician treats these conditions more than others. In fact, many illnesses are not found in the village. These include: rheumatic fever, malignancies of the buccal cavity and pharynx, lukemia, tuberculosis, diptheria, poliomyelitis, smallpox, and multiple sclerosis. In addition, death by suicide and homicide is so rare as to make it non-existent. Some diseases that were common in the past are no longer threats to the village. One such disease is brucellosis, which is carried through milk from cattle who have the disease. The symptoms included a fever accompanied by personality changes. The disease is cyclical with intervals between the cycles increasing until the symptoms disappear. Cattle are now tested for the disease and must be brucellosis free before their milk can be used.

Death Rates

A general measure of a population's health is death rate and age of death. In the first quarter of this century the death rate for the village was 9.72 persons per thousand per year. In the second quarter of the century this figure dropped to 8.84 per thousand, and from 1950 to 1974 the average death rate per year was 8.68. The average age at which people die has changed much since 1900. For the first quarter of this century the average age of death was 37.9 years. During the second quarter this figure increased to 58.7 years, and the most recent average is 66.6 years. This increase in average age of death is largely explained by decreases in infant mortality. In the

---

**bairns:children

early part of this century infants and young children accounted for almost half of the deaths. Those who survived these early vulnerable years were likely to live as long as people today. Home births were commonplace in the village through the 1950s. In the early part of the century, with poor medical facilities, women were aided in delivery by other women and sometimes a practical midwife. With the introduction of the National Health Service after World War II and the use of the maternity hospital in the early 1950s, infant mortality has almost disappeared.

Language

Language functions not only as a means for communication, but also as boundary marker between human groupings. Different cultures may be separated by language barriers as effectively as by physical or geographical barriers. And within a culture, specialized vocabularies and dialect variations serve as markers that distinguish occupations, classes, residences, and other significant social categories. In this section, some dialect and vocabulary characteristics of villagers are examined that serve both to distinguish this village from others and to link it to the surrounding area.

The village is located in a dialect region bounded on the west by the town of Buckie and the south by the city of Aberdeen. The dialect is spoken by both coastal and country people (Murison, 1963). The words come from Gaelic, English, French, Dutch, and Norse. The syntax is English and the speech rules derive from eleventh and twelfth Century Anglo-Saxon spoken in the North of England (Murison, 1963). This dialect is called "Buchan," the name of the region, or "Northern Scots," to distinguish it from Scots spoken elsewhere, or simply "Doric," meaning the Scottish dialect. Whatever the name, English speakers are likely to find it difficult to understand in spite of the fact that it shares a common origin with their own language.

In Buchan, a number of speech rules distinguish it from school English. For example, the "wh" sound in school English is pronounced "f" in Buchan. Thus, whiskey becomes fiskey and white is pronounced fite. Another consonant change is the "k" sound for "ch" and "gh" in English. Night is pronounced "nicht" and church is "kirk". Vowel changes are even more common. The English "o" is transformed to an "a" sound so that who becomes "fa" and "oo" is changed to "ee," which makes moon "meen", spoon "speen," and stone "steen." However, there are some exceptions. Look is "leuk" and book is "beuk." Sounds often disappear at the beginning, the middle, and the ends of words. Things are not small, but "sma," and "f"s and "g"s are seldom heard at the end of words. Having becomes "haein" and yourself is "yersel." To give the reader an appreciation for the spoken Buchan, I offer the following poem by Peter Buchan (1976:31) set alongside my translation:

THE PEEL	THE POOL
Twa-three heukies in his ganjey;	Two-three small hooks in his jersey;
In his pooch a penny line,	In his pocket a penny line,
Or, could he nae raise a penney,	Or, could he not raise a penney,
It micht be some barkit twine	It might be some barked* twine.
Owre the Queenie Brig, this loonie	Over the Queenie Brig, this boy
Watched a chance to scran his bait	Watch his chance to scrounge his bait
Far the gutter steemed their coggies,	Where the gutters emptied their coggies,**
Jist inside some curer's gate	Just inside some curer's gate.
Syne across the rocks he'd warstle;	Then across the rocks he'd struggle
Loons were there fae far and near,	Boys were there from far and near,
Shyvin' oot their hame-made lines,	Throwing out their home-made lines,
Aften raivelt, seldom clear.	Often ravelled, seldom clear.
O' the happy 'oors he'd spend there,	Oh, the happy hours he'd spend there,
Blithe an' cheery, young an' feel;	Blithe and cheery, young and foolish;
Jist a barfit, careless cratur,	Just a barefoot, careless creature,
Catchin' podlies in the Peel	Catching podlies*** in the Pool.
Dinna speir at me "Fa wis he?	Do not ask me "Who was he?"
That's a thing I couldna tell.	That's a thing I could not tell.
Steek yer een an' think a fyliee--	Shut your eyes and think a short while--
Could he nae ha' been yersel?	Could he not have been yourself?

While these dialect patterns are consistent within the region, there are some word variations that identify the speaker as coming from this or that village. For example, there seems to be as many different words for sea gulls as there are fishing villages. In Gamrie, the sea gull is called a "puhl," an old Norse word meaning to cry or complain. In the Moray area, the word is "gow;" in Fraserburgh it is either "myave" or "scurrie;" in Buckie it is a "maa;" and in Hopeman, a young gull is a "gru wullie" (Simpson, 1980). The use of one of these names quickly identifies the speaker's area of residence. Others words are even more local, being used only with other members of the speaker's community.

The use of broad Buchan in everyday conversation varies with the age of the speaker. Older villagers are more likely to converse in Buchan between themselves. Younger villagers are less likely to know many of the older local words. One cannot

---

*Barked twine: cotton twine that had been dipped in a solution made from tree bark to preserve the twine.
**Coggies: wooden buckets.

***Podlies: small saithe, a flat fish.

underestimate the influence of the media on local dialects. Younger villagers are exposed to radio and television. In addition, the education system deemphasizes Buchan. Older villagers often expressed their dissatisfaction about the younger villagers' ignorance of the old dialect words and pronunciation. Blame for this is attributed to television and moving the secondary school out of the village.

The use of Buchan or English depends largely upon the parties in the conversation. Villagers attempt to use the best Inverness English* when speaking to the local doctor or minister. Such code- shifting often happened when I spoke to villagers. For example, one day I was talking to a villager about the adjoining village of Crovie. Most villagers refer to the village as "Crivie." I also used the Crivie pronunciation in my conversation and was promptly given a lecture about how wrong it was to say it this way. The person to whom I was speaking was from a family in the village that prided itself in sending its children off to the university and generally presented an image of being better education than others. The lesson was clear. Those who are better educated pronounce words as they are spelled. The person knew I taught at a university and felt it proper that I be corrected. At another time I was standing in line at the village bank. Next to me was a local man who told me about parking his caravan (trailer) in a village down the coast. The village name is spelled Findochty. However, it is pronounced "Fin-nechty." When speaking to me, he pronounced the village name as it is spelled. He then turned to another local and told him the same story, except that he said his caravan was parked in Fin-nechty. Such code shifts occur when speaking to persons outside the area, I suggest, because Buchan has a class connotation. Persons with hereditary prestige such as the laird spoke school English or Scottish. Persons with prestige achieved through education eschew Buchan. Books written in Buchan are rare. And modern works that use some Buchan often present the Buchan speaker as ill educated but with a native craftiness and wit. A recent BBC-TV production about two children who were mentally retarded presented the Buchan speaker as from a humble working-class background, while his fellow student, who did not have a Buchan accent, came from a middle-class professional family.**

While there may be a discouragement of Buchan on land, it

---

*Inverness enjoys a reputation for having the best spoken English in Scotland.

**After reading this section, the writer of this BBC production told me that the decision to use English as the speech of the middle-class child was not his. It was suggested by one of the show's producers, who is not Scottish.

can be very useful at sea. If skippers from the village wish to converse with each other over the radio and do not wish their conversation known to others they will slip into the broadest Buchan they know. If they are fishing in an area where even broad Buchan may be understood, they will devise code words that only a limited number of skippers know. Thus, language codes are shifted to suit the needs of the speaker and to reflect the varying situations in which speakers find themselves.

Gamrie: A Summary

In this chapter a number of changes have been noted for Gamrie. The most striking of these has been population. The number of villagers increased up until the turn of this century and then began a period of decline primarily because of out-migration. There have also been changes in both birth rates and age of death. The average number of children per marriage has decreased and the average age at death is older. An increase in the number of housing units, beginning in the early part of this century, decreased population density and increased the geographical size of the village. Beginning with the original settlement in what is now Seatown, the village spread up the brae.

The village has remained a village of fishermen since its founding. Until the beginning of this century it was a self-contained community, providing all necessary services to its citizens. The local harbor was used both for fishing and for receiving goods from the outside. The various occupations of villagers from eighteenth and nineteenth century records indicate adequate services for both fishing and living. Since the turn of the century the number of service occupations has decreased and today the village is, for all practical purposes, a bedroom community for commuting fishermen and their families.

What had been locally provided services have been assumed by government agencies. Education, health and sanitation are all now under national or regional government control. The only service that reflects local influence is religion.

Having described these changes, it is now necessary to explain why they occurred. In the next chapter I review changes in fishing technology and their possible influence on Gamrie.

Main Street 1982

IV: TECHNOLOGY:
HISTORICAL CHANGES AND CONTEMPORARY ORGANIZATION
OF FISHING

Introduction

The history of the village is ultimately related to the history of fishing in the North Sea. Changes in boat design and fishing technology are linked to changing demographic characteristics of the village, as well as to changes in social interaction and cultural patterns. The founding of the village itself can be traced back to an attempt by George I to encourage Scots fishermen to adopt the fishing methods of the Dutch (Wilson, 1965). During this early period, the market for white fish caught by villagers was basically local, although some was salted and sent to the Firth of Forth (Wilson: 470). The coming of the railroads in the nineteenth century increased the markets for fish. In response to these increasing markets there was an increase in the number of fishermen and the number of boats in the village. The replacement of sail-powered fishing craft by steam- driven boats in the early part of the twentieth century extended the range of fishing beyond the inshore areas that had been fished by villagers. These larger boats could stay out longer and hold more fish, but they were too large for the small harbor in Gamrie. After an abortive attempt to enlarge the harbor in 1913, local fishermen had no other choice but to berth their larger boats at nearby harbors such as Fraserburgh, Macduff and other towns and villages with adequate harbor facilities. As a result, many fishermen and their families moved to places with larger harbors. Those who remained in the village had to commute to their boats. Thus, what had been an active, self-contained fishing village was transformed into a residential village for fishermen.

This series of changes affected a large number of villages along the Moray Firth. What makes Gamrie unique among them is the fact that it has remained a village of fishermen. The other villages can only claim to have once been fishing communities since few, if any, active fishermen still live in them.

Changing Boat Designs and Equipment

In this chapter the historical changes in boat design and fishing technology will be reviewed in some detail in order to link these changes to the social organization of the boat. In addition to the historical analysis there will be an examination of the present-day Gamrie fleet in terms of boat characteristics, recruitment of fishermen, composition of crews, and work cycles. Using this information as a data base, modifications of the initial ecological model will be suggested.

59

The earliest boats along the Moray Firth were similar in design to Norwegian boats of the period.* They were of light construction, clinker built,** with considerable sheer toward the bow and stern (Wilson, 17). Depending upon the number of oars, they were either "Sixterns" or "Fourerns." Their length ranged from 22 feet to 37 feet; they had a modified Norwegian square sail and a short straight tiller. A somewhat smaller version of this boat, the North Isles Yawl or the Westray Yawl, was also used on the Moray Firth. These boats had a more elaborate sail system--two standing lugs and a jib--and they carried two pairs of oars. Toward the end of the eighteenth century, the "Scaffie" made its appearance. Small at first, they were increased to lengths up to 60 feet during the nineteenth century. The Scaffie had a tall lug sail and was said to have maneuvered well for its size. By 1790 there were 10 fishing vessels and 6 boats less than 60 tons registered in Gamrie and Crovie. The crew size for these boats ranged from two to six men and boys. They fished from the harbor daily, using the long-line method to catch white fish--ling, cod, haddock, turbot, and skate.

During the eighteenth century there had been encouragement by the Crown to catch herring for the European market. But it was not until 1812 that the drift-net method used for herring fishing was introduced to the village (H.B., et al). The boats used by the Gamrie fishermen for herring fishing were the small scaffie type, that could be berthed in the local harbor. Other fishermen from ports with larger harbors were adopting a new boat, the "fifie." The scaffie was an open-decked boat. The new fifie was fully decked. By the middle 1800s, a number of these boats were being built along the Moray Firth. For example, the first decked boat built in Fraserburgh was in 1850; in 1872, 64 were built in Buckie (Wilson, 22). The decked boats offered a number of advantages to fishermen, the most obvious of which was protection against high seas and the elements. There was no set design for the fifie. The larger ones were carvel built,*** and there were some changes in sail arrangement. They were distinguished from the scaffie by an almost vertical stem and stern, deep heel and forfoot, long horizontal keel, and hollow rising floors (Wilson, 23). This design made the boat safer when running before the sea, but they were less maneuverable in small harbors such as those in Gamrie.

In 1879 a new boat was launched that combined design features of both the fifie and the scaffie. It had the vertical

<hr>

*For a comprehensive account of fishing in Scotland from 1790-1914, see: Gray, 1978.
**clinker built: built with overlapping boards.
***carvel built: having hull planks layed edge to edge.

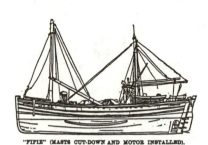

"FIFIE" (MASTS CUT-DOWN AND MOTOR INSTALLED).

"SKAFFIE."

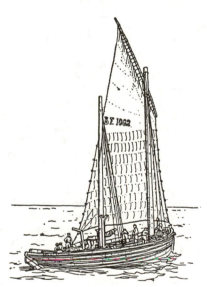

"ZULU."

Early Boat Designs
(From Anson, 1950)

stem and deep forfoot of the fifie and the raking stern of the scaffie. This combination made it faster than the scaffie and gave it better handling than the fifie. Because 1879 was the year of the Zulu War, the boat was given the name, "Zulu" (Wilson, 26). This design soon became popular among fishermen along the Moray Firth. They ranged in length from small "zulu skiffs" that were used for line fishing to 80 feet in length that were used as drifters for herring. The reliance upon human power to bring in the heavy herring nets was reduced by the steam capstan, which had been introduced a few years earlier. And in 1891, wheel steering appeared. The layout of the zulu was the same as the fifie. Crew quarters were aft, storage was forward, and the fish hold was located amidship. These boats were built in large numbers until 1906, when the last large sailing zulu was launched in Macduff (Wilson, 37). Many of the smaller zulus and fifies are still seen today. They have been motorized, usually have a small wheelhouse, and are used for line fishing and lobstering.

While Scottish fishermen were busy incorporating zulus into the fleet, events were happening in England that would eventually revolutionize fishing on the Moray Firth. In 1872 the first steam-powered trawler was built. Ten years later a steam-powered line-fishing boat was built in Leith (Wilson, 29). The first steam drifter in Scotland sailed from Wick in 1898 (Hamilton, 82), but Buckie was the first port to adopt the steam drifter in large numbers. Between 1901 and 1907, 168 steam drifters were added to the Buckie fleet, and by 1914 the number had risen to 298 (Hamilton, 82). Steam-powered boats have a number of advantages over sail powered boats, the most obvious being that they are not dependent upon the wind. The steam-powered boat could set a straight line course to the fishing grounds thus saving time over sailed craft, that had to tack.

In spite of the advantages of steam-powered craft, not all the Moray Firth fleets were able to adopt this kind of boat. Places like Gamrie were still restricted to smaller boats because of the harbor size, and so the Gamrie fleet continued to rely on sail power. The typical steam drifter was carvel built, usually between 75 and 90 feet in length. It differed from the fifie and zulu by having less beam and bluffer bow (Wilson, 30). The steam drifter had a wheelhouse located amidship, and many had a galley behind the wheelhouse. For the first time, skippers and those standing watch were protected. The increased adoption of steam-powered craft decreased the market for large fifies and zulus. As a result, few were built after 1900 (Wilson, 31).

The number of steam-powered fishing boats in the Scottish fleet increased until World War I. The war disturbed the fishing industry, since many of the larger steam drifters were pressed into the war effort and hostilities in the North Sea restricted fishing activities. Many of the steam drifters were sunk during the war. After the war, seasoned wood to build boats was difficult to obtain but plate steel was not. Thus began the era of steel- hulled boats, which proved superior to wooden boats, because they were both faster and stronger.

Steel-hulled boats used either steam or diesel power. The Gardner diesel engine was introduced in 1894, but it was not until 1902 that it was installed on a fishing craft (Wilson, 37). The first Moray Firth boat fitted with a diesel engine was in 1908. The adoption of diesel power among Moray Firth fishermen was not as rapid as the adoption of steam power, but gradually, more and more zulus and fifies were fitted with diesel engines. The move to dieselization proved prophetic. Following World War I the Russian market for herring was closed, the purchasing power of Germany and the Baltic States was decreased, and there was growing competition from Norway and Holland (Hamilton, 87). A coal strike in 1921 resulted in increased fuel costs for steam-driven boats. That same year a new fishing method was introduced, the Danish seine-net. The Moray Firth fishermen, the first to adopt this method, found that by building mid-sized diesel powered boats they could fish year-round. When not using their boats to fish for herring with the drift net they could use the seine-net for plaice, sole, and haddock just a few miles offshore from their home ports. By the mid 1920s the steam-powered drifters were being replaced by these smaller multi-purpose diesel-powered craft.

The year that signaled the end of steam power was 1926. That year another coal strike resulted in coal being rationed at 25 percent of its normal consumption. In addition, the price of foreign coal increased. With increased prices and uncertain availability of coal, many steam drifters were forced to stay in port or operate at a loss. Because of these problems, many older wooden sailing craft were converted to motor power. Usually fifie boats were converted because the rake of the zulu stern left insufficient room for the engine room, fish hold, and crew's quarters (Wilson, 46).

The Second World War disrupted fishing. Many fishing boats were commandeered, thus reducing the fleet size. Because fewer boats were fishing and fish was never rationed, the war years were prosperous to those willing to risk fishing in conditions that were sometimes hazardous. Able-bodied males and females were drafted or enlisted in the Armed Forces, so most of the fishing was done by older men and boys using older and smaller boats not suitable for military work. After the war, many of the fishing boats were returned to their original owners. Some had been converted back to their pre-war condition; others were returned along with a sum of money, so the owner could make the conversion. In addition, some boats that had been built for wartime use, but could be used for fishing, were made available to fishermen. In order to rebuild the fleet, government grants and subsidies were offered to fishermen. Most of these monies were used either to build new boats or convert old boats to diesel power. And most of these boats were meant for use with the seine-net. The conversion to seine-net fishing by the Moray Firth fleet was almost complete. Only one fleet was a notable exception--the Gamrie fleet. In 1955, 270 of the 378 fishermen from Gamrie were herring fishermen. Not only was this the highest proportion of herring fishermen by place, but the 270 Gamrie fishermen represented 70 percent of the total number of herring fishermen in the Macduff and Buckie districts of the Moray Firth. I shall return to the question of why the Gamrie fleet remained herring fishermen later. Suffice it to say, they hold this same distinction today.

After World War II, an increasing number of boats were equipped with labor-saving devices such as the power block.* In addition, navigation aids like the Decca navigator and radar became common. The Decca navigator is a position locator that works from radio signals transmitted from land. This enables the fisherman to locate fishing "spots" that were productive in the past. When linked to the steering mechanism, this unit will navigate the boat back to port even under the worst weather conditions. Radar enables one to locate other surface vessels under conditions of poor visibility. Another apparatus found on all modern fishing boats is the echosounder. First introduced in 1925 (Wilson, 81), it came into general use after World War II. The receiving unit of the earliest devices outlined the bottom, as well as shoals of fish, on chemically treated paper. Modern versions use a cathode receiving tube like a television screen. The tube type was first black and white; the most recent are in color so the bottom can be distinguished from fish. The echosounder has two functions. First, it makes it possible to read the sea floor configuration and to determine depth, and thus to avoid collision with submerged objects or the bottom itself. Second, it is used to determine whether one should fish in an area and the approximate size of the shoal.

The most recent addition to the Moray Firth fleet is the purser. These steel-hulled boats are over 100 feet in length and present the image of a luxury ocean liner. Inside they are quite unlike other inshore fishing boats. They are powered by one or two large diesel engines, and many have an additional engine amidship to enable the boat to be powered sideways or to hold the boat steady when the large nets are brought alongside. Smaller engines provide electric and hydraulic power. In many

*The Puretic power block was introduced in 1963 from America via Iceland (Goodlad, 1971).

pursers, crew members have individual quarters, and there are large dining and recreational areas. They have showers and facilities for washing and drying clothes. Most are fully carpeted in the wheel house and the commons areas. The purser is a special purpose boat, used to catch either members of the herring family or mackerel. The nets are of such enormous size that they are capable of catching whole schools of fish. When caught, the fish are brought alongside and pumped into refrigerated holding tanks.

The general trend in the evolution of fishing boats along the Moray Firth indicates a move from small wooden craft dependent upon wind and muscle power to large steel hulled craft powered by multiple diesel engines. Accompanying these changes has been the addition of navigational and fish-finding devices which rely less and less on learned skills and chance and more on sophisticated sensing apparatuses. Together, these changes have increased productivity, but not without a cost. The capital necessary to purchase and operate a fishing boat has increased dramatically since the turn of this century, and this has meant a change in ownership and control of fishing craft. In the next section, these changing patterns will be reviewed.

Capitalization and Ownership

Prior to the nineteenth century, fishing was largely controlled by local lairds or town councils. Lairds and councils had the capital to purchase boats; so fishermen either rented the boat or were employed to fish. Even when boats were purchased by a fisherman or a crew, they were often required to give "binnage freights" (Hamilton, 77). The boat could be called upon to carry freight such as wood or stone at the wish of the laird or council. Lairds and councils also had jural rights over residents. For example, in Buckie, if the laird felt that the fishermen were not going out to sea often enough he could have them placed in "joogs"* or manacled with irons. In nearby Banff the council rented boats and gear to fishermen, who were then obligated to fish for white fish for a period of seven years (Hamilton, 77). Those who violated their indenture were subject to fines and imprisonment.

This pattern of laird and council ownership of boats and gear, with fishermen in their employ, changed during the 1700s because the capital necessary to purchase the small boats and the hand-lines eventually came within the financial ability of fishermen. Studies of fishermen elsewhere who use similarly simple fishing technologies show that boats tended to be crewed by kinsmen who were also partners (Nemec, 1972; Faris, 1966;

*Joogs or Jougs: An instrument of punishment, of the nature of a pillory, placed on the offender's neck.

Firestone, 1967; Blehr, 1963). The costs of the boat and gear was equally distributed between persons who share kinship obligations, e.g. brothers, fathers, and sons. As long as capital investments for boats and gear were small, an ownership system by kin partners worked very well, but changes in fishing and fishing craft in the 1800s changed this pattern.

Fishing for herring with nets began in the early 1800s. In order to finance the boats and nets essential to enter this lucrative market it became necessary to obtain outside capital. This help came in different forms. We are told of one such form in Neil Gunn's historical novel, The Silver Darlings (1945).* The time is 1815. The place is the northern coast of the Moray Firth. Young Roddie, a crofter-fisherman, has been approached by Mr. Hendry, the inn-keeper, who has just bought a boat in Wick with a 20-foot keel. Anxious to become a curer, Mr. Hendry asks Roddie to take charge of the boat and then explains alternative financial arrangements.

> "I'll hold the ownership of boat and gear and take half your earnings; the other half you'll divide between the crew and yourself, keeping of course, a bigger share for yourself, because you'll not only be skipper but responsible to me for the boat. . ."

> "The second course is this," said Mr. Hendry, "I'll make over the boat to you now at exactly the same price as I paid for her. You'll be her sole owner and you'll owe me the money. That money will be the first charge on the boat and will have to be paid before you and your crew draw anything. When it's paid, the boat is yours--and you'll owe me no more" (74-75).

Roddie accepts the second alternative, but there is a catch. Mr. Hendry will not pay Roddie as much as the curer from Wick for his herring. Under this arrangement, Mr. Hendry cannot lose his investment money. The purchase price must be paid by Roddie even if the boat is lost. In addition, Mr. Hendry has a source of herring from which he can realize a handsome profit. For Roddie, this is the only way he can own his own boat. Similar arrangements must have taken place all along the Moray Firth. There was money to be made in herring but the proper boats and equipment were necessary. Not having

*For another fictional account of curer-fishermen relationships set at about the same period, see: Neil Paterson's Behold thy Daughter (1950).

capital of their own, fishermen had no recourse but to form alliances with merchants, curers, and others who would finance fishing.

Gamrie was the first port on the Moray Firth to use nets for herring fishing. According to H.B., et. al (1968):

> The Laird of Troup and Mr. John Watt, a merchant in the village were jointly engaged in the enterprise. A fisherman, named William Nicol, was sent to Queensferry to learn how to shoot, haul in, and manage the nets at sea. Nicol remained six weeks among the Queensferry fishermen, and, returning home in February, 1812, reported favourably of the likelihood of success. A boat was accordingly built by Mr. Garden, Rosehearty, after a model of the craft employed in fishing from the ports in the Firth of Forth--of 26 feet of keel, and capable of floating only 24 crans* of herring. Specimen netswere obtained from Greenock and Glasgow. Five of a crew went in the boat, who were paid half the produce of their labours, the other half going to Mr. Garden and Mr. Watt (40-41).

In this case the fishermen were employed by the Laird and the merchant, who incidentally was also a curer. This boat was the only herring fisher in the village for four years. By 1841, there were 34 boats from Gamrie that regularly fished for herring and 24 from Gamrie and Crovie that went for white fish (Wilson, 1845). Given this increase in the number of boats one can speculate that some of the fleet was locally owned.

During the 1800s, herring fishing began to replace long-line white fishing. One of the incentives to pursue herring was the introduction of the bounty system. Under the bounty system, curers contracted with boats to become their exclusive buyers. The contract would be for a fixed amount of herring at a guaranteed price. Upon completion of the contract, fishermen could contract with other curers. An important feature of the bounty system was that the fishermen could predict income for the season. Assuming that there were enough herring, it was possible to know what the boat's earnings would be and hence be able to borrow funds to purchase a boat. This system proved very lucrative to fishermen until 1884 and 1885. So many

*Cran: 3 1/2 cwt, between 900-1000 herring.

herring were caught those years that the international prices dropped and curers who had signed contracts to buy at the higher price at the beginning of the season could not fulfill the contracts without going bankrupt. In fact, many did go bankrupt, and in 1893 the bounty system was replaced by the auction system. The auction system meant that prices for fish varied according to supply and demand.

Under the auction system, it was impossible to predict what a boat or its crew would earn during the season. Given low predictability of outcomes, there was a greater reliance upon kin as crew members. During periods of economic fluctuation, crew members may be difficult to find since their wages are some share of the boat's earnings. Under the bounty system it was possible to guarantee a wage for the season. Under the auction system, it was not. To solve this dilemma, a number of methods were devised. One was to give each crew member an equal share in both the profits and losses of the boat. With each crew member an owner, it would be easier to justify working longer and harder. Another alternative was to rely upon persons with kin affiliations and obligations as crew members. It is more difficult to quit working for one's father, especially if one lives in the household or community of one's father, than to quit working for a stranger, to whom one has no obligations other than as an employee.

The cost of a Zulu with gear was around £ 600 (Deas, 1981). However, this cost could be distributed between crew-owners. Fishing requires two types of equipment--the boat and the nets. One or two crew members could own the boat; the others could own sections of net. This made boat crews dependent upon each other. Without nets a boat cannot fish; without a boat, nets are useless. The fact that fishing has property that is partible makes this kind of relationship possible. It also make possible partnerships that do not require vast amounts of individual capital. So long as boats were small in size and relied on sail power, fishermen could be individual entrepreneurs and escape financial dependence upon others.

The introduction of the steam drifter changed the independent financial status of fishermen. The steam drifter, with gear, cost around £ 3,000, and the costs of running the boat were significantly higher than sailed craft (Deas, 1981). Hamilton (1961) notes:

> ...fishsalesmen soon came to play a prominent part in the industry and a great deal of the capital required by fishermen to purchase steam drifters came from them. They often were agents for coal and other supplies, and a condition of assistance was

usually that the boats would deal only with their agents. The banks also came to the assistance of the fishermen and in many cases the engineers and boat-builders were content to leave balances on the purchase price of boats, while the number of private owners on land who had shares in fishing craft was greatly increased (83).

So high were the costs associated with the steam drifter that fishermen often had to depend upon a number of different sources of capital. It might have been a local merchant-grocer who had a "share" in the boat. This meant that the "stores"--food items--had to be purchased from the grocer, often at higher prices than other sources. The fishsales companies were also ship's chandlers and were often suppliers of coal. They also were responsible for auctioning the fish caught, for which they charged between three and six percent of gross earnings. With one or more such entrepreneurs "owning" the boat by having shares in the profits, the fisherman became little more than an employee until the debts were paid. And the rate of payback was still dependent upon fluctuating prices paid for fish through the auction system.

The introduction of diesel power brought with it even greater dependence upon outside capital. By 1939, a dual-purpose motor craft cost between £ 8,000 and £ 10,000. It was not until after World War II that the government became monetarily involved in the financing of boats and gear. The White Fish Authority and the Herring Board were empowered to offer grants and loans to build new boats and modernize older ones. The amount of grant and loan monies varied, depending upon governmental funding. The costs borne by the boat owner might be as low as 30 percent of the purchase price of a new boat, but boats cost between £ 40,000 and £ 60,000. Some or all of the costs by the fisherman/owner might be offset by selling his old boat, but there was no guarantee that the market for one's boat would remain the same from the time one ordered a new boat until it was completed two or three years later.

The prices of boats have continued to rise. Not only has the price of materials and labor increased, but the addition of modern electronic technology has resulted in some of the larger purser-type boats costing between £ 500,000 and £ 1,000,000. Because of the cost, rather complicated financial packages have to be negotiated that may involve the Herring Board, banks, investors, and now the E.E.C.--Common Market. And what had once been a skipper-owner who spent most of his time at sea catching fish is now a land-based financier negotiating financial "deals" to keep and maintain a boat with the task of fishing left to a mate or someone else on the boat with a skipper's ticket.

Fishing Technology: From Hand Line to Purse Net

Changes in fishing technology roughly parallel changes in boat design. The earliest technique used along the Moray Firth was line-fishing, either hand-line or long-line, which differ basically in the length and number of lines used. The hand-line technique was used in villages like Gamrie, where the fishermen went fishing in the morning and returned each night. When the boat gets to the fishing grounds a buoy with a flag is thrown overboard. The buoy is attached to an anchored line and the hand-line is fastened to the buoy. As the boat moves along, the hand-line is let out. Attached to the hand-line are "snoods," shorter lines that hold the baited hooks. The distance between the snoods and the number of snoods depend upon the species of fish caught. The hand-lines were approximately 300 feet long, and when they have been played out, the boat returns to the buoy and the line is hauled in. The fish are removed, the hooks rebaited, and the line is carefully coiled in a "scull" or basket. Each man has his own line, the number of men depended upon the boat's size. It was common for women and children to help bait the hand- line hooks at the end of the day, and women were also responsible for selling the fish. At present, this technology accounts for less than two percent of the fish landed along the Moray Firth. In Gamrie only a few retired fishermen supplement their income with this method, although I knew of two or three young fishermen who were both line fishing and catching partan (crab) and lobster. In the village, up to the early 1800s, this was the only method of fishing for cod, ling, skate, and haddock.

In Gamrie, the first drift net was used in 1812. It is used to catch pelagic fish (fish that swim near the surface) such as herring, mackerel and pilchard. Unlike line fishing, which could be carried out by a crew as small as two using a row boat, drift netting requires a larger boat and a larger crew. Larger boats are required because nets take more room than a hand-line. The larger crew is necessary because more muscle power is needed to handle the nets.

One casts a hand-line; one "shoots" a net. Once the fish are located the net is shot in their pathway and allowed to drift, hanging a few feet below and perpendicular to the surface. On top of the net are corks and buoys that hold it vertical. Along the bottom is a messenger rope or leader. Usually two crew members shoot the nets, one being responsible for the corks and buoys, the other for the net itself. Another crew member attends to the "strop-ropes," the ropes between sections of net, to make sure they are not tangled. A warp rope connects the boat to the nets. The boat drifts along with the nets until it is decided that they be "heaved"--brought back into the boat.

The drift-net is a gill net. If the fish are large enough, the net's mesh will trap them by the gills Thus, only the mature of the species is taken. This is an important consideration if there is a concern for maintaining fish populations. This concern was not, however, the original reason for the mesh size in a drift- net. Rather, curers wanted herring of a certain size for salting, kippering, or pickling for both domestic and foreign markets.

The process of hauling takes more manpower than shooting. According to Anson (1975):

> After three or four hours the process of hauling begins. The warp, or "bush-rope", is led through a block fixed on the bulwarks, near the capstan, and down into the rope-room, where a boy coils it down so as to be ready for running out when it is again wanted. One man, the "cast off," disconnects the nets from the warp, two others take charge of the buoys and seizings, and four more stand in the hold and shake out the fish from the nets...Should there be a good catch the process of hauling takes several hours. (172-173)

Thus, the typical crew size for a herring boat was eight, if the skipper also worked at hauling. Further, the number of tasks and hence the boat's division of labor became more differentiated. It is with drift-netting that one notes the beginning of social differentiation and specialization in fishing. In line fishing, each man cast and hauled his own line. With drift-netting, each man was responsible for one well defined set of tasks.

Not only did fishing for herring change shipboard interaction, but it meant following the shoals of herring as they migrated around Britain. Herring were at one time caught in the Moray Firth and the North Sea, and boats from the village traveled as far south as Yarmouth and Lowestoft and as far north as Lerwick in Shetland in their pursuit. Now, most of the herring are gone from the East Coast and are found in the Northern Minch (the Northwest coast of Scotland) south to the Isle of Man in the Irish Sea. As a result, less than one-half percent of the fish caught in the Moray Firth are herring and mackerel captured by drift-net.

Herring, or "Silver Darlings," as they are called, captured the imagination of fishermen. Idealized in song and verse, they were to fishermen what gold had been to those seeking their fortunes during the gold rush in America. Stories are told of the extreme hardships when out at sea, for months at a time. And they were told of men who made their fortunes or filled their nets with incredible hauls. So mythologized were these fish that the herring became a prestige fish and those who fished for them took on some of that prestige. I would suspect that a partial explanation for why Gamrie men are still herring fishermen can be attributed to this mythology.

Danish seining, or seine-net fishing, was introduced after World War I. This method accounts for 33 percent of the total Moray Firth catch. It is used primarily for cod, haddock, and whiting. In order to use this system, it is necessary to have a motorized craft. The net has a wide mesh along its outer extremities, then it narrows to a smaller mesh at the "cod end." At the top of the net are strung cork floats; at the bottom, weights. At either side of the net are warps. The net is shot in the following manner: one warp has an attached buoy; this end is thrown over the side; the boat then starts a circle route back to this buoy, first letting out the buoyed warp, then the net, and finally the second warp. The boat stops and picks the buoyed warp out of the water, fastens it to the boat and begins a run at full speed. After a few moments run, the warps are pulled in with winches or rollers. The boat continues its run while the net is heaved. Once alongside, the boat stops, the net is brought onboard, and the contents are emptied from the cod end. In general, the size of the seine-net is determined by the amount of power the boat has. Most seine-netters are smaller boats that are permitted to fish within the three-mile limit, and many are overnighters or day trippers that return to market every day. The crew may be as few as three. One person is needed in the wheelhouse to control the boat. Two crew members can control the two winches that bring in the warps.

Trawling is the most productive technology on the Moray Firth. Over 60 percent of the fish are caught by this method. Like the seine-net, it is used for white fish. In the seine-net, the net begins to close as soon as it is shot. The only thing that keeps it open is the forward motion of the boat. In trawling, otter boards, or "doors," have been added to keep the net open while it is being towed. The net is shot beginning at the cod end. The boat moves forward, pulling the net behind it until it is fully extended in the water. Then the doors are released. They are attached by a single warp to the boat. The warp is coiled on drums that are played out as the boat moves forward. After the warps are out, the boat tows the net for four or five hours. The process is then reversed, and the net is unloaded in much the same way as the seine-net.

Because of the size of these nets and the fact that they must be towed for extended periods of time, the boats and their engines are larger than in seine-netting. Most trawlers are also week-trippers. They leave the harbor "the back o' Sunday"-- Monday soon after midnight--and do not return home until Friday or Saturday, although they may come back mid-week to auction their fish. The typical crew size is 6 to 8. One usually finds the skipper, a mate, an engineer or mechanic, a cook, and one or two deck hands. The skipper is usually in the wheelhouse when the net is shot and heaved. The mate supervises the activities on deck. He, along with the engineer, the cook, and the hands are all busy during shooting and heaving. Once the fish are on board, the hands do most of the gutting and boxing of fish. The fish are first sorted by species and size into boxes. Then the fish are gutted, washed down with seawater, and placed in the hold, where they are iced. Before gutting, the net is shot again and the trawling continues.

Sorting, gutting, and icing of fish is not done with herring. Herring are put directly into the hold. Gutting and what little sorting is necessary is done by the fish processor or curer. This is another prestige dimension to herring. Once the herring are on board and in the hold the search begins for another shoal, and the men rest until the nets are shot again. In white fishing there may be little time between gutting and sorting and when the net must be heaved again.

The most recent technology, purse seining, combines features of both the seine-netting and drift-netting but on a more grandiose scale. The net, the boat, and the crew size is larger than any other method of fishing. Once a good "mark" of fish is found with the aid of the echosounder, the boat literally surrounds a whole school of fish with its nets. The nets have a depth of 450 feet and are over 1500 feet in circumference. As soon as the fish are surrounded, the net is drawn together like a purse and hauled alongside the boat. The fish are then pumped into the hold, where they are refrigerated. The only fish caught by the pursers are of the pelagic variety. Because of the size of the nets, fishing is not continuous but instead occurs only when the mark is good. Thus, a purse-netter may spend days searching for fish and only one day filling the hold. One consequence of this is that fishermen are often physically idle for days at a time. However, Goodlad (1971) suggests that this may cause psychological anxiety among purse-net fishermen.

There has been a growing resentment among many herring fishermen toward the purse-netters. Herring are becoming more scarce, and recently there have been governmental bans and quotas on catches. Many fishermen believe that the pursers

Figure 4
Methods Of Fishing*

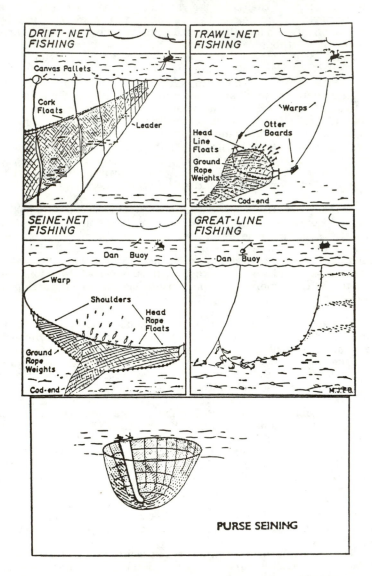

will eventually deplete herring resources, and they would like to see quotas on catches. Many fishermen believe that the pursers will eventually deplete herring resources, and they would like to see this technology stopped. Part of this resentment is also a reaction to the fact that many of the pursers are foreign flagships, mostly from the Scandinavian countries, that are able to fish in areas off the coasts of Scotland prohibited to Scottish fishermen. More will be said about this later in the section on collective actions by Scottish fishermen.

The Market

The market is where fish are sold at auction. Starting in the early morning, boats unload their iced boxes of gutted and sorted fish. The boxes are arranged in straight rows, each box having the name of a fishsales company. At the white-fish sales there are boxes of whiting, lemon sole, haddock, skate, ling, cod, monk, prawn, shrimp, and the occasional large halibut. Just before the morning market is scheduled to begin, usually around 8:30, the area begins to fill with sellers and buyers, occasional visitors or tourists, and a few retired fishermen or fishworkers who come to the market for a "fry"* and a "news" with their friends. Auctioning usually begins at one end of the market and works down to the opposite end where boats may still be unloading fish. The auctioneers are employed by the fishsales company and are paid a percent of the sales they make. The auction begins when one of the auctioneers stands on the top edges of a fish box and signals he is about to begin. In a semi-circle around him are the buyers, some from fish factories nearby, some who are distributors to local fish merchants and restaurants, and some who buy for other fishsales companies. The fish are sold by the box, by species, and by size. Buyers and sellers know each other, so the auctioneer is familiar with the subtle signs used by buyers to indicate their bids. The auctioning continues at a rapid pace with auctioneers changing when the box names change to another fishsales company. Those who buy follow the movement from row to row, putting tags with their names on the boxes they purchased.

The market floor soon becomes slippery from the fish, and both buyers and sellers walk carefully on the top edges of boxes to avoid slipping. As the auction proceeds the purchased fish are taken to trucks, which carry them to their destinations. By 10:30 or so the fish have been sold, the market floor is being washed down, the buyers and sellers have dispersed, and the retired fishermen have returned home, their fry protected in a plastic bag at their side. The same procedure is followed if the market has an afternoon sale.

**Fry: a small number of fish that are given away.

The prices paid for fish vary according to local and international demands and the amount of a particular fish that is available. There is, at present, legislation guaranteeing a minimum price paid for a box of fish. Some fish is sold "off the market." Fishermen may sell directly to consumers such as restaurants, or they may negotiate with fish-meal companies to sell "rounders"--fish, usually whiting, that have not been gutted. Fish sold in this way avoid the auctioneer's fee and, in some cases, avoid being taxed as income.

The sale of herring is somewhat different. Buyers will examine a sample of the herring in the boat's hold. The bid price is for a weight unit such as a tonne, a metric ton.

How Fishermen are Paid

There are, at present, two systems for paying fishermen, depending upon the ownership of the boat: the "wage" system and the "share" system. The wage system is practiced by the off-shore trawler fleet, which sails out of large ports such as Aberdeen. These trawlers are large in size and fish further from their ports than the smaller in-shore fleet. They usually stay at sea for at least three weeks and up to a month or more. Unlike the in-shore fleet, the boats are owned by land-based corporations and are viewed as another business interest of these corporations. The fishermen who sail on them are "hired hands" who work for wages plus some percentage of the catch. This means they have a guaranteed income regardless of how successful the fishing has been. They enjoy the same legislative protections as land-based workers. The only exceptions to this are the skipper and the mate, neither of whom has a guaranteed wage. Their contracts are for each trip and their incomes are some proportion of the catch.

Gamrie fishermen are all share fishermen, and their income is directly related to the amount of fish caught and the price paid for those fish. Thus, their incomes vary from week to week. The distribution of the boat's income follows a rather simple formula. The gross income of the boat is the amount received from the sale of fish. From this amount is deducted all operating expenses such as fuel, ice, and food stores, rental of radios, radar, echosounder and navigator, and any costs associated with operating the boat's van or car. The remaining amount is the boat's profit for that week. The profit is then divided equally between the boat and the crew. The boat's half goes to the owner or owners and is used to pay for any capital investments, such as repayment of loans, purchase of equipment, or boat maintenance. If there are no capital requirements this amount becomes the investor's profit. The other half is divided equally among the crew, which may or may not include the skipper-owner. The only exception to equal division among the

76

crew is when a crew member is paid part of a share. Usually novice fishermen are paid a "half share," or half of what the other crew members receive. This amount may be increased to three-quarters when the skipper decides that that person is making a greater contribution to the boat. Ultimately the novice will receive a full share. The amount paid to a crew member is his gross income. From that amount he is responsible for paying income taxes as well as health and unemployment payments.

Most fishermen are reluctant to talk about their salaries. When they do, it is most likely to be in reference to a good week. From what information I was able to gather, incomes have decreased slightly between 1974 and 1981. In 1974, a deck hand's income was between £130 and £170 per week. Estimating a 30 percent reduction for taxes and other obligations, the net income ranged from £91 to £119. This was a very good wage for workers in Britain. For example, Fricke (1974) reported that crew members on cargo ships were being paid £26 per week gross. By 1981 these same deck hands had an average net income between £56 and £70. These figures may be somewhat misleading. Fishermen are only paid for the weeks they work. If the boat is down, they may collect unemployment, but this is far less than they would make even on a poor week. In addition, it is usual for boats to be put in drydock for a week or two in order to have yearly maintenance done, and if the weather is bad enough, the boat will also stay in port. Thus, while fishing is a year-round job, it is rare that one works a full year.

The structure of the share system requires that crews trust the skipper. It is possible for share fishermen on one boat to be paid less than those on another boat, even though the gross earnings for both boats are the same. The largest deduction from a boat's earning is typically the boat's expenses. If one rents equipment, that is a deduction. If one buys equipment, that is a capital investment and that expense comes from the owner's share of the profit. Silent agreements with suppliers to purchase equipment and then pay for that equipment as rent result in the crew members receiving less pay.

Another example of how incomes of crew members may be reduced is in a second meaning of the term "share." Persons who invest in boats are often given a share of the boat's income. These may be retired skippers, merchants, or others who have lent money for capital expenditures. Shares may also be given to experts or specialists, e.g. the mate who skippers a second boat or an engineer whose services are defined as valuable. During the year they are paid the same as any deck hand, but at the end of the calendar year, usually around Christmas, they receive a bonus. The bonus comes from businesses such as grocers, chandlers, fuel and ice suppliers, mechanics, and

77

fishsales companies whose income is derived from fishing. Some pay a fixed amount; others pay some percentage of sales to that boat. This percentage varies between 9 and 20 percent. A person who has a share in the boat will receive some proportion of these monies, which have the attraction of being "off the books" and not subject to taxation. During the year, of course, bonuses are calculated as part of the boat's expense and result in lowered incomes. Just how widespread these practices are is impossible to estimate. Most skippers pay their crew some kind of bonus at Christmas. Whether this is done will depend upon the debts the owners have. Those who do not pay such a bonus or pay only a small bonus are generally regarded as "greedy" by their crews and others, and they often encounter problems in keeping or recruiting crew members.

The actual mechanics of wage payments are the responsibility of the boat's fishsales representative. Most fishsales companies have offices in ports where fish is auctioned, and most boats are represented by one of these companies. It is the fishsales company's responsibility to auction the fish caught by its customers and to keep the boat's records of income and expenses. At the end of the week the skipper will receive a statement of the boat's earnings along with individual pay packets, in cash, for each crew member. For being the boat's representative and keeping its records, the company charges a fee of between three and six percent of the boat's gross earnings.

Legal Status of Fishermen

The variability of wages and the rather unique relationship between crew members and skippers has had interesting implications for the legal status of fishermen. In Napier's (1976) review of employment and social legislation concerning fishermen, he points out that until recently the courts had consistently ruled that fishermen are essentially partners in a business rather than employees and therefore not covered under labor legislation. Fishermen were excluded from the 1906 Workmen's Compensation Act, the 1911 National Insurance Act, and the 1920 Unemployment Insurance Act. It was not until after World War II, with the major restructuring of the welfare system, that share fishermen were extended the same rights and privileges as other workers.

One effect of these exclusions has been mentioned in the section on health and illness. But there were others. Widows of men lost at sea while fishing either had to rely on relatives or friends or to declare themselves paupers and appeal for help from the county council. Fishermen who could not go to sea because of the weather or because their boats were damaged either had to seek employment on land or to rely on others.

Descriptions of Gamrie in the past (Watt, 1974) and conversations with older residents confirm that families and individuals had to cope with many personal misfortunes because of the lack of social legislation. At the same time, villagers will say that there was more cooperation among villagers in the past than there is now. Being subject to the same sorts of misfortunes may indeed have led to increased community solidarity. Through a spirit of generalized reciprocity, one can anticipate personal problems. Helping someone who is out of work or sick establishes a debt that one may expect to be repaid at a later date. Such a debt is not specifically the obligation of an individual but, rather of a moral community--a family, a kinship group, or the village itself. Further, these obligations and expectations are shared with people with whom one interacts on a daily basis. Today, however, if one is sick an outside agent or agency takes responsibility. If one is out of work, one goes on the dole.* Widows and orphans are supported by the state. The net effect of such social legislation is a loosening of village responsibilities and an increase of individual independence. Survivals of these past forms of obligations have already been cited in reference to the boat launching and the search for the lost fishermen. This does not in any way imply that the quality of life of people in the village has not benefited from this legislation. It most certainly has. But the organization of the village has changed, and part of the change can be explained as the consequences of social legislation.

*Being on the dole: collecting unemployment insurance.

The Gamrie Fleet

The Gamrie fleet is defined as all fishing boats that are registered to skippers living in Gamrie. At present, none of these boats sails from the harbor in Gamrie. They are all registered as being from either Banff (BF) or Fraserburgh (FR). The Gamrie fleet size has been decreasing since 1890, as illustrated in Table 4.

Table 4
Number of Boats Registered to
Skippers living in Gamrie and Crovie, 1890-1978

| Year | Number of Boats | |
	Gamrie	Crovie
1890	92	54
1901	89	44
1914	66	34
1920	56	28
1938	43	23
1957	44	--
1978	33	--

The boats in the Gamrie fleet in 1890 were all sail-powered and must have been small, as there were only 195 fishermen in the village, or 2.1 fishermen per boat. Given their size, they could use the local harbor facilities. By 1901 there had been little change, though the number of fishermen per boat had increased slightly to 2.4 per boat. The figures for 1920 reflect changes in the Gamrie fleet. Of the boats that year, 25 percent were powered by sail, 43 percent had been converted to motor, and 32 percent were steam-powered. By 1938, there were no sail boats over 30 feet in length. The number of motor-driven craft in the 30 feet and above category increased during the next decade. In 1948, 46 percent of the larger craft were motor-powered.

When I went into the field in 1974 there were no more steam-powered boats. Of the 37 boats registered to Gamrie skippers, 33 were over 50 feet in length. Most were dual purpose, being used for both herring and white fish. The median age of the boats in the fleet was 13 years. Eight boats had been built within the last five years, and four were over 30 years old. Almost all the boats had both radar and Decca navigators and all had echosounders.

The fleet decreased to 33 by 1978. A number of older boats had been replaced, and some had been refurbished through grants from either the White Fish Authority or the

80

Herring Industrial Board. By 1981 a few more new boats were added, including two purse-netters.

Between the years 1978 and 1981 there had been a few foreclosures on Gamrie boats. A number of events had happened in those years that increased the running costs of boats. In order to conserve fish stocks there was a total ban on herring and an increase in the area where fishing for certain species of fish was prohibited. Fish prices generally decreased during this period, and there was a marked increase in the price of fuel. Many fishermen had placed orders for new boats based upon the profitable years prior to 1976. Part of the purchase costs for these new boats was to be paid by the sale of the old boat. However, the prices for used boats declined as more and more boats went into receivership. Given these circumstances, owners and skippers had few options. The old boat could be sold at a loss in the hope that the new boat's earnings would cover that loss. Or the old boat could be kept and used for fishing until the prices on older boats increased. This would mean that someone would have to be found to skipper the old boat during the waiting period. Either of these options might lead to losing both the old and the new boat, depending upon fish prices and the success of the boats. For a few local fishermen this is what happened. The total ban on herring was removed in 1981, but quotas on catches were established. It is quite possible that these changes will result a modification of Gamrie's reputation as the herring village of the Moray Firth. In the future, the Gamrie fleet may be in the white fish business along with the other villages and towns along this coast.

Residency and Age Characteristics of the Gamrie Fleet

In 1978 there were 226 crew members on the 33 boats over 50 feet registered to skippers living in Gamrie. Of these crew members, only 99 were presently living in Gamrie. Thus, the Gamrie fleet, if defined as all those boats registered to skippers from Gamrie, is not the same as Gamrie fishermen, who would be all the fishermen living in Gamrie. However, it is possible that many of the non-Gamrie fishermen were born in Gamrie and because of that connection, have become crew members on Gamrie boats.

In order to ascertain how many of the Gamrie crew members had been born in the village, but were no longer residents, I constructed Table 5. It is clear from these data that present residency is related to where one is born. Fishermen tend to be living in their birth place. It is also clear that a "Gamrie connection," insofar as birth place is concerned, is not a factor in the recruitment of fishermen for the Gamrie fleet.

The present residency of crew members living outside the

81

village is concentrated in two places. Fifty-seven percent of the non-resident crew live in the Fraserburgh area east of the village and 34 percent live west of the village in the Macduff area. The remaining nine percent live in other coastal towns or villages.

Table 5
Place of Birth and
Present Residency of Gamrie Fleet

| | | Present Residence | |
		Gamrie	Not Gamrie
Place of Birth*	Gamrie	77	15
	Not Gamrie	16	88

*Total is less than number in the fleet because of missing data on place of birth

The average age of fishermen on Gamrie boats is 37.1 years. However, there are some differences in average ages if one considers the type of work one does on the boat. The oldest average age was for cooks. On the 16 boats where someone was given the designation "cook", their average age was 45.6. Skippers were somewhat younger with an average age of 43.1 years. Engineers, where listed (15 boats), had a mean age of 40.7, and mates were the same average age as the remaining crew, 37.1.

Using individual boats rather than the whole fleet, one finds that most skippers are older than the boat average. Seventy-three percent of the skippers were older than the crews on their boats. The age of mates was equally distributed. Half were above the average age, half below. Sixty-seven percent of the engineers were older than the boat average. Seventy-five percent of the cooks were older than the rest of the crew.

From these age differences, one may infer something about careers and age of fishermen. Assuming that one goes to sea at about the age of 15 or 16, it takes approximately 27 years before one becomes a skipper. Engineers have an average of 23 years experience at sea and mates about 19 years. Cooks are a special category; they tend to be either the youngest or the oldest

82

person on a boat. Traditionally, the youngest and least experienced person was assigned the job of cook. This was at a time when boys of 13 or 14 went to sea. They were responsible for preparing all the meals and were given small tasks associated with fishing. Once they had proven their competence as a fisherman and a berth became available, they were given a share and other young boys took their place. Much of the "seasoning" of young fishermen in traditional technologies had to do with physical maturation. Before mechanization, a fishermen's work required physical stamina to shoot and haul nets. Today, such physical stamina is not required. Rather, the young fisherman must adjust to working around the clock. The work-sleep cycles on a boat are erratic. They may get to sleep only a few hours before the next catch of fish is brought aboard, then it may be hours before the sorting, gutting, and packing is complete and they can return to their bunks. There are no shifts on a fishing boat. The crew works if there is a good "mark" and, if no fish are spotted, then one can sleep. This modern fishing cycle is often difficult for older fishermen, and to legitimatize their receiving a share they are given the cook's job. The cook works during the daytime preparing three meals a day. In addition, he is responsible for ordering stores, washing dishes, and, on the large pursers, cleaning the commons areas. It is interesting to note that almost half of the boats did not specify a person as cook. Nevertheless someone on the boat had that responsibility. Usually smaller boats do not have a full-time cook; rather, someone does the cooking as well as some other task.

Of all the jobs on a fishing boat, that of cook has the least prestige.* In reviewing the residency of various positions on the boat it was found that only 19 percent of those noted as cooks lived in Gamrie. In a sense their marginality on the boat was reflected in their residential marginality. Mates, who are integral to the running of a boat, tended to live in the village. Fifty-four percent of them lived in Gamrie. The engineer is a crucial member of the boat's crew. He has the job of keeping the boat and the equipment in order. If the boat breaks down or equipment fails this can mean lost income and, in some cases, loss of life. Yet, only 13 percent of those fishermen with the title engineer reside in the village. This finding seems to contradict the suggestion that marginality on a boat is reflected in residential marginality. Yet the engineer is anything but marginal. I would suggest that the engineer is the only technical "expert" on a fishing boat. Being an engineer requires knowledge of diesel engines, hydraulics, and electronics, and those who have this kind of expertise are

---

*For an analysis of how differences in age prestige and occupational prestige is resolved on a Hebridean fishing boat see: Prattis, 1973.

recruited from wherever they live. Deck hands, cooks, and even mates can be trained by skippers. Engineers cannot. Therefore residency is less important as a consideration for hiring an engineer than for any other job on a fishing boat.

Thus far I have examined the attributes of age and residency separately. However if one combines these two, another dimension of the Gamrie fleet is revealed. Chart 3 shows the age and residency distribution for the fleet. The most striking observation is the under-representation of village fisherman in the 25-29 year old category. In none of the other categories is the difference more than two percent, but in this category it is nine percent. In order to test whether this under-representation was simply a reflection of a lack of males between the ages of 25-29 in the village, chart 4 was constructed. This chart reveals that the proportion of males in this age category living in the village is only three percent more than the Gamrie males fishing on Gamrie boats. And with the exception of those in the 40-44 and 55-59 age categories, the age distribution of the village is similar to the age distribution of Gamrie fishermen in the fleet. Thus, while the number of local fishermen are under-represented in the Gamrie fleet, they are, nonetheless, representative of the village age structure.

Chart III
Age Distribution of Gamrie Fishing Fleet
By Residence of Fishermen

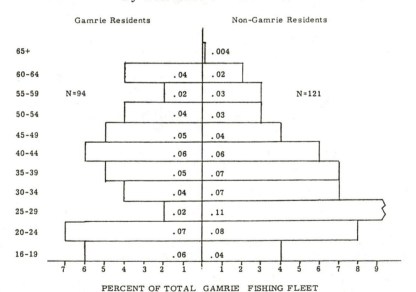

PERCENT OF TOTAL GAMRIE FISHING FLEET

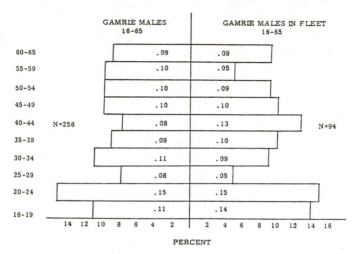

Chart IV
Comparison of Male Gamrie Residents, Ages 16-65
To Gamrie Males in the Fishing Fleet, Ages 16-65

	GAMRIE MALES 16-65	GAMRIE MALES IN FLEET 16-65
60-65	.09	.09
55-59	.10	.05
50-54	.10	.09
45-49	.10	.10
40-44	.08	.13
35-39	.09	.10
30-34	.11	.09
25-29	.08	.05
20-24	.15	.15
16-19	.11	.14

N=256   N=94

14 12 10 8 6 4 2   2 4 6 8 10 12 14 16

PERCENT

Recruitment: Getting a Berth

The characteristics of any given crew are the product of the recruitment process.   In single-occupation communities like Gamrie, where people are bound together by overlapping kinship networks, it comes as no surprise that many crew members are related to each other.   Whether those kinship ties involve occupational obligations is reviewed in this section.

In the village, males either become fishermen or they move away and take up other occupations.   If a young male indicates a desire to become a fishermen he will be given an opportunity to work on a boat.   This opportunity may be to work for a part share until he is ready to take full responsibilities as a fisherman, or it may be to fill in for a fisherman who is not going to sea because of some commitment on land.   The main prerequisite to being given an opportunity to try fishing is that the person be a resident of the village.   For example, a young man and his wife moved into the village in 1974 to set up a pottery.   He had obtained a grant to build a kiln and had set up his shop in an old store on the Main Street.   Needing money to get the business going, he made it known that he would like to go to sea, and he was soon asked to fill in for a fisherman who could not go out.   He worked off and on until he had the capital he needed to work full time in the pottery.   Neither this man nor his wife was locally connected, but because they lived in the village he came under the general expectation that males

85

living in the village should be given an opportunity to try fishing.

Being given this opportunity does not guarantee that a fisherman will be given a "berth"--a permanent position on a boat. There are a number of instances of local males who were taken on a boat and then were either "put ashore"--terminated--or quit. The frequency of these instances, however, is small. Most fishing novices eventually become fishermen, and those who cannot adjust to fishing usually move away.

There is no formal process of recruitment. One does not find ads in the newspaper seeking fishermen for the in-shore fleet. The process is very informal. If a berth becomes available the word spreads rather rapidly. Those seeking a berth will talk to either the boat's skipper or a crew member about the possibility of obtaining that berth. Crew members may recommend people, but the authority to hire rests with the skipper.

Studies of fishermen in small fishing communities generally find that kinship plays an important role in the recruitment of fishermen or fishing partners (Faris, 1966; Firestone, 1967; Nemec, 1972; Blehr, 1963; Poggie and Gersuny, 1974). In order to determine what influence kinship had in a skipper's decision to hire a crew member in the Gamrie fleet, genealogies for each of the skippers were constructed and then compared with the crew lists. It was found that on two-thirds of the boats at least one of the crewmen was related to the skipper. On ten boats that relative was the skipper's son; on two it was the skipper's father. On six there was one brother of the skipper; on three there were two brothers. Eight boats had other kin, including three sister's husbands, two father's sister's sons, one sister's son, one mother's brother, one brother's son, and a wife's brother. Whether a boat's crew had a kinsman of the skipper was related to the size of the crew. On boats with four or five in a crew, only half had a skipper's relative. Seventy-one percent of the boats with six or seven crew members had at least one related to the skipper, and on boats with eight or more the percentage increased to seventy-eight. Thus, it appears that the larger the boat, the more likely it is that the skipper will have relatives as crew members.

One notes other pairs of relatives on Gamrie boats. Nine boats had fathers and sons working together, and on two of these there were two pairs of father-son crewmen. On seven boats there were brothers working together; one boat had three brothers and two had four. When considering all these relationships for all thirty-three boats in the fleet, one finds that approximately forty percent of the crew members sail with

86

persons to whom they are related. The forty percent figure is probably an underestimate of the relatedness of crew members because the focus for this analysis was father-son and brother relations.

What explains this apparently high reliance upon kinsmen in this occupation? The first, most obvious, explanation is that the pool of labor from which fishermen are drawn is made up of persons already related. This relatedness is not just within the village, but to the nearby villages as well. It would be difficult to find a villager who could not name relatives in Macduff, Fraserburgh, and other villages along the coast. In this sense, kinship is a constant. People are hired who happen to be kinsmen; they are not hired because they are kinsmen.

Another consideration, suggested earlier, is the rather unpredictable economic nature of fishing. Skippers are almost unanimous in their condemnation of crew members who, after a few weeks of poor fishing, find a berth on another boat. This not only suggests a criticism of the skipper's fishing talents, but it also means that a new crew member has to be hired and then go through a period of adjustment on the boat. A relative of the skipper is more likely, because of their kinship ties, to stay on a boat that is not doing well. With sons, this is further reinforced by the fact that the boat will eventually become theirs.

The practice of having crews of closely related kin has been questioned by villagers. Almost every year one reads of a fishing boat being lost, and with it members from a single family. One way to avoid this is a simple exchange between skippers. Your son fishes with me; my son fishes with you. One does find this practice occasionally when a skipper's son first goes to sea. However, these sons almost invariably end up on their father's boats.

One might predict that the Gamrie in-shore fleet will continue to be characterized by crews of persons related to each other. But if current trends toward larger and more technologically sophisticated boats continue, one should expect to see a greater reliance upon technicians who have gone through specialized training. That already happens with engineers, who are less likely to be relatives of skippers and who do not live in the village. The traditional methods of recruiting fishermen from among kinsmen worked well when technologies were simple and fishing was a labor intensive kind of work. With each change in technology, however, came a new specialist, with a resultant change in the organization of the boat. With steam power came the fireman; with diesel came the engineer. Changes in the size of boat changed the size of the crew and altered the division of labor. It was one thing to fish with a brother or father on a fifie, but it is quite another to carry out a limited number of specialized tasks on a purse-netter. In the future, skippers might hire relatives if they have the appropriate skills needed to operate the newer boats, and indeed relatives with necessary skills may be preferred crewmen. But given a choice between a relative without the skill and a non-relative with the skill, the skilled person will be the crewman.

Work Cycles: Seine Net, Trawl-Net, Purser

Three basic work cycles followed along the Moray Firth: the "day tripper," the "week tripper," and the "extended tripper." Each is associated with different technologies. The "day tripper" is a smaller boat, usually under 50 feet, that uses the seine-net method of fishing. The crews on these boats range from two to four men. Boats under 50 feet are permitted to fish closer to land and hence closer to markets. But this makes the the skipper more dependent upon the migration behaviors of fish species. Depending upon the time of the year and the available species of fish, the day-tripper's day begins in the evening or the early morning. Although there are no day-trippers in the Gamrie fleet, I was able to get out on a boat from Fraserburgh. The skipper was one of three brothers each of whom had a similar boat and with a similar name. The skipper, a man in his mid 50s, did not have any sons. His crew of two consisted of his son-in-law and his future son-in-law. The son-in-law was from the area but was of country background. His future son-in-law was from England, and his most recent job had been as a lorry driver. The skipper had been a fisherman all his life and was one of the few fishermen in his age category who still wore an earring. Earrings have been worn by fishermen from the sixteenth century (Anson, 1965). Some believed that the earring would protect them from drowning as well as being a cure for, or protection against a number of diseases. Occasionally one still sees young fishermen with earrings, but the practice is no longer commonplace.

The trip on this seine-netter began on Sunday evening at 6:00. This is rather unusual because most fishing boats will not leave the harbor until "the back o' Sunday." After getting on board and checking the engines and the equipment, the boat left its berth about 6:30. After an hour and a half steam from the harbor, but still in sight of land, the net was shot. The skipper had gotten a mark on the echosounder and decided it was large enough to make the shot. The sequence followed the description for seine-netting given earlier. A lighted buoy was dropped off the side; the boat steamed in a wide circle and the warp, then the net, and finally the other warp were played out until the lighted buoy was reached. The two warps were fastened down and the net was towed as the warps were winched back into the boat. Each of the crew members operated a winch for each warp. The speed of the winches was regulated by the skipper. As the boat steamed ahead he could look out of the wheelhouse and see if the warps were being winched evenly. If they were not, he would shout to one or the other of the crew to either speed up or slow down the winch. Actually, the warps can be winched at the same rate by visual cues. Attached to each warp at fixed distances are pieces of brightly colored material. So long as these markers stay aligned with each other the net is being heaved properly. Once the metal wires become visible, the boat is stopped, the rope warp is detached and the net is pulled alongside with the aid of the power block. As the net is brought alongside, the cod end floats to the surface and the crew can see how successful the shot was. With the help of a derrick to which a rope is attached, the bag is lifted out of the water and swung over the deck. The cod end of the net is untied and the fish drop on the deck into what is called a fishpond. A fishpond is created by boards held in place by vertical metal channels. The boards are about two feet high and are usually only in place when fish are brought aboard. On this boat there were two of these fishponds. The catch brought in by the net was placed in the larger of the two. In addition to fish there were starfish, mussels, and other shell fish. The fish were shoveled from the larger fishpond into the smaller, and there was some preliminary sorting of fish as well as throwing away of some of the more obvious rubbish. If the haul is large, only part of the net is emptied at one time. The process of bringing the fish aboard is repeated until the net is completely empty. From shooting to hauling took about one hour. The gutting and sorting time varied by the size of the catch.

As the crew was sorting and gutting the fish, the skipper began looking for another mark. This type of fishing often yields a variety of fish. On the night that I spent on this boat they caught lemon sole, cod, haddock, skate, monk, and whiting. The fish were gutted and then placed into boxes by species and size. After the gutting was completed, the deck was washed and sea water was sprayed on the gutted fish to further clean them. If a mark was found before the fish were gutted, the crew shot the net and then returned to gutting and sorting. The net was shot and hauled five times before it got too dark to fish. Between 11 p.m. and 1 a.m. the crew went below for a "piece"--something to eat. In addition to eating the sandwiches and sweet rolls they had brought along, tea was made. The rest of the time was spent talking or listening to the boat's radio. The seemingly constant conversations between fishermen were punctuated here and there by hymn singing. And while I had difficulty understanding what was said, the reactions of the boat's crew to these conversations clearly indicated they were more recreational than inspirational.

Between one and two o'clock in the morning it got lighter

and the fishing began again. Three more shots were made and we were back at the market by 6 a.m., in plenty of time for the morning auction. After the fish were unloaded, the boat was berthed and the fishermen went home to sleep. I was told that this was not a typical week day. On Monday evening they would go back to sea between 5 and 6 p.m. and fish until midnight. This would permit them to be home by 2 a.m.

These small seine-netters fill a gap in what otherwise is an unequal production of fish for the market. The larger weekly trippers will leave Monday morning and are not likely to return to the market until mid-week. The day-trippers fish in time for the Monday market and Monday night's fishing will supply fish for the Tuesday market. If the market relied only on the larger week-trippers there would be little need to have the Monday and Tuesday markets. There are also some advantages for the fishermen. Being only a few miles off land means that there is less risk to the boat and the crew in case of bad weather. The work cycle itself makes it possible for the fishermen to return home each day rather than being at sea for a week. The major disadvantage to this type of fishing is that the fishermen are not likely to become wealthy. The earnings are adequate, but skippers often have the same living standards as the deck hands.

In this type of fishing the division of labor is rather simple. The skipper has responsibility for the boat. The decision where to fish and when the nets are shot is his. In addition, he operates the power-block that brings the net alongside the boat. Back at the market he operates the derrick, used to lift the boxes of fish from the boat to the market floor. The deck hands have responsibility for the mechanics of shooting and hauling nets, as well as gutting and sorting fish.

The trawler on which I spent time was a week-tripper. It was fishing for pout, a small fish in the herring family that is used for fish meal and oil. Normally this boat leaves on Sunday evening but because of gale warnings we did not go to the boat until Monday afternoon. After storing my gear--a sleeping bag and "oilskins"--in the berth to which I was assigned, the cook made tea. We waited until the 6 p.m. forecast. It turned out to be bad--gale force 6 to 8.* The next forecast was not until 9 p.m., so it was decided that some of us would walk into Fraserburgh.

Three of the crew and I went to the movies. The others went elsewhere. We returned to the boat a little before nine. The weather report was somewhat better so the skipper decided to sail. As soon as we got underway, the cook prepared

---

*Gale force 12 is a hurricane.

"breakfast," fried eggs, baked beans and blood pudding. The trip out on the day tripper had been calm. The trip out that night on this boat was quite different. The boat pitched up and down and side to side. After eating my eggs I began to feel a little sick to my stomach. I attributed this at first to the closeness of the crew's quarters and the smell of diesel fuel. The crew's quarters were aft, behind the engine room. Along the sides of the quarters are the bunks, two high and three long, to accommodate 12 crew-members. A low bench ringed the quarters, and in the center was a table. To get from one end of the quarters to the other it was necessary to walk on this bench. So I sat between two fishermen eating fried eggs that had been cooked in lard, on a boat going out in less than ideal weather, breathing fumes from the diesel engine only a few feet away. It wasn't long after finishing breakfast that I excused myself to go up on deck. At 11:30 p.m. and again at midnight I returned to the sea what my gracious hosts had fed me for breakfast. I returned to the crew's quarters, crawled into my sleeping bag, and fell into a sound sleep.

I awoke early the next morning to a loud metallic banging on the deck above. Seeing nobody in the crew's quarters I got out of my berth and went up on the deck to see the net being shot. On a trawler, the net is shot first and is then followed by danlines and steel wired sweeps attached to the "doors". The net is thrown over the stern and spreads out as the boat moves forward. When the net and the danlines are fully out, the doors are removed from stands on either side of the stern. As soon as they are in the water, the boat picks up speed and the wire warps are released from winches located forward of the wheelhouse. Once these are played out, they are made fast. The forward motion of the boat pulls the net, the mouth of which is held open by doors. The net was towed about three and one-half hours and was heaved in a similar fashion to the seine-netter, with some exceptions. On the boat were the skipper and five crewmen, including the engineer, the mate, and the cook. In the hauling operation, the deck hands worked the winches for the lines; the mate and the engineer secured the doors, and the cook ran a drum winch that brought the net aboard. All of this was coordinated by the skipper, who could see the forward winches from the wheelhouse and could speak to the crew members on the stern through a two-way speaker system.

When the net was emptied on the deck, the white fish that had been caught were separated from the pout. They were gutted and sorted as on the seine-net boat and they were then iced. Because the boat stays out longer it is necessary to ice any white fish that are caught. The pout were put directly into the hold and care was taken to equalize the weight in the various compartments in the hold. On Tuesday night we ran out of ice. More white fish had been caught than had been anticipated. The skipper tried to make the 9 a.m. market but we were too late. The fish was unloaded for the 2 p.m. market instead. The pout were removed from the hold by an elevator to a truck on the quay. This elevator was hand loaded by the deck hands. They shoveled what was by then rather rotten fish onto the elevator in about two hours. After this, the deck and the hold were washed down with water. As soon as the unloading was completed, the boat moved to the ice house, where it took on another load of ice and then steamed back out to sea to finish the week's fishing.

The division of labor on this boat is more complex than on the seine-netter. The mate is second in command and usually has skipper's papers. If the skipper does not go to sea for some reason, the mate will take the boat. The mate has responsibility for the nets and the deck activities. The engineer is responsible for maintaining the main and auxillary engines and motors, as well as the equipment on deck. The cook prepares all the meals and the deck hands work the winches, gut and sort white fish, and load pout. However, with the exception of the skipper, none of these positions a full-time specialist. The engineer, the mate, and the cook are all involved in shooting and hauling the net. Thus, while these positions do demand specialized skills they also carry responsibilities that are shared with all other crew members except the skipper.

In spite of increasing specialization in the division of labor associated with the change from seine-netting to trawling, this boat, like so many others, had kinsmen as crew members. The engineer on this boat was the skipper's brother and one of the hands was his son. Two other members of the boat were related, but more distantly.

This boat is an example of what happened when the market for used boats fell. The skipper had bought another boat and had it completely refitted with the aid of grants and loans. He expected to be able to pay off part of the loan for the new boat with the sale of this one, but by the time the new boat was launched, the old one could not be sold. Therefore he decided to keep the old boat running along with the new one. At present, the mate acts as skipper. The engineer, who is from the Highlands, is not related to any of the crew. Still on the boat is the skipper's son and a deck hand who is unrelated. The position of cook has been eliminated and the skipper does the cooking. While this decrease in personnel increases the amount of work every member of the boat has to do, it can also increase their earnings. Of special note is the fact that the engineer's position was not eliminated and an "outsider" with the prerequisite skills was employed.

92

The "extended tripper" is the purse-netter. These boats have crews of ten to fifteen men. At least two people are certified and are able to skipper the boat. On crew lists one notes two or more mates, an engineer, and a cook. Some of these boats have a search-boat handler to pilot a small boat with the purse-net around the shoal and a net boss who controls the shooting and hauling of the net. Because these boats are specialized and are so large, they may have to stay out for weeks at a time in order to pay expenses. Their range is greater, so they are able to maximize the profits from the catch by selecting from a number of markets, in both Scotland and Europe. Wherever the prices are higher for herring or mackerel is where they sell their fish. Depending upon the season and the market, these boats will stay out two or three weeks at a time. They may also be tied up in the harbor for two or three weeks at a time.

Even on large specialized boats one is sure to find some relative of the skipper. However, relatives are less likely to be among the trained technicians, as on other smaller boats.

A major social consequence of changing fishing technologies is an increasing differentiation between skipper and crew. This change was already cited in the discussion of capitalization of fishing boats where the role of skipper changed from fishermen to that of land-based financier. It is also seen in residence patterns. The movement of skippers to exclusive neighborhoods clearly marks them as more affluent than other crew members. These differences are also indicated by the sleeping arrangements on newer, larger boats. Most of the newer boats are designed with the skipper's berth separate from those of the crew and behind closed doors. Thus, social distinctions are translated into spatial distinctions.

That changes have occurred in capitalization and shipboard interaction as a result of changing boat design and fishing technology is clear. However, these are not the only changes. In the next section the consequences of these changes for beliefs, namely fishing magic, will be examined.

Fishing Magic

There is no practice so universally observed in fishing communities as some form of what might be called "fishing magic." Some type of proscriptive or prescriptive practice relative to the abundance of the catch or the weather or personal safety has been recorded among fishing peoples in all parts of the world. Folklorists like Anson (1965) and Gregor (1881) catalogued many such practices among fishermen in the North-East of Scotland during the late 1800s and early 1900s. Central to fishing magic was the avoidance of certain words

93

thought to bring misfortune. According to Anson (1965):

> On no account could reference be made on a
> Scottish fishing vessel to a minister, kirk,
> pig, salmon, trout, hare, rabbit or dog. . .
> Before hauling lines it was strictly forbidden
> to mention a horse, cow, dog, pig, hare,
> rabbit, rat, and certain other quadrupeds
> (131)

Cove (1978) observed that tabooed words in Cornwall were clergy, women, and rabbits. Poggie and Gersuny (1974), in their study of Rhode Island fishermen and lobstermen, found that the three most standard customs were: "Don't turn hatch cover upside down"; "Don't whistle because it whistles up a breeze"; and "Don't mention pig on board." Similar practices are reported by Löfgren (n.d.) for Swedish fishermen in Noorland and Scania.

My first encounter with proscriptive words was on the seine-netter. In a conversation with the deck hands I mentioned the word "pig." Their reaction was first to look at each other, then laugh. They made it clear that I should not say that word on board or the skipper might get angry enough to steam back to port and put me ashore. They thought the practice was silly, but they were not willing to test the tolerance of the skipper and therefore avoided its use. On the trawler I asked about this practice and not only did they review the words that the "old time" fishermen avoided, but they also insisted that modern fishermen don't believe this any more.

The most frequently mentioned tabooed words by Gamrie fishermen were: salmon, pig, and rabbit or hare. They also mentioned not whistling on board and avoidance of a minister or "women of a certain kind." Having mentioned these avoided behaviors or words, they often went to great lengths to demonstrate that these practices are no longer meaningful. They pointed out that bacon was eaten frequently while out on the boat, and salmon, when they are occasionally caught, would be put on the menu. Rabbit and hare are not eaten frequently by villagers although reference was made to their being rather popular before an outbreak of myxomatosis in the area some years ago.

The tabooed practices and words suggest four categories of concern--the catch, weather, the boat, and personal safety. The prohibited words listed above would avoid against the catch being poor. However, there are no words which insure a good catch. The avoidance of whistling is an obvious reference to the weather. Some breeze was necessary to operate a sail boat; too much wind, and a sail boat is in trouble. Thus the reference here is to whistling up a gale-force wind, not just a breeze. The avoidance of the minister and "women of a certain kind" reflects a concern for the boat because if either one was seen prior to going out to sea, the fishermen were suppose to go home and wait until the next day. The belief was that something would happen to the boat if this practice was not followed.

In only one of these categories--the catch--did I find any modern practices one might classify as magic, but magic that was idiosyncratic rather than collectively recognized or practiced. This I call "net magic." Most boats carry a spare net that can be used if one is badly damaged. On trawlers, one notes that with almost every haul the net has been torn. Between shots the net is mended. Occasionally the net will be so badly torn that the spare net is used in its place. Some skippers feel that some nets catch better than others, even if those nets were made of the same material and by the same manufacturer. This belief can result in a long time spent mending the "lucky" net and therefore missing a shot.

Another instance of idiosyncratic magic was related to me by a fisherman from another village. I was told of a skipper who would not change his clothes after he had a good haul. While it is usual for fishermen to wear the same clothes throughout the week, they usually take their clothes home on the weekends to be washed. In this case, the skipper continued to wear the same clothes from week to week so long as the fishing was good.*

Where personal safety was concerned I did note some practices even among young fishermen. A few young Gamrie fishermen wore earrings and some wore religious medals. But I suspect that these are more ornamental than protective.

If the reports by folklorists of magic among fishermen along the Moray Firth represent widespread practices of the eighteenth and early nineteenth century, what accounts for their disappearance among contemporary fishermen? One explanation comes from Malinowski (quoted from Gmelch, 1971):

> We find magic wherever the elements of chance and accident, and the emotional play between hope and fear have a wide and extensive range. We do not find magic wherever the pursuit is certain, reliable, and well under the control of rational methods (39).

*For a similar practice see: Gmelch, 1971.

95

The technology of fishing practiced by the early Moray Firth fishermen was not predictable. Herring fishermen relied on natural signs--the diving Ganet, the humpback whale, or surface disturbances in the water--to tell them when to shoot their nets. Under these conditions, outcomes could not be predicted. When this method of fishing is replaced by modern technology such as the "echosounder," which "sees" fish, there is no need to use avoidance magic. If something goes wrong with the echo-sounder it is not because someone said pig or hare or salmon; it is because something in the circuitry of the machine is amiss. To correct that, an expert is called in. There is little need to avoid a practice like whistling to guarantee good weather. Rather, all that has to be done is listen to the weather forecast over the wireless. If the forcast is poor, then the boat does not go to sea or the skipper takes it home. And if fog rolls in, collision with other boats is avoided by using the radar. To find his way back to the home harbor under adverse weather conditions, the skipper switches on the Decca. This is not to say that fishing, even modern fishing, is without its perils. But when a boat is lost at sea, fishermen do not explain it as a result of a violation of ritual. Rather, it is because of poor judgment on the part of the skipper. If a skipper does not do well at fishing, it is attributed to lack of knowledge or poor equipment. The changes in boat design and fishing technology have brought with them a greater amount of certainty in fishing, and with increased certainty has come a decreased reliance upon the use of magic.

Another way of understanding such practices is by structural analysis. Structural analysis attempts to reveal hidden structures through an examination of cultural practices. Cove's (1978) analysis of the objects avoided by Cornwall and Nootkan fishermen suggests an underlying set of binary categories; land:sea; productive:non-productive. Thus, animals belonging on land should not be mentioned at sea. Hence, pig and rabbit are tabooed words at sea. Women and ministers are non-productive; fishermen are productive. Therefore women and ministers are words to be avoided while at sea. From this analysis, Cove implies that Cornwall fishermen "think" in terms of these categories. There is a small problem using this system for Moray Firth fishermen. What about salmon? The salmon is a fish and therefore part of the sea. One might suggest that salmon are caught in nets close to shore and also in fresh-water rivers during their spawning season. And this makes them somewhat different from the fish caught by the in-shore fishermen. They are obviously not land animals, but one might argue that they stand somewhere between land and sea and hence are "liminal," do not belong to one category or the other. This not only makes them difficult to categorize but according to Mary Douglas (1966) would result in their being defined as polluted, dirty, and dangerous. Since things that are polluted, dirty, or dangerous are to be avoided, the taboo on the word salmon is explained.

While the above explanation for tabooed words seems reasonable in structuralist terms, I would suggest an alternative explanation. Words are symbols and symbols are metaphors for experience. A word is not the thing, it is a symbol for the thing. Two of the tabooed words--salmon and minister--may be thought of as metaphors for the experiences of fishermen from small villages and communities all along the Moray Firth. Fishermen have traditionally come from communities that are neatly divided into two categories, outside:inside. The fishermen are the insiders. The outsiders include the minister and that which the minister represents, the kirk. This is obvious. But what of the salmon? Salmon has been and still is a prestige fish. Along with the sturgeon, its consumption has been regulated by the crown or by civil authorities. In the local community, such as Gamrie, salmon rights were controlled by the laird. The laird was not a fisherman. He was a representative of the landed aristocracy who had ties to the outside. He was not subject to local informal sanctions and controls. Most outsiders can be gotten rid of by villagers if their behavior violates local expectations. It is possible to replace the minister, the school master, even the physician. But you cannot fire the laird! Good or bad, sympathetic or unsympathetic, the laird's position of authority is fixed. I would suggest that the salmon is a symbol of the laird, and a symbol of that which makes fishermen different. At sea, fishermen were the same. They shared a common world of experience away from land. It was only when they returned to land that their differences became apparent. The avoidance of the word salmon was an avoidance of that world of difference. But, changes in fishing technology have resulted in an organization of the boat that is characterized by differences. Fishermen today live in a world of differences on both land and sea, and the reminder of those differences cannot be evaded, even metaphorically.

An explanation of the practice of avoiding "women of a certain kind" also proves problematic for structural analysis. Who is a "woman of a certain kind?" When I would ask villagers they would usually respond with a wink and the statement, "ach, you ken."* If I read these gestures and words correctly, the reference was to women with a certain moral character, e.g. unmarried mothers, the sexually active, or those that were peculiar or odd. The names of these women are not only avoided on the boat, but in the village as well. Because of this, they do not belong to any special category of names avoided only at sea and in the case of this village do not

---
*Oh, you know.

97

represent the sea:land binary opposition.

Whatever the explanation for the words or actions that were avoided by fishermen in the past, it is clear that such avoidances and practices no longer exist among those fishermen who employ modern fishing technology. Malinowski's observation that as technologies make environments more predictable there will be less reliance upon magical and ritual practices is amply documented for the Moray Firth fleet. There is, at present, more control over environmental factors in fishing than ever before. Only one other aspect of fishing is still subject to control from outside, and that is the marketing of fish. Fluctuations in market prices make it difficult to predict incomes. The fishermen of the Moray Firth are responding to these conditions of uncertainty not by magic but by social action. It is to this change that we turn next.

Getting Organized: Changing Relationships Between Fishermen

The organizational unit of fishing, up until the recent past, has been the boat. The designation "fleet" refers to a number of boats that share a harbor or a common residence of skippers. The linkages that existed between boats in the past were largely based upon friendship or kinship ties between skippers and crew members. The everyday concerns of fishing required skippers to concentrate on immediate needs, and when markets changed and competition became keen those personal, cooperative ties between boats were replaced by secrecy and further insularity of the boat. Given these conditions, it is not difficult to understand why Scottish fishermen earned the reputation of being fiercely independent. Their independence came not from their self-reliance, but rather from market situations that selected the skippers who were best able to compete for scarce resources. Scots fishermen had never been independent. From the very beginnings of fishing in Scotland, they were bound to one authority or another. First it was the laird, then the curer, and now some combination of fishsales company, bank, or governmental agency. However, a series of events in the recent past suggests a growing spirit of collectivism among fishermen.

One of the first accounts of a collective action by Scottish fishermen occurred at the end of the last century. This was in response to a new fishing technology--ring netting--that had been introduced on the West Coast of Scotland.* Similar to the purse-net technology, two boats "herded" herring into large nets. According to Wilson (1965), fishermen believed that this type of fishing would sweep the seas clean of fish. So strongly were they opposed to it that they rioted, and in some areas the

*For a detailed history of ring-netting, see: Martin,1982.

militia had to be called. Such instances of collective responses by fishermen were rare among Scottish fishermen, however, and it was not until the end of World War II that such activities were noted again.

During World War II herring fishing was extremely curtailed. The Scottish fleet was reduced by fifty percent. The Ministry of Food controlled the herring fishing and the marketing for home consumption. Because of the war, the amount of herring landed and the place of landing was shifted according to need. In spite of this, Fraserburgh was the main herring port in Scotland. Soon after the war in 1946 the herring fishery was jointly administered by the Herring Industrial Board and the Ministry of Food. During the summer season of 1946 there were a number of disputes between buyers and fishermen in the North Sea-Shetland area (Anson, 1950:81). These disputes centered mostly on prices paid by the curers. In autumn of that year the Scottish fleet went south to East Anglia. Along with the fleet went Scottish women who had contracted with the curers. A number of strikes broke out among both fishermen and the female fish workers. The fishermen wanted full seamen's food rations and the women demanded higher wages. This was primarily an action by the English fishermen. The majority of the English fleet was corporate-owned, as opposed to the individually owned boats of the Scottish fishermen. The English fishermen had only wages to lose by going on strike; the Scottish fishermen could have lost their boats.

I talked to women in Gamrie who remembered the fall of 1946. They recalled not having participated in the strikes. Women from villages and towns all along the Moray Firth were in Yarmouth and Lowestoft for the gutting. They had made the long trip with the promise of work, but being far away from home they were vulnerable. If they did not work they could not pay for their "digs."* Without an income, it might be difficult to get home. The curers told the women that if they continued to work they would be paid any additional benefits derived through the strike action. So they went back to work.

The strike action moved the Herring Industrial Board and the Ministry of Food into action. Guaranteed prices were established for the herring caught and the season turned out to be a moderate success.

A more recent action that had a marginal effect on Gamrie fishermen occurred in 1970. This was the boycott of Aberdeen harbor by the Scottish in-shore fishing fleet. The Aberdeen market had the reputation for high fish prices, so some Gamrie

---

*Digs: accomodations

boats involved in white fishing would occasionally land fish there. Prior to 1970 there had been some disputes between the large ocean-going trawlers and the smaller seine-netters. These disputes focused on two issues. One was the charge by the seine-netters that the larger steel-hulled trawlers often damaged them when maneuvering alongside the market quay. The second was that the trawlers were given preference in unloading their catch. All boats using the Aberdeen market had to be unloaded by unionized porters, or "lumpers" as they are called locally. The porters were paid by the number of boxes they unloaded, and it was far easier to unload the trawlers than the seiners. In addition, trawlers contained many more boxes of fish. The cost of unloading the catch was borne by the boat, and in the case of the seiners it was another expense taken from the boat's earnings. But because the prices paid for fish in the Aberdeen market were higher than any nearby port, the costs associated with unloading did not significantly alter the boat's earnings.

In the later 1960s, the porters initiated increased disputes which resulted in their receiving more money per box unloaded and being given greater preference in what type of boats would be given priority unloading. The consequence for the in-shore fleet was that they had to pay more to unload their catch and they often had to wait long periods before unloading. One way of solving this problem was for the fishermen from the in-shore fleet to unload their own fish. But, even if they did this, the porters had to be paid as if they had done the unloading. This situation was so intolerable to the in-shore fishermen that they boycotted Aberdeen and moved their home port to Peterhead. Peterhead had a number of advantages. The harbor board was dominated by representatives of the in-shore fleet who were able to secure funding for a new market area. And there were no unionized porters. While it was true that the average prices for fish in Peterhead were lower than Aberdeen, there were no fees to pay porters and time was not lost waiting for the trawlers to unload. On balance, therefore, it was more profitable in Peterhead than Aberdeen.

According to the analysis of this boycott by Brand and Kort (1978), the movement from Aberdeen to Peterhead was organized by the in-shore fishermen. This is one of the first examples of Scottish fishermen acting as a collective body in opposition to policy established by an outside agency. The action itself was atypical of past Scottish fishermen's reactions to displeasing situations. If they disliked the treatment they received from a curer, they moved on to another. If they found authorities at one harbor difficult, they changed the registration of the boat. But those actions were taken on an individual basis. This action was different because the Aberdeen in-shore fleet acted as a unit. Typical of past behaviors was that the action was not an attempt to change anything; they were simply expressing their displeasure. But what they did, I suggest, offered a model for collective action that was to lead to a massive demonstration of solidarity by Scottish fishermen--the blockade.

Beginning in the late 1960s and into the early 1970s there was a boom in fishing. Catches were up and so were market prices. And even though the cost of boats, nets,and gear had escalated, profits from fishing increased. This presented a dilemma for owners and skippers. They could either pay increased taxes on their profits or invest the money in newer replacement boats. In order to compete with foreign vessels fishing in Scottish waters, many elected to invest in new boats that would more effectively compete with their competitors modernized fleets. Although the new boats were expensive-- between £ 100,000 and £ 150,000-- a number of funding combinations were available. Grants and loans could be obtained from the Herring Board or the White Fish Authority. There was also the possibility of grant monies from the EEC, which the United Kingdom had joined in 1972. And there was the sale of the old boat. The prices for used boats were up in the early 1970s, so when making an application for a grant from an agency these higher prices were used in calculating the amount needed to purchase a new boat.

In 1973 the price of diesel fuel increased 25 percent as a result of the Israeli-Arab war. In 1974 there was a drop in landings and the price of fish. Cargill (1976) suggests that the dwindling fish stocks were probably due to some combination of three factors. First was changing fishing technology, in particular purse-net fishing, which yielded more fish. Second was the increase in industrial fishing for species such as pout, sand eels, sprats, herring, and mackerel, which were used for pet food and fertilizer but were also food for cod and haddock. The third factor was an increase in the number of foreign boats. Because of decreased landings and prices, the demand for older boats was dramatically reduced and prices fell. To add further to these problems, the prices on the new boats that had been ordered in the early 70s also increased. These new boats had been ordered for a fixed price, but with increasing steel prices and increasing labor costs, many boat builders were unable to complete boats at the original fixed price. The choice was clear. Either the purchasers of the new boats had to pay the increased costs in order to save what they had already invested or the builder went bankrupt and the purchaser lost his investment. Most fishermen elected to pay the increased cost, which in many cases was three times the original fixed fee. Not only did the additional money have to be borrowed at higher interest rates, but additional money had to be borrowed to compensate for losses on the sale of the old boat.

101

To add to the gravity of this situation, the government introduced a quota system for herring in July, 1974. The North East Atlantic Fisheries established quotas for herring based upon the amount of fish caught since 1964. The proportion of the total amount of fish permitted was based upon all fish caught, not just herring for human consumption. The Scottish fishermen had traditionally fished for herring for human consumption and had only recently begun industrial fishing. As a result of the quota system, the Scottish fleet was allocated only a small proportion of the total quota. Thus, when Scottish fishermen caught their quota, the Danish, Norwegian, Russian, and Icelandic fleets were still out catching fish.

The quota system had the effect of reducing the income of the Scottish fleet. And this evoked feelings of national pride. These feelings were translated into the ballot. In October, 1974 the Scottish National Party won a number of parliamentary seats that had traditionally belonged to the Labor Party. The SNP had waged a campaign among the fishermen of the Moray Firth that placed special emphasis upon the quota system and the other problems of fishermen. The SNP's campaign throughout Scotland had stressed devolution, the withdrawal of Scotland from the U.K., or at least greater autonomy for Scotland. The implication of devolution for Scottish fishermen was that the coastal waters of Scotland would be under Scottish control, rather than the national government which was dominated by the English. If Scotland had an independent government, it would establish fishing boundaries that favored the Scottish fleet. Even if fishermen did not favor the idea of devolution, the election of SNP ministers would give them spokesmen in government.

Encouraged by the election of representatives whom they felt would present their case to Parliament, fishermen began meeting under the aegis of the Scottish Fishermen's Federation. Founded in September, 1973, the SFF incorporated the regional fishermen's associations together with the two major fishing interests--herring and white fish. Of the two fishing interests, the herring fishermen are somewhat better organized. Herring fishermen from different parts of Scotland tend to interact more because they move from port to port following the herring. The white fish and shell fish interests fish in different areas and are less likely to come in contact with each other. These meetings resulted in the decision to send a delegation of fishermen to London so that their grievances could be presented personally to their elected representatives. One hundred and twenty-five fishermen flew from Aberdeen to London at the end of January 1975. They met with their representatives, set forth their demands for changes, and gave the government one month before they would take further action.

A model for this action had been formed by French fishermen earlier in January. After staging an unproductive sit-in in Paris, they blocked the harbors at Boulogne, Dunkirk, Calais, Dieppe Le Treport, and Bordeaux. The French government responded rapidly to their demands, and the fishermen went back to sea.

The success of this action was an encouragement to English fishermen. Fishermen in Grimbsey were having problems with porters that were similar to the ones the in-shore fleet had encountered in Aberdeen. They were also faced with the same high costs and low prices as the Scottish fleet. On March 19, 1975, a blockade of Grimbsey and Immingham harbors was formed, and it spread to North Shields and Tyne. This blockade ended one week later with promises from the government to do something about their grievances.

Representatives of the Scottish Fishermen's Federation were asked by the English fishermen to engage in a sympathy blockade. They declined because there was not enough time to organize the Scottish fleet, but they were clearly in sympathy with the English. More than a month had gone by since the Scottish fishermen had presented their case to members of Parliament. During this time, talks continued among fishermen on what action they should take, and they finally decided to carry out their own blockade. On March 31, 1975, 850 Scottish fishing boats left their home ports and blockaded 18 fishing ports on the east and west coasts, as well as Shetland. The only boats that did not participate in the blockade were boats belonging to members of the Brethren, who are forbidden from being members of any organization, including fishing organizations. But while they could not directly participate in the blockade, they did help with communication and in supplying stores. The blockade stopped all commercial trade in and out of harbors. The only boats permitted into harbors were those on which people needed emergency medical attention. The blockade ended four days later with a promise from the government to investigate the fishermen's grievances.

The significance of the blockade is not that it was successful in having demands met. It was not. Only a few of the demands were partially met. However, it was the first time that Scottish fishermen had acted as a collective body. A protest of this magnitude required strong central leadership, as well as a shared resolve on the part of participants. The organizational model for fishermen in the in-shore fleet is the boat. The division of labor on the boat is instrumental. Crew members are allocated functional tasks related to running the boat or catching fish. On a boat there are five to ten men and there are three or four positions in the division of labor. To organize over 800 boats and 5,000 fishermen demands a different organizational mentality than organizing a boat. Further, the organization of a boat in reference to corporeal things is different than the organization of a large group of people in reference to an idea having no concrete reference. But the crucial element necessary to organize an activity like the blockade was not available until the recent past. That element is time. With the modernization of the fleet, fishing has become routinized. The boat can be automatically steered to a predetermined fishing place. The echosounder spots the fish. A course is set in relationship to the movement of the fish; the net is shot and hauled and fish are caught. All these activities can be learned in a short period of time. The result is that skippers now can spend more time ashore than they ever could under the older technologies, which were dependent upon many years of experience, the reading of signs, and the use of magic. Simply put, one cannot organize a blockade if one is always at sea.

The 1975 blockade was not the last collective action. In February, 1980, again under the direction of the Scottish Fishermen's Federation, fishing boats tied up at the quayside for three weeks. The issue this time was inexpensive fish coming from the EEC and the resultant decrease in demand for fish caught by the Scottish fleet. Like the 1975 blockade, the benefits from this action were minimal--the government gave a cash subsidy to boat owners to compensate for high fuel prices--but the fact that the action took place at all further reinforced the viability of an organization that could mobilize owners and skippers in collective action against government policy.

Fishing as Adaptation: The Ecological Model

The point has been reached where it is necessary to make sense of the data on changes in fishing over the past 250 years and the implications of these changes for the village of Gamrie. In the Introduction, the basic ecological model used in this study was outlined. The question now is the applicability of that model to this case study.

To begin, one can say that fishing is a cultural mode of adaptation to a particular ecological niche. Further, I can agree with Anderson and Wadel (1972) that fishing, even modern fishing, is essentially a hunting adaptation. They argue that:

> Hunting as an exploitative technique is functionally controlled by the nature of the resource, and less by human management. It is necessary to seek out, pursue and capture mobile species; harvesting and

farming activities, on the other hand, imply control and managed production of resources (153).

This description of the hunting adaptation includes a number of cultures, from Bushmen and Eskimos to Gamricks. However, there is a fundamental difference between the kinds of behaviors one observes among the Bushmen and Eskimo and the fishermen of Gamrie. This difference is in the ultimate use of that which is hunted, not the fact that it is hunted. Dimen-Schein's (1977) distinction between "production for use" and "production for exchange" makes the ecological adaptations of technologically simple societies something different from the adaptations of industrial societies and "implies a fine, though inflexible, attunement between needs and the objects made to satisfy them (203)." On the other hand, production for exchange, "means that the objects made often have nothing to do with the needs requiring satisfaction (203)" and is associated with societies having markets. Thus, for the traditional Bushmen and Eskimo, the value of that which is hunted is in its direct use. One eats the giraffe or the seal. Conversely, the fish caught by Gamrie fishermen is valuable as an item of exchange. One does not fish in order to eat fish; one fishes in order to exchange fish for money, which is then used to purchase other commodities. This distinction is recognized by Anderson and Wadel in describing "modern" fishing:

> ...the technical equipment and work organization required in modern deep-sea fishing is complex and involve large capital investments, it is commercialized and necessitates "industrial" forms of mass processing and marketing. All these characteristics lead us to view deep-sea fishing as an industrial adaption...Thus, deep-sea fishing might be classified as industrial hunting (154).

It has been noted in this chapter that Gamrie fishermen have historically been involved in a market economy and that these markets have changed from relatively local to world-wide. Thus, any understanding of changes in fishing technology relative to environment must take into account the characteristics of markets. Further, it must be recognized that these markets were and are outside the control of fishermen. Unlike the rather simple models developed to explain the adaptations of relatively closed cultures such as the Bushmen or the Eskimo, the understanding of industrial hunting is confounded by its dependence upon factors many degrees removed from the actual fishing itself. Even with this consideration, there is one factor that makes industrial fishing a hunting adaptation. This is the decision-making process. While market conditions may dictate if one goes fishing, decisions at sea in reference to where and how one captures mobile species must be made while fishing. Fishing, in other words, cannot be controlled directly from land. These decisions must take into account the environment--the characteristics of the sea and the behavior of fish.

Environment◄─►Technology: The Basic Ecological Relationship

There are two environmental characteristics of importance in understanding fishing behavior. One is the water itself; the other is the behavioral characteristics of the species of fish. The two bodies of water utilized by the Gamrie fishermen are the Moray Firth and the North Sea (see:Map 1). Both of these are rather unforgiving and hazardous, because of the combination of sudden changes in surface conditions and wide weather variations. The Moray Firth coastline is rocky and has been responsible for many lost boats and men. However, for our purposes the sea and weather conditions are a constant environmental characteristics. These bodies of water have not changed since the first oared boat was launched from Gamrie shore over 250 years ago.

What have changed, however, are boat designs and power. The first boats were small in size and powered by muscle and sail. Their size and the source of power limited their range and hence the area that could be fished. Increases in the size of boats extended their range, but they were still dependent upon a single source of energy, namely wind. This dependency upon this "natural" power source was not broken until the early part of the 1900s with the introduction and then adoption of steam power, which increased the range even further. The adoption of more recent innovations such as diesel power, steel-hulled boats, decca, and radar have further decreased the fishermen's dependency upon the natural conditions of sea and weather. In broad evolutionary terms, the changes in fishing vessels have brought greater and greater amounts of energy under human control. Thus, while one can assume that the sea is a constant, it is only constant as a natural phenomena. Culturally, and more specifically, technologically, the sea has changed.

The other environmental characteristic, the behavior of the fish populations exploited by villagers, has changed, and it is more directly linked to changes in technology. The Gamrie fishermen of the eighteenth century sought a number of species of white fish. The seasonal migrations of these fish populations determined when and the potential number of any particular species that could be be caught. The species and the number of fish actually caught was determined by two technological considerations--boat design and fishing method. Open, oar-powered boats had a limited range which meant that fishermen

106

could only catch fish that came within that range. Further, the hand-line method restricted fishing to a time period of less than one day. Lines were baited at home, mostly by women, and were used for the day's fishing. After returning home with their catch, this pattern was repeated.

The dependency upon the migration of white fish species was altered by herring fishing. Herring did not appear in large numbers along the Scottish coast until 1790 (Gray, 1978), and then only along the Firth of Forth. By 1805 they had disappeared, but they were soon in abundance along the Caithness coast, where they were vigorously pursued starting about 1815. It was just a few years later that Gamrie fishermen began using the drift-net method to catch the "silver darlings." During this early period, herring fishing was seasonal, since the fish migrated along the Moray Firth only during the summer months. For the rest of the year, white fish were taken with the line method. This shift from the line to drift-net fishing demanded a change in boat design. Larger boats were needed to carry nets, as well as the increased number of fishermen needed to handle the nets. The behavior of herring also changed the time of day when fishing took place. White fish are caught mostly during daylight hours; herring come to the surface, where they can be caught in drift-nets, in the evening or early morning hours.

Herring and white fish also differ significantly in their physical characteristics. Herring are a highly perishable fish. Unlike the white-fish species, which could be air dried along a rocky shore line, herring must be processed soon after they are caught or they will spoil. It is this factor, a biological factor, that is problematic to all hunting populations. Those that engage in production for use simply consume that which has not yet spoiled. Whatever can be preserved helps to postpone a return to the hunt. Producers for exchange, on the other hand, must have some method for storing or preserving what they produce if they are to expand market areas.* Gamrie fishermen have always been producers for exchange. The market for white fish was local for fresh fish and both local and extended for the white fish that had been air cured. To be able to exploit herring, it was necessary to have a land-based specialist who could process them for extended markets. As noted, the land-based partner for the herring fishermen was the curer. The curer's ability to increase markets made the pursuit of herring worthwhile for fishermen, but only if they were to invest in larger boats capable of following the herring on their natural migration routes. In order to recover their investment, those fishermen who did invest in the more costly larger boats, would have to

---

*For a more extended discussion of the relationship between food storage and differences in hunting populations, see: Testart, 1982.

become full-time herring fishermen. This is apparently what happened. Herring fishing went from a part-year venture in the early 1800s to an almost year-round activity by 1880 (Gray, 1978: 154).

The consequence for Gamrie fishermen was the beginning of a period of transhumance, which took villagers, both male and female, away from home a part of the year. Men were needed to fish for herring; women were employed by curers to gut, salt, and barrel the herring for markets in many parts of the world. This migratory pattern was to continue up until World War II.

The technology for herring fishing changed little from its earliest form. Drift-net technology is simple and few improvement could be made. The system worked as long as one was able to predict the movement of herring. Variations in catch size depended upon the skill of the skipper and seasonal fluctuations in the herring populations. The crucial factor for the survival of fishing as an exploitative activity was no longer a matter of fishing technology; instead the characteristics of the market became the most important factor. If demand and price of herring was high and there was enough herring, fishermen enjoyed high rewards. If demand and price were low, it did not make any difference whether herring were available or not; fishermen would suffer a loss. Whether they continued to be herring fishermen was largely due to factors far removed from fishing itself, such as the eating habits of Russians, the availability and price of salt, the number of barrels of herring produced by the Dutch, changes in currency exchanges, and so forth.

Steam-powered boats gave herring fishermen a selective advantage over those who did not have them. Because of the perishable nature of herring, it was important that the boat return to port as soon as possible after a catch. Also, the fresher the herring, the higher the price. However, the adoption of steam, and later diesel-powered boats, meant greater capital investment and ultimately greater dependence upon outsiders--curers, merchants, fishsales companies, banks, and government. Some such costs-benefits consideration must have taken place in reference to herring fishing soon after World War I, when the fishermen of the Moray Firth began using the seine-net method of fishing for white fish. The only notable exception to this widespread change was the Gamrie fleet, which continued to fish for herring. The more recent adoption of the dual-purpose trawler by Gamrie fishermen as well as others along the East Coast greatly enhanced their adaptability. The ability to engage in both herring and white fishing without the necessity of having two boats gave them options to pursue whichever market had the highest benefits.

108

Thus far this discussion of the relationship between environment and technology has focused on the exploitative nature of technology, and little has been said about the impact of more efficient technologies on the fish populations themselves. With each increase in productivity there have been corresponding changes in fish populations. Such is the nature of fishing. As one local farmer stated, "fishermen reap, but never sow." There are no mechanisms for replacing what they kill. It has only been recently that systematic efforts have been made to regulate fish populations. In the past such regulation was largely unplanned. During the world wars, for example, the number of fish increased because fishing activities were curtailed. Even when efforts have been made to control the taking of certain species through governmental quotas, it has been in response to dwindling stocks and has often been started too late to ameliorate the situation. The relationship between the natural reproduction cycles of fish and the technological capacity to catch more fish does present a dilemma. More productive technologies require greater capital investment and that investment can only be repaid by harvesting more fish. The greater the number of fish caught, the less capable they are of reproducing themselves. The reduction in fish stocks eventually leads to greater competition among fishermen and provides a stimulus for adopting even more productive technologies. It is possible that this chain of events could lead to permanent depopulation of existing fish stocks in the North Sea.

Technology: The Social Organization of Fishing

The rather straightforward relationship between changes in fishing technology and the organization of the boat has been demonstrated in this chapter. Small open-decked, sail-powered craft using the long-line method only needed a few men and boys as crew members. Lacking in any specialization of the division of labor, each man was responsible for his own line. Partnerships on such boats were kinship based, and the fisherman's wife or mother contributed to this venture by gathering bait and then baiting hooks.

The change to drift-net demanded larger boats and larger crews. While boats and nets may have been separately owned and may have been the basis for dividing the rewards of fishing, shooting and heaving the nets necessitated cooperation among fishermen. Decisions concerning when and where to fish and when to shoot and heave the nets changed from collective decisions between partners to one-man decisions when boats and nets were owned by a skipper. In turn, the skipper was responsible to land-based investors insofar as he was indebted to them. In the early days of herring fishing, kinship played an important role in the recruitment and composition of the crew largely because of the unpredictibility of the economic outcome.

The introduction of steam-powered boats began a period of specialization of crew activity. The maintenance and care of the engine was crucial to the survival of the boat, in terms of both human life and economic success. This specialization was further increased with the adoption of power equipment and the diesel engine, and with the even more specialized division of labor associated with the modern purser.

One can conclude that the adoption of more productive fishing methods is necessary for the survival of fishing as an economic activity in a market economy. As one system of technology is replaced by another that has a higher adaptive advantage, i.e. is more competitive, there will be a change in the organization of the boat consistent with that new technology. But what is the impetus for the adoption of newer more productive technologies? The push to embrace technologies with higher capitalization costs comes from the demands of the market. Fishermen have little choice between utilizing more costly innovations and not being competititve in the marketplace. The record speaks directly to this issue. Since 1890 the number of boats registered to villagers has decreased. The same observation can be made for the Moray Firth in general. More productive technologies mean fewer producing units.

The Ecological Model Revisited

The basic ecological model proposed in Chapter I as a guide to the collection of data and observations in this study obviously needs revision if we are to adequately understand the evolution of fishing in Gamrie. Given the fact that Gamrie fishermen engage in production for exchange, it is necessary to include the influence of the market in the relationship between environment and technology. The adjusted model might look something like the following:

Model II
The Basic Ecological Model:
The Organization of the Boat

(Available curing and
distribution systems)
Market

Environment◄─────────►Organization of the Boat
(Appearance of Herring)   (Specialization in the
                                Division of Labor)

Technology
(Larger boats, steam
and diesel power)

110

The environment, under industrial systems, represents an opportunity structure. Herring provide us with an illustration of this. Prior to the appearance of herring along the Moray Firth, the fishing technology for white fish "fit" the market conditions. With the appearance of herring, the market encouraged the adoption of a new technology. Had the potential for expanding the market--and here I would include the methods for curing as well as the distribution system--not been available, there would have been little incentive to adopt a technology that would result in the catching of large numbers of herring. Once the technology was in place to meet market demands, however, the organization of the boat had to change. The relationship between the variables in the model can be formally stated as:

> In industrial societies, environments provide opportunity structures that, if technology and market characteristics permit, will change the organization of work.

In Steward's terms, this is what "core" culture is all about. For Harris, this is "infrastructure." However, we are not just interested in the effect of changing technologies on the people directly involved in the process of exploitation. We are also concerned with how these changes affect the survival of the community. The relationship between the organization of work and the community is summarized nicely by Arensberg and Kimball:

> A particular shift in industrial technique becomes a particular change in organization among persons of a specific community, to be at related at once to further, subsequent changes in other nonindustrial patterns of organization among the same men in their lives outside of work and in the same community (1965:291).

Technology: The Organization of Gamrie

Some ecologists suggest that the unit of primary concern as the adaptive survival measure is the human population (Dimen-Schein, 1977; Little and Morren, 1976). The measure of population is "carrying-capacity," or how many people can be supported by a technology. Taking Gamrie as our population unit, one notes from Chapter III that its population has changed and this change has been caused in part, at least, by changing technology.

From 1745 to 1841 the population of the village was small and stable. This corresponds to the period when hand-line fishing was the dominant technology. Beginning shortly after 1841, the population rose dramatically. This was the period when the drift-net method of fishing for herring became more widely used. The population continued to increase until 1911, when it began its present decline. The 1911 date is significant. It marks the beginning of steam power and larger boats. The early steam-powered fishing craft were converted sailing boats such as the zulu and the fifie, which could use the small harbor in Gamrie. However, the availibility of steam power made possible the building of larger craft capable of holding more nets and larger catches. The problem with Gamrie was the harbor size. If local fishermen wished to purchase these larger craft, they could not berth them in the local harbor. Thus, a decision had to be made. Stay with the smaller converted craft and live in the village. Adopt the larger craft and move away. Or adopt the larger craft, continue to live in the village, and commute to the larger harbored town. Apparently the choice to move to larger harbored towns nearby was made by many villagers. The more attractive town was Fraserburgh. It not only had enlarged its harbor, but it was a major herring center. This also made it attractive to women, who could work part of the summer herring season without leaving home.

The option to commute to nearby harbors deserves some additional comment. While Gamrie fishermen do this today, it would have been problematic in 1911. The automobile was not available to villagers, public transportation was non-existent, and the road system out of the village was primitive at best. Thus, the absence of available transportation precluded commuting as an option at that time. With improved transportation and the availibility of vans to carry crews to and from the boat, this option eventually could be exercised. The point here is clear. If one uses the concept "carrying capacity" to measure the success or failure of exploitative systems in industrial communities, it must take into account contributory factors other than the specific technological systems in which community members participate. In the Gamrie case, the change to steam-powered and larger craft was only possible when there were supportive facilities such as a larger harbor or transportation systems. Thus, while Gamrie lost population, places like Fraserburgh gained. One could speculate that if there had been an adequate transportation system, Gamrie would have maintained its size. In another time period this might have been the case; at that particular time, it was not.

In order to explain population changes in Gamrie, the basic ecological model would have to include more variables than in explaining the organization of the boat. Using the information above, the revised model is:

112

Model III
The Basic Ecological Model:
Gamrie Population Size

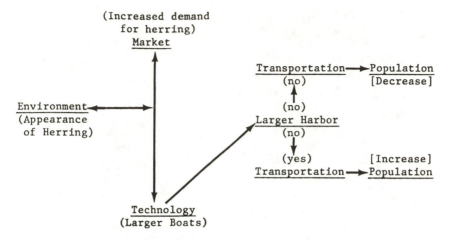

To view the community as simply an increasing or decreasing number of people is to ignore much of what distinguishes humans from other animals. What survives along with human populations is a wide variety of practices. And if the ecological model is to make a contribution to our knowledge about humans, it must be able to explain these practices, even though they appear to make no direct contribution to survival. Therefore, in the next three chapters, I shall examine two major institutions within the village--family and religion--and then discuss those social processes which serve to maintain the integrity of Gamrie as a community. In the last chapter that information is used to further evaluate the ecological model.

V. SOCIAL ORGANIZATION
FAMILY AND KINSHIP

Introduction

The main thesis of this study is that the relationship between technology and environment determines social organization. In the last section changes in fishing technology were reviewed. We noted that kinship was used in the recruitment process and that the reliance upon kinship had changed with changing technology. In this section we will review the organization of marriage and family to determine what influence changing technology has had on this dimension of community organization.

Courtship

Most young males in the village leave school when they are legally permitted, now at the age of sixteen. They usually go to work on a boat, which means that if they are to engage in court-ship behavior it has to be on the weekends.* Patterns of court-ship usually begin prior to going to sea. During the summer school holiday and on evenings when the weather permits one is likely to find young adolescents gathered at the "Braeheed," the corner of Main Street that overlooks the harbor. During the day this corner is used by the adult members of the village. Men and women gather to talk or just look out over the harbor. But at night, it is the children's corner. Males and females cluster under the yellow arc lights into unisex groups. There is no set area that is male or female. Sometimes males sit on the bench or the metal railing; sometimes the females are there. Occasionally a group of males or females will stand next to the Clysdale Bank across from the benches. The conversation between and within these unisex groups is light in nature and tends to be for the benefit of the grouping with which one is identified rather than for members of another group. Cigarette smoking, generally disapproved by parents, is surreptitiously

*This pattern of being home on the weekends is relatively recent for the herring fishermen of Gamrie. Up until the early 1960s, they would ride a bus to the fishing grounds on the west coast and return after two or more weeks away from home. In the early 1960s a few fishermen started taking their cars, and rather than staying, they would return home on the weekends. Thus began the present practice of the boat having a car or van to make the weekly commute to the fishing. The only exception to this is the Isle of Man herring season when crews will be away for up to a month.

115

carried out by both males and females. Crisps* and sweeties** are shared within and between groups. In this situation, adolescents can test male-female relations outside of the school, the kirk or hall, or the home. The size of these groupings will vary through the evening. During the early part of the evening one notes a wider variation in ages. Later, the younger participants will leave for home.

Occasionally one of the older adolescents who is already fishing will appear in his automobile. If he is successful, he may negotiate a "run" with one or more of the older females. This "run" may just be a ride outside the village into the surrounding countryside or to a nearby town or village. Until 1975 there might have been a run into Fraserburgh to the cinema, but that is closed now. Or it might be to pubs that serve underage patrons. The ability of younger fishermen to purchase automobiles has altered courtship patterns. Not only does it enable couples to escape the public corner, but it also makes possible the courtship of females in other villages.

The availability of possible courtship partners has also changed as a result of changes in schooling in Gamrie. Prior to 1970, children had all their schooling needs met within the village. Since 1970 the older children have gone to school in either Macduff or Banff which has increased the pool of potential courtship partners from the village to surrounding towns and villages.

The goal of courtship is marriage. Because the pool of courtship partners has increased to include persons from places outside, marriage has changed from the past practice of village endogamy, and more people are marrying outside the village. However, there continues to be a kind of occupational endogamy. Fisherfolk tend to marry fisherfolk, regardless of where they live.

What characteristics did fishermen seek in a wife? According to Anson (1965):

> The only sort of wife useful to him was one who had a good working knowledge of the jobs she would have to do once they set up a home together (55).

The work to which Anson refers is mending nets, baiting hooks, selling fish, and other activities directly related to fishing. But it was not just a female partner-helper that the fisherman sought, it was also a wife who could produce children.

---

*crisps: potato chips
**sweeties: candy

A fisherman could not be independent until he had a wife and children to help him with his job. He needed sons to go to sea with him if he owned his own boat. If he worked with lines he required healthy daughters to help their mother gather bait, prepare the lines, and to sell fish (Anson, 1965; 54).

This need, according to Anson, led fishermen to marry early. He observed that fishermen married and started to raise a family at seventeen or eighteen years of age. The time period to which Anson refers for early marriages was probably the late 1700s or early 1800s. Data on age of marriage for the county of Banff are available back to 1861. The average age of marriage for males that year was 29.1 years; for females 25.9. Data for the average age of marriage in Gamrie have been reconstructed from marriage records and are presented in Table 6.

Table 6
Mean Age Of Marriage By Decades 1900-1969
And The Years 1970-1974

Years	Mean Age		Number of Marriages
	Males	Females	
1900-1909	28.1	25.2	58
1910-1919	27.8	24.2	51
1920-1929	25.5	23.8	16
1930-1939	25.4	22.8	33
1940-1949	26.5	23.4	26
1950-1959	25.4	22.7	34
1960-1969	24.6	20.4	58
1970-1974	25.1	21.8	30

Data on average age of marriage for Banff county presented by Smout (1976) indicate an increase for both males and females from 1861 to 1901. Table 6 shows that the average age at marriage has slowly decreased since the turn of the century. If Anson's observation that males married in order to become fisherman at the time long-line technology was used, then something must have happened with the change to drift-net fishing (1812-1840) to change this. At the turn of this century it appears that one became a fisherman first, and then took a wife. With the shift to drift-net fishing and later to the steam-powered boats, village fishermen broke their dependency upon wives-as-partners in the fishing venture. At the same time, drift-net fishing took unmarried males away from the village and thus interrupted courtship. The later age of marriage

117

for both males and females in the village is probably due to the work cycle of fishing. Present-day villages would maintain that one marries for love. But "Falling in love" takes time. Being home only on weekends does not permit much time for courtship.

Premarital Sexual Behavior

Villagers were reluctant to talk about sexuality, either premarital or marital. However, one can make inferences about premarital sexuality by examination of antemarital pregnancy and illegitimacy. In the mid 1800s, the Registrar-General published figures on illegitimacy ratios* for Scotland. The highest ratios were found in the North-East, where approximately 13 percent of all children were illegitimate. However, there appeared to be some variation in these rates between coastal fishing communities and inland farm communities. The coastal communities had ratios between 10 and 14.9 percent. Some farming areas had ratios above 20 percent. This difference, according to Cramond (1888), is explained by the strong family organization in fishing communities which led to forced marriages between couples whose premarital sexual behavior led to pregnancy. This pattern of premarital pregnancy has become so much a part of the cultural configuration of the North-East that even today when a couple moves their marriage date back, it is assumed that she is "bairned."** The reaction by villagers to a woman's being pregnant before marriage is usually a smile and some mild gossip. If the woman has a child out of wedlock, she is treated in a much more serious manner. These women are included in the category "women of a certain kind," mentioned in the last chapter. The behavioral consequences for women who have illegitimate children often go beyond simple epithets. They are generally ill-treated, and if they have to work to support their illegitimate children they are given menial jobs in people's homes and often paid less than others.

The premarital sexual behavior that led to pregnancy is reflected in the village birth records. Until 1960, illegitimacy was frequently noted. Often the statement "father alleged to be _____ " was included. This statement would even be included on a person's death record. (I saw it on the death record of a man who was over 90 when he died.) The illegitimacy designation is no longer used, and father's name is simply left blank.

Table 7 shows the number of illegitimate births to women in the village from 1900 to 1974. I also calculated another category to estimate the percentage of births to women who had been married less than seven months. This I call: "premature births."

*Illegitimacy ratio: number of illegitimate children as a percent of all children born for a specific time period.
**Being bairned: being with child, pregnant.

Table 7

Number Of Children Born, Number Of "Premature" Births And
Number Of Illegitimate Births For The Decades 1900-1969 And The
Years 1970-1974

Decades	Total Births	"Premature Births" N	"Premature Births" %	Illegitimate Births N	Illegitimate Births %
1900-1909	330	20	6	10	3
1910-1919	301	11	4	4	1
1920-1929	212	5	2	8	4
1930-1939	189	21	11	4	2
1940-1949	121	10	8	1	8
1950-1959	125	7	6	4	3
1960-1969	124	10	8	2	2
1970-1974	58	4	7	2	3

If fisher females get married after they discover they are pregnant, this category should indicate that practice. In all but one decade--1920-1929--the percentage of premature births was higher than the percentage of illegitimate births. The ratios for premature and illegitimate births does not vary much over this 74-year period. The combined measure constitutes about nine percent of total births. What is clear from these data is that most pregnancies of unwed females result in marriage.

The illegitimate and premature ratios are underestimates of premarital sexual behavior. The ratios are a proportion of total births, not the first-born child. Since the average number of children born per female is somewhat over two, one could conservatively estimate that the figures for premature births would be doubled if they were percentages of all first born children. Therefore, I would estimate that approximately 13 percent of the marriages in the village are preceded by pregnancy.

The consistency of premature and illegitimate births over the past 74 years does not appear to be related to changing fishing technology or other demographic indicators. When rates remain constant, as these do, they suggest a cultural pattern related to the value of children. In the past, pregnancy could be prevented by celibacy. Today it can be prevented by the "pill." The local doctor, as far back as the late 1960s, counseled unmarried females on the use of birth control, and the pill is the most common form of birth control used by both unmarried and married women. The high number of pregnancies before marriage, however, indicates that women are not using the pill. One reason given for this is that the pill must be

119

obtained through a chemist,* which is staffed by local women. If an unmarried female has her prescription filled locally, it is suggested, everyone would soon know about it. Even if she goes to nearby towns, she still runs the risk of having this information become public.

While this reason for not using birth control is given by informants, I would suggest that one can understand premarital pregnancy as part of a larger set of cultural expectations related to the attainment of adulthood. In the past, children were economic necessities associated with a labor-intensive form of fishing technology. This is not true today. A successful skipper may pass his boat on to his sons, but sons are not necessary for his becoming a success or even survival as a fisherman. In all cultures there are expectations of what one should do in one's lifetime. For these villagers, the expectations are rather clear-cut. Males should leave school as soon as possible. They should go to sea and get a "good"--well paying, secure--berth on a boat. Females may go on further in school, but they are expected to get married and have children. Before marriage and before having children in marriage, they can work. Indeed they are expected to work, but not to have a career. After having a child they are expected to devote full attention to that child and any subsequent children.

Marriage and parenthood are thus linked. Marriage without parenthood and parenthood without marriage violate cultural expectations. Sexual intercourse prior to marriage may violate a moral code, but if it results in pregnancy and then marriage, it satisfies a more global cultural expectation. The indiscretion is forgiven. The male no longer stands at the braeheed with the children. The female no longer works. And they become recognized as adults by the community.

From Engagement to Wedding: Planning and Ritual

The engagement of the couple is a simple announcement by them that they intend to marry on some future date. This is usually done in consultation with the parents of the bride and groom. Sometimes friends of the prospective bride will give small gifts marking the occasion. There is no formal written announcement, but like so much other information in the village, news of it soon spreads. The prospective bride may wear an engagement ring, but this is not necessary.

After the betrothal the couple is expected to practice exclusivity in courtship, and there usually begins a "pseudo married" relationship. This includes meals with prospective parents-in-law and occasionally staying overnight at the house of

---

*chemist: pharmacy

a future spouse. This is sometimes extended to going on holiday together and even being alone for a week or two. Although no sexual license is given, staying overnight and going on holiday together tends to happen more frequently the closer the couple gets to the actual wedding date.

The wedding can occur anytime after the engagement notice. However, if the couple has not set a marriage date after a year of engagement, the sincerity of one or the other party may be called into question. The date may be difficult to schedule due to a number of factors. First, fishermen normally get married on a Saturday, which is a reflection of the work cycle. Fishermen are home on the weekends. To have the wedding during the week would exclude most of the male friends and relatives. A second difficulty is logistical. Members of the kirk or Open Brethren* must schedule their wedding date with the minister or someone licensed to perform the ceremony. If the kirk or hall is already being used on that date then it will be necessary to reschedule for another time. Another logistical problem is booking a hotel in which to hold the traditional meal and dance after the wedding. There is one large hotel in the area that is considered the best for this purpose, although most larger hotels have the necessary facilities. The prestige hotel serves a rather large geographical area and therefore it may be difficult to get a booking. Since there are only 52 potential Saturdays in a year and there are many more than 52 weddings a year in this area, some couples may have to wait more than a year before being able to book this hotel. Thus the sequence for determining the wedding date is first securing the hotel, then making arrangements with the minister.

An invitation list is then compiled by the bride and groom and their parents. Since the bride's family normally pays for the reception and meal, the number of guests is limited by their financial ability. This list contains persons one is obligated to invite, as well as persons one wants to invite. Among the obligatory guests are: members of the bride's and groom's nuclear family; extended kin such as grandparents, parent's siblings, and cousins; and crew members of the boats on which the bride's father, the groom's father, and the groom sail. Preferential guests include friends of the bride and groom and business associates--fish salesmen, boat builders, and so on. Invitations are sent for three events: the wedding itself, the reception and meal after the ceremony, and the dance after the meal. The number of people at the wedding and the dance tends to be larger than the number of people at the reception and

---

*Members of the Close and Exclusive branches of the Brethren are married in a civil ceremony by the county clerk. Since this can be done almost any time during working hours, scheduling is not a problem.

meal. The wedding and the dance are often considered semi-public events. Anybody can attend the wedding, even strangers, but it would be considered improper for a stranger to attend the dance.

The wedding itself normally takes place in the community of the bride. Gregor (1881) noted that the ceremony usually took place in the church, if it was convenient. Failing a convenient church, the schoolhouse or public hall might have been used. And if none of these was available the house of the bride's father would be used. Beginning in 1906, the wedding location was noted in the Gamrie marriage records. Unfortunately this information was not systematically included in the records until 1919. From these data it is clear that most village weddings took place in the Kirk until the 1960s. Since then there has been an increase in marriages by the county clerk, and this corresponds to the increased number of Brethren in the village. There has also been a slight increase in the number of weddings performed in the parish church. If a local male marries a female from a neighboring village or town, the ceremony will be performed by the minister of her kirk. If a local female marries someone from outside the village, the ceremony is performed locally. One of the few exceptions to this rule is that village males or females who graduate from the University of Aberdeen are entitled to be married in the university chapel. But because there are so few university graduates from the village, this is a rare occurrence. I knew of only one person during my field work who was married in the university chapel.

The time of year weddings take place has been changing since the turn of this century. This is one practice that reflects, in a rather direct way, changes in fishing technology. Traditionally, boats were not at sea during the worst winter months--December and January. Table 8 shows that December was the wedding month from 1900 through the 1930s. Since then, one notes weddings have been distributed throughout the year which corresponds to fishing becoming a year-round activity as a result of changes in boat design and fishing technology. One can imagine what the month of December must have been like at the turn of this century. There was a marriage almost every week, and in some weeks there were two. It must have been a carnival-like atmosphere with fishermen all home, and a constant series of meals and other associated activities to bring people out of their houses to interact with kinsmen and friends. December and January have the fewest hours of daylight, about four hours a day and without these kinds of activities, public interaction might have been severely curtailed, as they are today. Thus, the most difficult months were made tolerable.

Table 8
Month Of Marriage By Decades 1900-1969 And The Years
1970-1974 From Marriage Records

	Months											
Decades	Jan	Feb	Mar	Apr	May	Jun	Jul	Aug	Sep	Oct	Nov	Dec
1900-09	11			4		2	2		4		5	30
1910-19	1	1	3	2	2	1		2	1	3	1	35
1920-29	3		4						3			6
1930-39	2	1		4	5	1			5			15
1940-49	3	2	1	5	5	1			4	1	1	3
1950-59	1		7	3	1	4	2	3	8		1	4
1960-69	3	1	8	6		9	4	7	8	7	1	4
1970-74		3	2		2	3	2		3	5	4	6

At some time prior to the wedding, participants in the actual ceremony are selected. Usually this is done according to kinship affiliation. The best man is typically the groom's brother or cousin. The bridesmaid is typically the bride's sister or cousin. If there is a flowergirl, it might be a younger sister, a niece, or a younger cousin. The ushers are usually brothers of the bride and groom, or cousins in the absence of brothers. The bride is given away by her father; if the father is dead, then it is usually a male relative of her parent's generation.

Traditionally, both the bride and the groom brought something to the marriage. The bride was:

> ...expected to have a chest-of-drawers, otherwise a "kist"; also a feather bed, four pairs of white blankets, two coloured ones, two bolsters, four pillows, sheets, one dozen towels, a table-cloth, also crockery and kitchen utensils...It was the bridegroom's business to supply chairs, a table, and all fishing gear. (Anson, 1965:58)

These expectations do not hold true today. Starting about two weeks before the actual wedding, people begin to bring gifts to the households of the bride and groom. Usually the gifts are displayed in the house of the bride, but if the bride is not from the village, they may be displayed in both houses. Persons invited to the wedding are expected to bring a gift, but gifts are also given by persons not invited. The gifts are arranged in a room of the house, and anyone bringing a gift is invited to see what others have brought and is invited to have a cup of tea and something to eat. As the wedding date approaches, more people bring gifts, so that the mother of the bride is usually kept busy from early morning to evening with a parade of callers and gift givers. The gifts given are mostly household items--furniture, tea sets, lamps, irons, tea kettles, linens, pillows, and so on. Money may also be given so that the couple can purchase items they might not have received.

I mentioned earlier that during the 1981 field season I witnessed my first blackening. This practice apparently is very old in this region. According to Gregor (1888):

> On the evening before the marriage there was a "feet washing." A few of the bridegroom's most intimate friends assembled at his house, when a large tub was brought forward and nearly filled with water. The bridegroom was stripped of shoes and stockings, and his feet were plunged in the water. One seized a besom, and began to rub them lustily, while another was busy besmearing them with soot or shoe-blacking, and a third was practising some other vagery. (89)

Gregor does not tell us what "other vageries" were practiced, nor does he indicate if something similar happens to the bride. The present-day "feet washing" or blackening goes far beyond the feet and usually includes the bride as well. The blackening I witnessed occurred one week before the wedding and involved considerable planning as well and secrecy. The bridegroom was prawn fishing on the west coast. The only person on his boat who knew about the blackening was his father, the skipper. Soon after arriving home on Friday evening he was given his evening meal. Prior to his coming home, his bride was called and told to come to the house to sign some papers. In the meantime, a local truck had been decorated with the name of the bride and groom and a batch of blackening had been made. The blackening mixture has no specific ingredients, but it should contain substances that will get one dirty. This particular batch was made of dark and light treacle, dirt, and motor oil. Sometimes pitch or tar and shoe polish are added.

After eating, the bride and groom went into the living room. After a few moments some of his friends, dressed in costume, came into the room. He then realized what was about to happen and attempted to escape, but the door was blocked and he appeared to resign himself to being blackened. The couple was taken upstairs and dressed in old clothes. As they were being taken outside, the groom broke loose and ran down

124

the brae. Some of his friends ran after him, and another drove his car down the brae to aid in the capture. The bride was taken into the front garden (yard), where the barrel of blackening had been placed. The females took her over to the barrel and then scooped out blackening, which they smeared into her hair and on her face. In retaliation, she threw blackening on them. It soon became difficult to tell who was being blackened.

Just as the females were finishing blackening each other, the groom was brought back in the car by his friends. Still putting up a gallant resistance, he was wrestled down to the ground, and held fast by each limb, and the barrel of blackening was poured over him and his abductors. Once blackened, he no longer resisted. The truck, with the bride's and groom's name fastened to the back, was driven up in front of the house, the bride and groom and about 12 others climbed in the back. It was driven down the brae toward the Seatown, the driver blowing the truck's horn and the occupants in the back pounding metal pans and shouting. People came out of their houses to watch and wave and laugh. The truck drove down Main Street to the bake house, where the participants were given a bag of flour, the contents of which were thrown over the black sticky mixture, which by now covered everyone.

The truck then drove to Macduff to visit the family and friends of the bride, and then went on to Banff, where it circled the town much to the amusement of people on holiday and citizens alike. Finally, they all returned to the groom's house where his father served refreshments to everyone involved. The evening ended with the groom and his friends going out to the local pub.

This practice occurs less frequently now than in the past. Older informants told me that almost every male used to be blackened prior to his marriage. Whether or not a person is blackened depends upon the willingness of others to organize the activity. Some arrangement has to be made for the truck, someone has to make the blackening, and the costumes have to be readied. And all of this has to be done without the bride or groom suspecting anything. When the village residents all lived in the Seatown, people could be recruited to carry out the necessary preparations from among friends and neighbors who lived nearby. A truck was not necessary to take people from one end of the village to another, as it is only a short walk through the Seatown. Now because of changes in residence patterns, the orchestration of the blackening is much more difficult and therefore is less likely to be a regular part of pre-marriage ritual.

The Marriage Ceremony

There are a number of variations in marriage ceremonies. The close and exclusive Brethren are married by the county clerk in an administrative office. The open Brethren may be married in the local hall. Members of the kirk are married in the church. Within each one of these groups there are some variations in activities. What follows is a description of the marriage day of a couple who were married in the Church of Scotland. He was from the village, she was from a nearby fishing village. While the specifics of this wedding day may be different from others, the general sequence of activities is similar to what one observes in kirk weddings along this part of the Moray Firth.

The marriage ceremony was scheduled for 3 p.m. on a Saturday, in the bride's kirk. Starting a few days before, relatives of the bride and groom who were to participate in the ceremony went to stay in the bride's and groom's homes. Thus, on the morning of the wedding day, each household consisted of the family and the house-guests. During the morning there was much activity. People were taking baths and laying out their wardrobes for the afternoon. Someone went to the florist to pick up flowers, and meals were prepared.

Since the wedding was to take place in the bride's church, arrangements had to be made to transport guests from Gamrie. About 2 p.m. a bus arrived in the village and parked at the Braeheed where invited guests had already begun to congregate. They boarded the bus, which then left for the bride's village to pick up additional guests. A few minutes later two taxis arrived at the house of the groom, one taxi for the parents of the groom, the other for the groom and the best man. The taxis were clearly identified as part of the wedding party, having two pieces of cloth or crepe paper stretched in a "V" shape over the hood and the top. The arrival of the taxis was a signal for children, and some adults, to gather around the front door of the house. It is customary for the father of the bride and groom to throw coins to the assembled crowd. While they are scrambling for the money, the taxis leave with their passengers. This same sequence was followed in the bride's community, except somewhat later since she lived closer to the church.

The bus arrived at the church about twenty minutes before the service was scheduled to begin. Since a wedding is an important rite of passage, it is usually photo documented. Many professional photographers in the area derive a large part of their incomes from photographing weddings. As people enter the church they stop for a moment to be photographed. They are photographed according to social units. Single persons are photographed alone or with another single person. Married couples are photographed together, along with their children. Thus there is a record of all of those who attend the wedding. The bride and groom are the last to arrive at the church. The groom arrives first. A series of photos are taken--the groom and his parents, the groom and the best man, the parents, the groom alone, the best man, and the parents. After the photos they go into the church and down the aisle to the altar. The bride's entourage by this time has arrived; their photographs are taken and they enter the church. When the organist begins playing, the bride and her father, followed by the maid or maids of honor and the flower girl, walk down the aisle to the altar. The music stops and the minister reads the vows. After the vows are read, the couple, the minister, and witnesses go to the minister's study, where the official documents are signed. In the few minutes it takes to sign the documents the guests leave the church and congregate outside. When the bride and groom come out, photos are taken of the bride and groom along with their families.

The order for leaving the church to go to the hotel is the reverse of the order coming to the church. The taxis take the bride and groom, the best man and maid(s) of honor, the parents of the bride, and the parents of the groom. After the taxis leave, the guests' bus leaves. At the hotel, the wedding party goes to the lounge, which serves as a reception area. The wedding party forms a line at the door to the reception area and greets the wedding guests as they arrive. The guests are served refreshments, usually whiskey for the males and sherry for the females. The reception lasts about an hour. The end of the reception is signaled by the announcement that the meal is being served.

The dining area is divided into two seating arrangements. At a long table sit all the official members of the wedding party. The bride and groom are in the center. Next to them is the minister. On the bride's side are her family in closeness of relationship--mother, father, grandparents, and maids of honor who are also relatives. On the groom's side this same arrangement is followed. The guests sit at individual tables that seat five or six people. The minister opens the meal with a prayer, followed by a short statement, after which a toast is offered. With the exception of the minister and those who do not drink, everyone sips whiskey or sherry. This is followed by a number of toasts by various people--the fathers of the couple, the best man, and other special male guests. Once this is completed, telegrams from those who were invited, but were unable to attend, are read. Finally the wedding cake is cut by the bride and groom. After one cut, the cake is taken away to be cut into small portions for the guests and boxed for those who were not there. Then the meal is served.

At the conclusion of the meal a few words are said and the guests are asked to leave while the room is rearranged for the dance. The guests either go to the hotel lobby or into the lounge, where they may wait or purchase more to drink. It is about this time that those who were invited to the dance arrive. Once the room has been arranged for the dance the guests move out of the lounge and find themselves tables around the dance floor.

The dance begins with a "Grand March." The bride and groom are first in the march, and they are followed by the parents and other members of the wedding party and finally the guests. Arm in arm, they march to the end of the dance floor and circle around to the other end where they are met by others. Thus the line of marchers lengthens until it is as wide as the dance floor. After this, waltz music replaces the march music. The bride and groom are the first couple to waltz. After a few minutes the members of the wedding party join them, and finally the guests. Once the waltz begins a bar is opened at one end of the room and people may purchase their own drinks. It is usual for large amounts of alcoholic beverages to be consumed at weddings. The most obvious justification for this is that it is a festive occasion. Or perhaps it is a festive occasion because people drink a lot. Another reason is that those who drink do not have to drive. Being caught for driving under the influence of alcohol is a serious offense in Scotland. Since there is a bus to take the guests home at the end of the evening, this problem is avoided.

At about 10:00, the dance music stopped so a game could be played. This game involved the wearing of funny apparel. A box of clothing, mostly dresses and female underwear, was brought out on the floor. Those wishing to participate, arranged themselves in a circle. When the music started, an item of clothing was circulated from one person to another. When the music stopped, the person holding the item had to put it on. This continued until all the items had been circulated. The person judged to have the most comical combination of clothing was then awarded a small prize.

The dance lasts until 11 p.m., unless a special midnight license has been obtained. An hour or so before the end, the bride and groom change out of their wedding clothes. They say good-bye to members of the wedding party and leave to spend their wedding night elsewhere. The next day they go on their honeymoon, which lasts one or two weeks. The honeymoon destination is usually kept secret. At 11:00 the guests leave the dance floor and go to the awaiting busses to be taken home.

The symbolism of the wedding is rather straightforward. The wedding ceremony publicly marks an alliance between two family units and the formation of a new social unit. The day of the wedding begins with each family making similar preparations, but separate from each other. The ride to the church separates parents from the bride and groom. The wedding vows formally unite the representatives of each family and legitimatizes the formation of a new family unit. The passengers in the taxis to the hotel reflect this alliance, as well as separate the newly formed family unit from the old. The alliance and new formation are again symbolized in the grand march with the two families merging together after marching separately.

The wedding also reinforces another dominant theme--the authority position of males. A male is the best man, it is a male who "gives away" the bride, it is a male who performs the ritual, and it is males who speak at the meal. I shall come back to this theme later in a discussion of the division of labor in the village.

Post-Marital Residency

The preferential pattern for post-marital residency is neolocal. That is, the couple is expected to establish a household or domicile separate from either the bride's or the groom's family. However, a number of factors can influence where the couple will reside. One consideration is the availability of housing. If no housing is available in the village, the couple may have to find a residence elsewhere. A recently built housing estate in Macduff has drawn a number of younger married village couples and their families. Another consideration is the husband's occupation and his pre-marital residency. If both the bride and groom are from the village and he is a fisherman, they are likely to live in the village after they are married. If the wife is from the village and she marries a fisherman from another village, they are also likely to live in the village. But if the wife is from another village and the husband is a Gamrie fisherman, the residency is more likely to be the community of the wife.

This residency pattern can be explained in terms of the work cycle of fishermen. Because fishermen are gone most of the week, women are left to run the household. If the wife continues to work, she may live in her husband's community. She would be gone most of the day and would only return to the village at night. When she has her first child, she is expected to stay at home. Staying in the village means being cut off from her network of family and friends and having to rely on her husband's network within the village. This often results in difficulties for the wife-mother. One way to resolve this problem is for the couple to move to the wife's community. There she can use the networks that have developed during her pre-marital years for assistance or support. On the weekends when her husband is at home, they can visit his community. In purely descriptive terms, post-marital residency is neolocal, but with a matrilateral bias.

"Tee" and "By" Names

Soon after arriving in the village I became aware of a system of naming alternatively called "Tee" or "By" names. Chambers (1911) defines them as nicknames or names intended to distinguish persons who have the same name. Anson (1965) suggests that they were given to young fishermen when they were "brothered"--initiated--into fishing (52). I was never able to distinguish between a tee or by name, as the terms were used interchangeably by villagers. However, it did become clear that alternative names for people were contextually different. First, there were names that referred to individuals and their first name. Diminutives abound in Scottish and are applied to almost every imaginable thing, including first names. For instance, William becomes Willie or Billy or Will'm; David become Davie; Albert become Abb. Another system for naming involves identification of a person with someone else. Benjie's Billy referred to Benjamin's son William who might also be called "young Benjie." A similar linkage of names is sometimes found between husband and wife. Jessie's Johnny would be John, the husband of Jessie. Another category of reference names is individual-specific. Someone might be known as "Sargeant" or "Deef* Will'm" or even by a boat name. In all of these cases, the reference is to a single individual. However, there are other names for people that are more inclusive. And they are used in a different contextual manner. These are specific names used to identify a person in a conversation. One might say, "Go see Sargeant if you want to know more about fishing in the old days." One would never say that he is a Sargeant. To say that one is a Sargeant implies the existence of a named category of people. Thus there are two general categories of alternative names used in Gamrie. One refers to specific individuals, the other to categories that include a number of people.

The existence of systems of alternative names has not escaped the attention of scholars (Fox, 1968; Kaut, 1967; Synge, 1910). Dorian (1970), in her study of villages along the Moray Firth in Sunderland, refers to these names as "by-names." She describes five types. The basic genealogical type--the most common form--is when a person's christian name is paired with either the mother's or father's christian name and more rarely with a grandparent's christian name. She discovered that whole families might have a genealogical by-name. "Descriptive" by-names identify persons according to physical characteristics, occupation, or place of origin or residence. Sometimes these names will be passed on to children. "Derisive" by-names are

---

*deef: deaf

evaluative names that are intended to demean the referent person. "Nonsense" by-names are those that make no sense to the users or to this category schema. The last type, "secondary genealogical" by-names, are some combination of the other types.

Dorian suggests three functions of the by-name system. One is their use as a measure of social solidarity. The use of derisive by-names is usually by persons who share similar sentiments toward the subject of that by-name. The use of the derisive by-name directly to that person reflects personal license and familarity. The second function is to identify persons with identical names. In these Sunderland communities there were many people with the same surname. In one village, 90 percent of the population shared three names. To avoid confusion in identifying individuals, one or more by-names were used. The third function was to entertain. She found that the mere mention of some by-names would result in laughter and recollections of the named person.

In Gamrie one finds all these by-name types. And these names do have the functions that Dorian suggests. Derisive names are used by villagers to identify specific individuals. There are descriptive and genealogical by-names, as well as names that combine these categories. I did not note what she called "nonsense" names. However, nowhere in her analysis does she suggest a category for names that include people from different families. She suggests that some of these names are passed down from one generation to another within a family, but she presents no data to suggest that these names apply across families. Into what category would one place the following use of an alternative name?: "David has nosebleeds; that is a characteristic of the _____." In this context, the reference is not to parent-child, but rather to a more general category of people, one characteristic of which is a common ailment. The specific person referred to in this statement might have a derisive, a descriptive, or a genealogical name that would identify him or her as an individual. But this other name does something more than simply identify this individual. Thus, we are faced with the situation of having to explain this additional category of alternative names.

I would suggest that this type of "allonym"--alternative name--is related to two kinship practices--bilateral descent and village endogamy. In systems of bilateral descent children are related to people through both mother and father. This is reflected in kinship terminology.* Siblings of mother and father are called aunts and uncles with no distinction made between

*Anthropologically, this naming system is called Eskimo terminology.

131

mother's siblings and father's siblings. The same is true of grandparents. Both mother's parents and father's parents are called grandmother or grandfather. In a system of bilateral descent one doubles the number of relatives with each generation one moves back: one has two parents, four grand parents, and eight great grandparents. What enables this system to work is marriage, an alliance between two unrelated persons. Children trace descent through their parents, but the parents are not related to each other. This unrelatedness of parents is important. If parents are related, then their children would have shared ancestors. The same ancestor might be the great grandfather on both the mother's and the father's side.

In large populations with bilateral descent, the separation of mother's and father's line can be maintained if one does not go back too many generations. However, in small populations where spouses are taken from within the population the maintenance of separate lines of descent may be difficult to maintain. Gamrie is such a case. The village was founded in 1720 by persons with a limited number of surnames. As the population increased, up to the early 1900s, the number of people with the same surname also increased because marriages were taking place between persons from the village--village endogamy. Today, we find that almost half the people in the village share one of three names belonging to the original village settlers. Villagers recognize that if one goes back far enough, they are in some way related to each other. The word "freen" is often used to describe this relatedness. "He is freen to me" could be interpreted to mean that he is a friend of mine or that he is a distance relative.

This relatedness can be demonstrated mathematically. If two villagers marry today and they both claim non-relatedness to each other, they would each have 128 separate great, great, great, great grandparents.* This would go back only to 1720 when the population was less than 300. Going back that far would mean there would have to have been 256 unrelated persons in 1720 to whom one could trace one's lineage. Since this is not possible, relatives have to be shared when village endogamy is practiced. Village endogamy was cause for some alarm in the nineteenth century. In Wilson's (1845) account of the village he stated:

> Another peculiarity among the tenantry,
> which proceeds, no doubt, from the same
> cause, is an endless chain of connection,
> running through them by kindred and inter-

---

*I assumed that a generation is 30 years. Thirty time 7 generations is 210 years. Since parents are doubled each generation, the formula is $2^7 = 128$.

132

marriage. . . . This system of clanship is carried still farther among the fishing population in the villages; the most of whom in Crovie and Gardenstown are of the name of _____ or _____ , so that they are obliged to have recourse to nicknames for the sake of distinction. It is a rare thing for them to marry but among themselves, as the manners and habits, as well as the work of the rural population, are quite different from theirs. The influx of strangers, however, at the time of the herring-fishing leads both sexes to form connections with strangers, which will likely in time give more variety of names (295-6).

The names to which he refers are the tee-names or by-names. And he relates these to the limited number of names in the village.

One's legal surname is inherited from one's father--a patronymic system. This name is carried in the official records throughout one's lifetime. A female might be named Mary W1 at birth. If she marries John W2, her official name would be Mary W1W2. Thus, identity with the father's name is maintained. The official names are recognized within the village as being linked to the original settlers, and there is the assumption that people who share the same official name are related to each other. However, because of the unequal distribution of these names, it is difficult if not impossible for all people to marry others without their name, especially if one marries within the village. For example, if 60 percent of the villagers have one name and 40 percent have other names, it is only possible for 40 percent of the dominant named people to marry someone with another name. The remaining 20 percent will either not marry or will marry others with their name--homonymic marriage. It has been noted elsewhere that more and more marriages are between villagers and non-villagers. This is reflected in Table 9. Assuming that there is a preference for marrying partners with different names in order to maintain the structure of bilateral descent, and assuming that given no alternative, one will marry others with the same name, I calculated the frequency of homonymic marriages from 1900 to 1974. The decades at the beginning of this century and again starting in the 1960s had the lowest proportions of homonymic marriages. A number of factors explain these findings. The steam drifter was introduced in the 1909-1919 decade. As a result, fishermen were gone for extended periods of time. This meant that there was little time at home to engage in courtship with persons other than those one knew from school. Thus, one either married within the village or not at all.

Table 9
Number And Percent Of Homonymic Marriages
For The Decades 1900-1969 And The Years 1970-1974

Decade	# of Homonymic Marriages	Total Number of Marriages	%
1900-1909	3	59	5.1
1909-1919	7	52	13.5
1920-1929	2	16	12.5
1930-1939	5	34	14.7
1940-1949	3	26	11.5
1950-1959	6	34	17.7
1960-1969	4	56	7.1
1970-1974	1	29	3.5
	31	306	10.5

Starting in the early 1960s, the practice of commuting to and from the fishing grounds on the west coast with hired busses was replaced by use of a car or van. This enabled fishermen to spend more time in the village on weekends and hence to engage in courtship more actively. Coupled with this was increased affluence, which made possible the ownership of automobiles by unmarried fishermen and which increased the area within which courtship was possible. But time and space increases are not the only factors. In order to marry outside the village, one must become acquainted with eligible courtship partners. The crucial event that increased the pool of potential marriage partners from which one could select a mate was the closing of the local secondary school in 1966. The interaction between local children and children from outside the village in the consolidated school at an age when serious courtship was beginning provided an opportunity structure for extra-village marriage. Thus, these three factors--time, space, and opportunity--all increased at about the same time. The result was a decrease in intra-village marriages between persons with the same name.

But what of the tee-names and by-names? I would suggest that these are names that have been used to create fictive lines of descent. Officially Mary W1 marries John W1 and becomes Mary W1W1. However, in the village, the tee-name or by-name is used to identify the couple. It is Mary (tee-name1) who marries John (tee-name2). In this way different descent lines are maintained and alliances can be formed between persons who are now defined locally as unrelated. I would further suggest that the use of the tee-name is in response to a situation in which marriage is endogomous. When the community becomes more open to the outside, the reliance upon an alternative name system will disappear. This is precisely what I found. Older persons had more knowledge of tee-names and by-names of this

134

type than did younger persons. For younger people, the probability of marrying someone with the same name has been reduced and there is little need for the tee-name or by-name. For older informants, the probability for homonymic marriage was greater, not just for themselves but within their families. Thus, their knowledge and use of tee-names and by-names was reflective of a problem that was real to them.

In summary, it appears that the terms "tee-name" and "by-name" are inadequate to describe the many functional consequences of alternative names. Allonyms are used to identify individuals where there are a limited number of available names and where their use has significance for the maintenance of social group boundaries. They also have cultural consequences. The maintenance of an orderly system of descent and alliance is made possible by the inheritance of names that create differences between same-named people. This latter function is important for the organization of the village as a unit, especially when kinship was the organizing principle. The former function is important because all individuals have identities that distinguish them from others.

Parent-Child/Child-Parent Relationships

The number of children per married couple has been slowly decreasing over the last half century. Families with eight or nine children were common at the turn of the century. The large number of births was largely offset by high infant mortality. Couples with large families might have expected that only half of their children would survive to have families of their own. It has already noted that having children under the hand-line fishing technology could be an economic benefit. Children could help bait hooks or gather bait. When a boy was old enough, he could help his father in the boat. A female child could diffuse some of the burdens of her fishwife mother.

However, having a large number of children had consequences for interaction within a household. Older informants told me about living in two roomed houses in the Seatown and sleeping four or more to a bed. At that time villagers rarely slept alone. Infants slept with their mothers. When children were a little older, they slept with their siblings. And once married, they slept with their spouse. The average number of children per married couple today is 2.4. And, as noted, there has been a corresponding increase in number of houses. Today, children might share a bedroom with their siblings, but is rare that they would have to share a bed.

Responsibility for children, both male and female, is with the mother. Mothers are expected to assume full responsibility for early socialization until the children reach school age, at

135

about five, when part of the responsibility is shifted to the school authorities. Mothers are also the chief liaison with the school. They visit teachers, and it is they who are contacted if there are any problems. Most school events are held during the week, so it is mothers who attend these events. Mothers are direct authority figures for children. Fathers have indirect authority. Behaviors may be rewarded or punished in reference to the father, but sanctioning must wait until the father is at home on the weekend.

Fathers begin to take a direct interest in male children at about the age of twelve or thirteen. Although they have heard about fishing from early childhood, it is not until early adolescence that males have their first experience on a fishing boat. Usually during the summer school holiday a boy will be taken out on his father's boat for a week's sail. There, it is the father's responsibility to watch him as well as teach him some rudimentary boat etiquette. Although the experience of going out on a boat for the first time is significant for the young male, like so many other experiences, it is treated with a controlled indifference. When asked about the event, the young male is as likely as not to simply say "nae bad" and continue what he is doing. Yet, I never met a fisherman who did not remember that first experience.

There is no similar significant experience for women. Young females will help their mothers do "women's work" from an early age. There is no abrupt point at which they are introduced to cleaning, washing, and other household task, only a slow accumulation of information and knowledge about running a household. Males are seldom responsible for this kind of information. Cooking, cleaning, washing dishes, and even shopping are activities young males try to avoid, and most are not encouraged to learn these tasks by either parent.

At the beginning of adolescence there is a "push" from parents and others to become a full participant in the religious community. This is marked by both the kirk and the Brethren by taking communion. Both the kirk and the Close Brethren baptize children when they are young, but neither permits children to take communion until they have reached an age at which they are presumed to have the ability to understand religious beliefs and practices. Whether one goes through the training and instruction that permits one to take communion is largely due to parental influence. Parents who are active in religious affairs are likely to have children who will become members of the kirk or meeting.

Once children leave the local school at the age of 12 there is a lessening of parental control, especially for males. At this age, there begins a period of male bonding. One notes this bonding at the Braeheed. Males stay out later at night than females. What little vandalism there is in the village is often carried out by small groups of young males. It is in these groups that they first experience smoking and drinking. At this age, mothers begin to lose control, and there is a general expectation that local boys will go through a period during which they are excused for much of their errant behavior. The bonds established between males during this period of social experimentation often last a lifetime. Some of these age mates sail on the same boat or continue their friendship in such activities such as religion or recreation. Though there is no strict age grading system, both males and females of similar ages share common life experiences, some of which are interpersonal, others more general. These experiences act both to separate the generations and to weaken kinship obligations. The changes in technology that have resulted in increased affluence over the past two decades have also increased the gap between the experiences of parents and children. And the resultant bonding between males or females who share those experiences serves to further reinforce those differences.

In general, what one notes in the process of maturation is that the move away from parental influence and control is sex differentiated. Males tend to move out from under their mother's authority and rely more on fathers, who are away most of the time. Females tend to remain more closely controlled by their mothers, who are role models for what most females will become--wives and mothers. In spite of these differences, one notes that neither males nor females move out of their natal homes before they are married. Young unmarried males and females continue to live at home if they live in the village. Living alone is observed only in the elderly.

If providing a home for unmarried children is an obligation of parents, are there reciprocal obligations for children to provide a home for their parents? One way to answer this question is by analysis of the residency of older villagers. Table 10 shows those with whom villagers 65 years of age and older live. Most persons 65 and older live with their spouses, although the proportion decreases above the age of 69. This reduction is probably due to death. From these data it appears that as spouses die widows or widowers tend to become part of a relative's household. An examination of the relatives with whom one lives shows that it is likely to be a child or a sibling. In the 70+ category three persons lived with sons and their families, three with daughters and her family, two with siblings and one with another relative. In the 65-69 age category, two lived with siblings and one with a daughter's family. The sex of the parent is not related to the sex of the child with whom one lives. Siblings who live together are most likely to be sisters.

137

Table 10
Residential Status Of Villagers
65 Years Of Age And Older

Age	With Whom One is Living					
	Alone		Spouse		Relative	
	N	%	N	%	N	%
70+	8	27	13	43	9	30
65-69	11	27	27	66	3	7

Older villagers who either live alone or with a spouse tend to live in the Seatown. Those who live with their children are more likely to be found in council housing. Five smaller units in the council housing section of the village were built for older citizens. At present, these are occupied by five women who live alone. Living alone can be problematic, especially if one is sick or infirmed. Aid is available to older villagers through "Home Help," "Meals on Wheels," and the local nurse. Local women are paid a small amount to deliver meals and to clean house for older citizens. The local nurse makes visits to those who must take medication or who have other health problems. For those who are unable to live alone and whose relatives are not able to take them in, there are nursing homes in the area.

Many of the older villagers do not have children living in the village. Because of the large out-migration, their children have moved away. Therefore, they must rely on neighbors and friends to help them with daily problems. Residential propinquity appears to be as much an obligation to help older citizens as kinship. To answer the question posed at the beginning of this discussion of the aged, it appears that the husband-wife bond remains the strongest among older citizens. If a widow or widower has children living in the village, they can usually be prevailed upon to take him or her in. For those who live alone, there is a greater reliance upon neighbors, especially if one has no children living in the village.

The Sexual Division of Labor

The worlds of men and women are clearly divided by the tasks they perform. Men are fishermen, identified with the sea and the boat, and they are away from land most of the time. Women are identified as part of the village with responsibilities for the household and children. While the image of males has not changed much since they first went to sea, the image of females has.

138

The earliest written reports on fishing villages describe the "fishwife" as physically strong, financially shrewd, and firmly in control of house and husband (Anson, 1965;137-145). They carried their husbands and sons to their small fishing craft lest the fishermen's feet get wet; they collected mussels to bait the long lines; they traveled long distances selling fish. At the same time, they took care of their children, sewed, washed and mended clothes and did all the cooking. The role of women changed with a change from hand-line fishing to drift net, when women began migrating with the fishermen to work in curing yards, gutting and packing herring. Since World War II, this has changed. Now women stay in the village to tend house and care for the children; they do not help their husbands with the fishing. They have gone from a partnership role with their fishermen husbands to a dependency role.

The weekly household cycle is unequally divided. Monday through Friday women go shopping, clean the house, and tend to the needs of children. Beginning Friday afternoon there is an air of expectation in the village. In the morning, last-minute shopping is done. The women, who might normally be talking to each other in the street or having a "fly cup," stay at home to make preparations for their husbands and sons to return. Even businesses in the village make special preparations. On Friday and Saturday the local bake house makes the most expensive pastries. The second part of the weekly cycle begins when the fishermen return, and it ends with his leaving.

There is a general expectation that when a fisherman returns home, the evening meal will be prepared, or almost prepared. After eating, it is common for the fisherman to fall asleep on the setee or "go to his bed" for a rest. For most fishermen the land sleep cycle is out of synch with his work-week cycle. On the boat, they sleep when the work is finished; this varies according to fishing technology and species of fish caught. Thus, sleeping may occur at anytime during a 24-hour period. Almost the only time a fisherman gets to sleep for six or eight hours straight is during the steam out to the fishing grounds or the steam back to the harbor. Normally, the sleep periods between work cycles are two to three hours in length. This sleep pattern continues on the weekends. They may be wide awake when their wives are ready for bed; they may have a "kip" in the morning or afternoon. But whatever the pattern, the wife is expected to adjust to the husband's schedule.

On the weekends, as during the week, women are expected to do all the cooking. The kitchen is part of the women's world. The only exception to this definition of space is related to the "fry" brought back by the fisherman-husband. Each man on the boat can take home fish for himself and his family. If

139

this fish needs preparation, either for freezing at home or to be eaten on the weekend, it will be done by the fisherman. Otherwise, the woman is expected to be in control when food is concerned. She makes and serves tea when there are guests in the house, and she brings out a plate or plates containing a variety of "sweets" --small cakes, biscuits,* pieces of cake, and/or sweeties. Not to offer something to a guest, even though he or she may refuse, is considered a breach of etiquette for the female. Women are not, however, expected to offer guests beer or spirits. This is a male responsibility.

As a part of the definition of a "good" wife there is the expectation that she keep a clean house. Because most of the floors in Gamrie houses are covered with carpet, women must continually "hoover."** As a local wag once said to me: "If Gamrie had a flag, it would contain a hoover." When the husband comes home on the weekend, the house should be clean and in order.

Most weekend recreational activities are dictated by the husband. Going out for a meal, going shopping, or going to a dance are initiated by the male. These activities are often viewed as rewards by the wife for a job well done during the week. It is rare that local women go out together during the week. The only activity they might do jointly with other local women is to shop for groceries, which is considered a female activity.

On Sundays most businesses are closed in this area. There is one small grocer in the country and a news shop in Macduff where one can buy the Sunday newspapers. The only other activities are religion and eating out.** For those who are active participants in religion, much of the day is spent in either the kirk or the meeting hall. This is usually a family activity. For others, the day might be spent visiting relatives in the village or in nearby communities. Since fishermen often leave on Sunday evening, any meals eaten out would most likely be in the late morning or afternoon.

In addition to cooking, cleaning, and other household activities, women are usually responsible for the house itself. Most house maintenance is taken care of during the week when the fishermen are away. Women are expected to engage workmen to make minor house or appliance repairs if they are necessary. This decision-making concerning the house does not, however, extend to such major purchases as appliances, furniture, or

---

*biscuits: cookies
**hoover: vacuum
***There is a golf course nearby, but only two or three fishermen from the village ever play golf on Sunday.

extensive renovations of the house. These are either done jointly or by the husband alone. The same holds true for the purchase of an automobile. Usually this is a male decision.

Because of the work cycle of fishermen, there are a number of activities that are difficult for them to do. For example, making deposits in the bank, paying the health stamp or unemployment insurance or local rates, and paying post office taxes on the radio or T.V. are done by the wife during the week. Any repairs on the automobile must be done during the week, and it is the wife who has this responsibility.

In spite of having such responsibilities, women enjoy little prestige. The work of males is more highly valued than the work of females. This differential prestige within the village reflects a more general observation concerning the relationship between prestige and exchange. Friedl (1975) suggests that greater sexual prestige is accorded the sex that participates in wider exchange networks. Exchange is the process by which commodities produced are distributed. The larger the exchange networks over which one has control the greater prestige one has. The housewife has control over a household. She is responsible for the exchange of goods and services within that unit. The fisherman is part of a much larger exchange network that links his activities to regional, national and international markets. In this sense, he is part of an activity structure that links households. The popular image of the old fishwife suggests that women's prestige might previously been higher. In the past, the fisherman had control over an individual boat, but it was the fishwife who linked that boat's activities to a broader market network. One must be very cautious about making such statements concerning changing social prestige. Much of our knowledge about the fishwife comes from folklore, which may be historically inaccurate. However, the notion of the fishwife does represent an idealized type, if not a specific person or persons. Real or imagined, the fishwife has attributes that define sexual prestige in terms of control over exchange networks. Thus, as an historical fact, the fishwife may never have existed. But, as a lesson about the value of men's and women's work she illustrates the principles by which prestige is accorded.

Death and the Funeral

Death is a biological fact. Upon death the body ceases its normal functions and the process of decomposition begins. It is therefore incumbent upon the living to dispose of the corpse in some manner. The funeral is a cultural fact. People are part of status and interaction networks, the patterns of which are interrupted when death occurs. In order to mend those networks a series of rituals is performed. Through observation of those rituals one can learn a great deal about those networks

141

and the position the deceased held within them. The ways people treat their dead tell us something about how they treat their living.

Kinship plays an important role in the death ritual within the village. The funeral reflects community definitions of age and sex as well as religious participation. Thus, the funeral is a kind of social microcosm bringing together and displaying publicly some of the definitions and rules that characterized the village as a social unit.

Upon biological death, a standard set of procedures are followed. If a person dies at home, the local doctor is called to certify death. If the person dies in a hospital, the death is certified by an attending doctor. Soon after death, the local joiner,* who is also the undertaker, is called. He will order the coffin and see that death notices are printed. Death notices are published in the newspaper. Small, black bordered notices are also placed in the windows of local shops. The notice in the newspaper will usually indicate the place of death, the age of the deceased, the nearest surviving kin, and the place and time of the funeral. An additional responsibility of the undertaker is to hire a bus that will take mourners from the funeral to the burial in the parish church yard.

If the deceased is a male, the undertaker takes responsibility for bathing and dressing the body for the funeral. If the deceased is a female, it is usual for female friends, relatives and neighbors to take this responsibility. It is a common practice to have the funeral in the house of the deceased, although occasionally funeral services are held in the Kirk or the meeting halls. Before the funeral, the deceased will lie in the living room of the house. The coffin is often brought in and taken out through a window, especially in the Seatown houses, because the doorways are too narrow. It is the responsibility of the joiner to "grease" the window frames to ensure that they can be opened when necessary.

In a death notice some reference is made to callers. If callers are welcome, they come to the house and sit with the family of the deceased. This period is no longer than a few days, since embalming is not practiced. When the funeral is held often depends upon how quickly relatives of the deceased can get to the village and how soon other arrangements can be made, such as digging the grave, when the bus is available, or in the case of the Brethren, when a speaker can be obtained.

Who officiates at the funeral and the burial depends upon the religious affiliation of the deceased and the deceased's

*joiner: a carpenter

142

family. Those who are members of the kirk will have the minister. Those who are members of the Brethren will have a representative of the meeting. Funerals are usually held in the afternoon. Immediate family members and women stay inside the house of the deceased. Men who are not members of the family stand in the street outside the house. The minister or meeting representative usually stands in the doorway so that both those outside and inside can hear. This service usually lasts about one hour. After the funeral, the coffin is taken, by hearse, to the church yard for burial.

Burials are male events. After the funeral the males leave, either by bus or by car to the church yard. Most of those attending the burial are already at the grave site when the hearse arrives. The coffin is carried from the hearse and placed on wooden boards over the grave. Pallbearers are determined by the family of the deceased. Cards, with the shape of a coffin, are given to each pallbearer to indicate which of the "cords" he will hold. Illustration 5 shows the number positions of pallbearers. Number one cord goes to the closest male relative--a father, a son, a brother, a grandson. The next cord goes to the next closest relative and so on. If the deceased is a female, number one cord would normally go to her husband, then to her father, and on through sons, brothers, cousins and other relatives.* After the burial service, the boards over the grave are removed and the coffin is lowered into the grave with the cords.

Illustration 5
Facsimile of Coffin Card

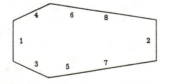

Women friends and relatives of the deceased stay at the house where the funeral took place. After the burial, the males who were close relatives or friends of the deceased return to the house, where they are given something to eat, usually tea and sandwiches or sweet rolls and cakes.

*Age is sometimes a factor in allocating cords. Older or younger males who are physically incapable of handling a cord may be excluded, in spite of the fact that kinship affiliation to the deceased entitles them to a cord.

143

The mourning period varies. As previously stated, mourning is indicated by closed window curtains or venetian blinds. It is seldom more than two weeks before the curtains and blinds are open and the mourning period ends.

Since the sequence of steps from biological death to cultural death is fairly routinized in Gamrie and does not vary with the age, sex, religion, or prestige of the deceased, funerals and burials are judged qualitatively by the number of people who attend. And the number of people who attend is reflective of the general expectations and sentiments of villagers. As a general observation, attendance varies by the age, sex, occupational status, and religious participation of the deceased. Young people below the age when they would enter the work force and older people beyond retirement age have fewer people in attendance than persons inbetween those age categories. Females have fewer mourners than males. Skippers have more than deck hands. The number of people at the funeral and burial is influenced by skippers. If an individual fisherman wants to attend a funeral during the week, he would be unable to go to sea that week. If a skipper wants to attend a funeral during the week he can decide to bring the boat back for that day. The only exception to this would be when a crew member dies. It is considered proper that the boat stay home the week of the funeral.

The number of people who attend a funeral varies considerably. At the extremes are two funerals I observed of older people. One was a male age 72; the other a female age 82. Between 25 and 30 people attended the burial; there were approximately twice as many people at the funeral. At two funerals of skipper's sons the number of participants was over 200. Neither one of these males was married and both served on their father's boats. One obvious difference between these cases is prestige. Skippers enjoy high prestige, and this is transferred to their immediate families--sons, daughters, wives. Another difference is age. The 72-year-old male and the 82-year-old female had fulfilled the expectations of a "normal" lifetime. Both had married, had had children and even had become grandparents. The older male had been a fisherman all his life and was retired. In contrast, the young males had only just begun to fullfill the cultural expectations for a male. Neither was married, but both were working fishermen in a situation where they were likely to become skippers someday. They had not established separate households and they had no procreated heirs. Their lives were but promissory notes, the payments on which could not be paid because of death. The number of people who attended their funerals and burials and the intensity of public bereavement were expressions of those cultural expectations.

One additional factor associated with attendance at funerals is religious affiliation and participation. If the deceased is an active member of the kirk or Brethren, others from the kirk or the particular division of the Brethren are expected to attend the funeral and burial. If the deceased has a position of honor or prestige within the kirk or meeting, the expectation to attend is more imperative. Thus, prestige within a religious organization gets translated into the prestige of the funeral.

The Importance of Kinship in Everyday Life

Anthropologists have been intrigued with kinship systems ever since the discipline began over 100 years ago. And it may very well be that kinship is as much an anthropological invention as a social reality. The question that must be asked eventually is whether kinship has behavioral consequences. Do people act in ways that are determined by the characteristics of the kinship in their culture? Gamrie provides us with a situation within which it is possible to examine this question.

It has been noted that villagers acknowledge their inter-relatedness. Ask a villager how he or she is related to someone else and the reply may be specific--"He is my cousin" or "She is married to my nephew." Or it may be more general--"Some W____'s married R____'s and since I'm a W____ and she's a R____, we are related." This inter-relatedness of villagers can be corroborated by analysis of birth, death and marriage records. But the question still remains whether it has any behavioral consequences.

Because most villagers are all related to each other in one way or another, interaction between villagers is between kinsmen. If a person buys something from the grocer and that grocer is related, is it because of kinship ties that the purchase was made? If a skipper hires crew members who are kin are we to conclude that kinship connections carry with them obligations for recruitment? If kinsmen attend the same kirk or meeting can one conclude that religious behavior is determined by kin attachments? The answer to these questions is no. It is no on two grounds-- logical and observational. Logically, variations cannot be explained by constants. On observational grounds one notes that persons within the village do not behave similarly with similar kinsmen. Not all brothers are members of the same kirk or meeting, nor do they all have berths on the same boat. Persons who are related but are separated by great genealogical distance may be friends, while persons who are immediate consanguinal kin may be bitter enemies. It is difficult to predict friendship and organizational affiliation through kinship. Thus, while kinship is pervasive, it is not the characteristic that determines all relationships.

145

A number of factors other than kinship explain the behaviors of the villagers. For example, one of the grocers in the village is a member of the Brethren. His clientele is made up of other Brethren, many of whom are not closely related, and of people who live nearby who are neither Brethren nor related. This particular grocery is located "up the brae," close to the council houses and the bungalows. It also has the only petrol* pump in the village. People patronize him because it is convenient or because they are in need of petrol, not because they are kin. The two grocers on Main Street both have bakeries.* One sells newspapers, the other does not. Comparisons of these two are often made on the basis of which one makes the better loaf. Although each is related to other villagers, their customers are not all direct kinsmen. The utilization of local shops, therefore, is based on a number of considerations. It might be propinquity or pecuniary or religious or some combination of these factors.

Another factor influencing interaction is a distinction that marks the boundary between the village and the adjacent countryside. This is the fisher-farmer or village-country distinction, which is a reflection of different work cycles and interests. Fishermen who are gone all week have little opportunity to interact with farmers. Wives of both fishermen and farmers are home during the week, but they interact infrequently. The distinction between fisher and farmer begins for children when they enter the local school. During the school day, children from the village interact with children from the country. After school, they return home. The distinction continues on Sundays. Children from the village may attend the village kirk; farm children attend the country kirk. There are no country Brethren. Because of the residential and occupational gulf between these two populations, very few marriages occur between them. Thus, the ties that do exist between them are based on considerations other than kinship.

There are occasions that bring fisher and farm people together. One is the funeral. Depending upon who the deceased is, one is likely to find farmers at the burial of a fisherman. One is not, however, as likely to find fishermen at the burial of a farmer. This is due to the work cycle. The farmer's participation in a funeral means that he will miss an afternoon's work. For the fisherman, a whole week is lost. Therefore, farmers will attend the funeral of a fisherman with whom they might have had little interaction whereas fishermen are found only at funerals of farmers with whom they enjoyed a close relationship.

---

*Petrol: gasoline
**One of the bakehouses closed in 1981.

146

Another example of overlapping interests was a party to commemorating the departure of a very popular local doctor, who served both the country and the village population. The event, held in the village hall, was organized by the RLNI, an organization of village women, and the WRI, an organization of country women. The event was a success. Both fisher and farm people attended, and the hall never held so many people at one time. After gifts were presented to the doctor and speeches were made, tea was served by the two organizations. As the crowd dispersed, representatives from each organization began picking up cups and saucers and spoons that had been left around the hall. Thus began the closest thing to gyno-warfare the village had ever seen. There were shouts of, "These are our cups," or "Leave those plates, they belong to _____." The battle raged until each organization had safely put away its own chinaware. But despite this, the event had marked an integration between farmer and fisher. The village organization had served tea to country people. The farm organization had served tea to fisher people. For a brief moment there was no distinction between the two. At the end of the evening it was time to put the symbols that distinguished them back into proper order. A cup was no longer a container for a liquid, it was a symbol of a fundamental distinction between two separate ways of life. The boundaries between the two populations were re-established and the symbols were locked into cupboards.

In this section I have noted the declining influence of kinship on the everyday lives of villagers. This is not to say that kinship structures are totally unimportant. One might think of kinship for those in Gamrie as an available, rather than an imperative structure. In times of need or crisis, kinship provides support facilities. For ritual purposes--weddings and funerals--it provides personnel. Kinship creates groups responsible for nurturing and training children to become adult members of the community. The declining influence of kinship is marked by the size of available kinship structures. What were once large, extended networks of kinsmen have shrunk to nuclear families with loosely knit ties to other nuclear families. Within those nuclear units, kinship is just as imperative as it was in the past.

A Couple After a Blackening

VI: SOCIAL ORGANIZATION: RELIGION AND CHURCHES

A village is not just a place with people. It is a moral community held together by shared beliefs, values, and expectations. Some of those beliefs have been codified and organized into what we call church. In this section the history and organization of the village churches is reviewed.

The Kirk: The Church of Scotland

Christianity came to what is now Scotland sometime in the fifth century as a result of missionaries representing the Christian Roman Empire. The churches, monasteries, and universities founded by these missionaries were sanctioned by papal authority, but they were largely under the control of the crowned heads of England and Scotland. The early churches held vast amounts of land and were able to extract rents from those who used the land. Many monks and priests were independent entrepreneurs who were as concerned with collecting rents as they were with saving souls.

The uneasy relationship among the church, the state, and the population was resolved in 1560, when Parliament repudiated Rome, forbade the celebration of mass, and adopted a reformed "Confession of Faith" (Donaldson, 1980:185). The results of this reformation were largely organizational. The priesthood was no longer appointed by the crown or pope, but rather by the congregation, and financial responsibilities were shifted to "elders." In 1561, a General Assembly was established that had an organization similar to Parliament. Three groups were represented in the Assembly--the nobles and lairds, burgesses chosen by town councils, and superintendents and such ministers as they might select (Donaldson, 185).

The redistribution of power from the bishopric to the parishioners was reflected in a number of changes. One was language. The Bible and the service were to be in the language of the people. Another change was in increased participation by the laity in the service and communion, as well as more control in selecting and overseeing the ministry. In spite of the reformers' intentions to decentralize power in the church through the General Assembly, ministers were still appointed to vacant bishoprics and were able to exercise a great deal of power in the selection of clergy. The response to this situation was divided between the Presbyterians, who pressed for the equality of ministers, and the Episcopalians, who favored an office of bishop. These two systems alternated power in the Assembly until 1690, when the Presbyterians prevailed in Scotland and the Episcopalians triumphed in England.

The establishment of a Church of Scotland with an identity independent from England, however, did not result in a church with ideological and organizational consensus. There were ideological distinctions between the "Evangelicals," who were Calvinists, especially with reference to the doctrine of predestination, and the "Moderates," who emphasized religion as an ethical and moral system, with little reference to the supernatural (Donaldson, 194). The organizational differences were between those who felt that the Assembly, in a modified form, should be reinstated and those who supported parliamentary control, but not by the Parliament at Westminster.

Thus began a period of furcations. In 1733 the First or Original Secession Church broke away. It was conservative in theology and supported the Assembly. It split again 11 years later over the issue of whether the burgesses had power to acknowledge the true religion of a region. This split resulted in the "Burgher" and "Anti-Burgher" divisions. A further split at the end of the 1700s was precipitated by the question of the state's obligation to enforce church law, and it resulted in the "Old Light" and the "New Light" sections. In 1761, the issue of patronage resulted in yet another division. Ministers who identified with their congregations refused to take part in admitting ministers who were presented by patrons. This led to the Second Secession or Relief Church which refused state support and formed churches that were supported by congregations.

Throughout the 1700s, the Assembly had been controlled by the "Moderates," but by the middle 1800s the number of "Evangelicals" had grown large enough to break away and form the Free Church of Scotland. This period in church history is called the "Disruption." The issues during the Disruption were basically the same as they had been in the 1700s, but one new issue was added--missionary activities in foreign lands and in the growing towns of Scotland. The Free Kirk was able to obtain enough financial support to build churches and schools that paralleled those of the existing church. It also attracted 39 percent of the clergy and almost one-third of the parishioners (Donaldson, 195). Further divisions and schisms occurred in the latter half of the nineteenth century, so that by the late 1800s there were three major groupings--The Church of Scotland, The Free Church, and the United Presbyterian Church.

In 1900, the United Presbyterian and the Free Church joined to form the United Free Church. This alliance resulted in the Free Church being larger than the Church of Scotland and hence in a position of power during negotiation in matters of theology and administration. Negotiations between the United Free Church and the Church of Scotland were intensified between 1921 and 1925. The result was the formation of the Church of Scotland with the doctrine of the United Free Church. The Parliament abdicated its power over church matters. Power was placed with the presbytery. Ministers were elected by the church elders, who were also the lay ministry. Church business was controlled by an elected vestry, clerity and laity elected bishops, and the laity was represented on councils and synods. Thus the administration of church matters was placed under local control.

The history of churches in Gamrie reflects this history. The earliest church, St. John's, was originally Roman Catholic. After the Reformation it was taken over by the Established Church (the Church of England). According to Wilson (1745), the minister in 1732 was a crown patron. By 1837, the Established Church had the largest membership, although there were a small number of families who were Independents and United Secessionists (Wilson, 1845). The church buildings and manses in the parish during this period were donated by the laird and other benefactors, who, one would suspect, exercised some control of the ministry. The present Church of Scotland building in the village was originally built by the Free Church in the late 1800s at the same time the Established Church maintained a building just a few yards away. With the alliance of the churches in the twentieth century, the Free Church building became the Church of Scotland building.

The organization of the Church of Scotland in the village today is presbyterian. Elders are elected by the parishioners as a governing board and a lay ministry. They have responsibility for electing the minister and have the power to dismiss him if they see fit. This local control of church matters means that Churches of Scotland will reflect local interests in matters of belief. Hence, one notes vast differences in religious emphasis from community to community. For example, the nearby country Church of Scotland is considered much less conservative than the village church in matters of belief and practice.

Revivals

If anti-clericalism was a concern of the Reformationists and the leaders of the Church of Scotland, it was even more of a concern among the evangelists who appeared along the Moray Firth in the mid-1800s. Some of these evangelists were representatives of the Free Kirk. Others were part of a charismatic evangelistic movement. From early accounts, the populations in places like Gamrie were a "rough, uneducated, and immoral set of men, professional smugglers, and everywhere addicted to drink" (Anson, 1975:89). The writer of the Second Statistical Account on the parish of Gamrie, while otherwise praiseful of parish residents, made it clear that, "Low public-houses have been a great nuisance in this parish and neighborhood, for a considerable number of years. There are far too many of them yet in the town of Macduff and the villages" (Wilson, 1845:295). It must be kept in mind that in 1846 there was a serious potato blight. A large number of people bordered on starvation, and there were riots in Macduff and Fraserburgh. Ships of war patrolled the Moray Firth to prevent the citizenry from stopping boats with food from going south (Johnston, 1946:276). This blight, coupled with the failed herring fishing three years before, resulted in social conditions that made the population susceptible to social movements. There is little wonder that between the economic conditions and the "Disruption" in the Church, people were willing to listen and even join those who promised better conditions.

The Brethren

One of the best known evangelists along the Moray Firth was James Turner, a cooper and herring curer from Peterhead (Anson, 1975:89). Turner is attributed with converting more than eight thousand people along the coast, first in the towns and later in the small fishing villages. Soon after Turner began his revival, the Salvation Army came to the region. However, the Army concentrated its attention on people in towns and cities and never gained strength in the smaller fishing villages. There is some evidence that Turner was familiar with Gamrie. According to Adams (1972), Turner, who died at the age of 100, gave Gamrie the epithet "The Non-Swearing Village," based upon a complaint made by the local pub owner that two patrons had said "bloody" and "damn." Anson's reference to Turner suggests that he was part of a religious movement that began in America and then diffused to Britain via Ulster (89). His reference was probably to the religious movement that began in Dublin in 1827 under the influence of John Nelson Darby and that later became known as the Plymouth Brethren.

The early Brethren were similar in theology to the evangelical Protestants of the time. They accepted literal interpretations of the Scriptures, but they rejected revivalism (Wilson, 1967:288). They differed from the evangelicals in organization, rejecting all but minimal organization. The central belief was that all members of the Brethren were saints and as such could have no formal clergy or leadership.

The early Brethren were rather open about membership. But in 1848, under the direction of Darby, the Exclusive branch of Brethrenism developed. The Exclusives rejected all but the most personal type of evangelism and along with that, all but the most necessary ties to secular society. This included membership in any unions or associations, as well as participation in government, including voting. The early Brethren, now the Open Brethren, moved rather rapidly over Britain through independent evangelism at the local level. With no strong leadership, charismatic or otherwise, they formed loose-knit confederations of meetings.

The Exclusives, in spite of their renouncement of any leadership, nevertheless were characterized by a sense of unity through a succession of informal but influential leaders. Assemblies within a region met once a month at what was called "care meetings." At these meetings, matters of doctrine were discussed and decided. Local meetings or individuals who disagreed with decisions made at the care meetings were excommunicated. Those who agreed were received into fellowship.

As a result of these procedures, a number of schisms developed among the Exclusives in Britain and North America. These schisms often focused on two issue--exclusiveness and evangelism. There were those who felt the teachings of the Exclusives should be restricted to a select few. Others felt that evangelism should be practiced to recruit new membership. The resulting splits led to greater exclusiveness, even to the point where Exclusives would not permit Open Brethren to participate in their meetings while they admitted other Christians to become members.

Soon after the turn of the century, James Taylor,Sr., became the acknowledged leader of the Exclusives. Taylor was a linen merchant from New York who regularly did business in Britain. Taylor's dominance over Brethren theology and practice was complete. His writings on theological matters were spread rapidly through the care meetings. Questioning of his doctrine, either by individuals or whole meetings, resulted in prompt excommunication. Taylor continued a trend among the exclusives. From Darby on, the leadership had consisted of persons with the financial means to devote full time to the ministry. Under Taylor there developed the idea that Exclusive practices were to take precedence over any and all competing expectations. Members were expected to abandon job, family, or anything else that contradicted the will of the assembly. Members of a meeting thus had to submit their lives not only to their local meeting, but also to the care meeting itself. Taylor died in 1953. After his death a number of prominent Brethren vied for the leadership role, but six years later it was clear that his son, James Taylor, Jr.--"Big Jim"--had taken the reins.

Under the rule of James Taylor, Sr., the Exclusives had not penetrated the North-East of Scotland. His son, however, traveled all along the Moray Firth, visiting and preaching in fishing towns and villages, and preached in Gamrie at what is now the Close meeting hall across from the Kirk. This event attracted a wide audience of fisher folk, many of whom became converts to exclusive practices and beliefs.

Many of these converts were from the Open meeting, which had moved into the Moray Firth area from England in 1921. The fishing had been bad in the summer of 1921 and had become worse as the year elapsed. Herring fishermen from along the Moray Firth were on their summer cycle of herring fishing in Yarmouth and Lowestoft. The herring fishing was as poor there as it had been elsewhere, but the revival spirit was not. As Anson (1975) observed:

> Wandering round the streets of Yarmouth during those autumn evenings, I often came across groups of fishermen gathered under a lamp-post, singing hymns with intense fervour or listening with hungry, eager faces to the fiery, passionate words of some young evangelist, whose preaching was interrupted by frequent ejaculation of "Amen" and "Hallelujah!" Within some of the Non-conformist chapels one found it difficult to obtain standing-room, every corner being filled with fishermen and fisher-lassies. After much hymn-singing, endless prayers and petitions for those whose hearts were still hardened, recent converts would stand up and give their "testimony." From every part of the building you saw middle-aged, weather-beaten skippers, young deck-hands, and countless lassies making their way to the penitents' form. And when at last the meeting was over some of the more enthusiastic would carry on their offensive among the crowds that were still loafing round the marketplace after the public houses had been closed. Sudden "conversions" took place, men would doff hats and caps, and, joining hands, sing together such stirring hymns as Throw out the life-line or Will your anchor hold? (93-94)

After that summer in Yarmouth, the revivals were brought back to the Moray Firth.

The Open Brethren in Gamrie trace their local meeting beginnings to 1921, the year the revivalist Jock Troup from Wick came to the village. A number of fishermen were converted by Jock Troup but remained members of the Kirk. Three of the converts practiced a lay ministry, preaching wherever and whenever they could on their travels around the coast of Britain. These three were converted to the Open Brethren quite independently of each other. In 1946 they discovered their independent conversions and decided to start a meeting in the village. For ten months they met at the public hall. Then in 1947 they moved into their present location in the "bog."

The history of the Open Brethren in the village is very typical of Open Brethren structure. Three men simply decided, on the basis of common experience, to start a meeting. The Open have no formal federation other than their support of Muller's Orphanages and, more recently, some missionary work. They are locally organized and locally run. They rely upon each other for their ministry, but they do bring in speakers from other meetings. What links various local meetings to each other are informal ties of friendship and sometimes kinship.

The membership of the Open meeting is made up of those who are "gathered out"--persons saved and baptised--and is collectively known as the "company," or the meeting family. The Open have three worship services on Sunday. The morning meeting at 11:00 is attended by the "company." At this service, there is communion for members of the family. The 3 p.m. service is the ministry. At this service there is a word for "believers," those who believe but have not been "gathered out." Members of the "company" also attend this meeting. The evening service at 6:00 is the "word for non-believers." Persons at this service would include members of the company, the believers, and guests. Thus, the world view of Brethren is made up of three categories--the company, the believers, and the non-believers. The way that one can move from the believer to the company category is a feature of Open Brethrenism that distinguishes it from the Close and Exclusive branches. Membership into the company is marked by full immersion baptism at the age of 12 or so. The Close and the Exclusives practice "home baptism" of children by sprinkling rather than immersion.

The Open Brethren, like the Close and Exclusive, is a male-dominated religious practice. Females are members of the meeting family, but they play no part to in the services. They are, however, responsible for keeping the meeting hall clean. Each meeting has a number of males called "overseers" who are responsible for the sacred and secular activities of that meeting. The secular decisions include matters such as improvements and maintenance of the meeting hall and paying visiting speakers. The sacred decisions involve the admittance of new or transferred members and selection of guest speakers for Sunday or for funerals and weddings. These overseers may be further divided into "teachers" and the "exercised." Teachers are those who understand scripture and doctrine, and are able to help others understand. The exercised are those having talent for speaking from the platform. The exercised do the actual preaching.

James Taylor, Jr.'s evangelism had consequences for Moray Firth fishermen converts quite different from land based converts. Big Jim's exclusiveness required members to attend all meetings. For fishermen on a weekly fishing cycle this sometimes meant making a choice between following Big Jim or giving up fishing. Many chose to give up fishing. Fishermen were also expected to withdraw from any fishermen's cooperatives or associations. The only compensation given to fishermen was permitting them to listen to the radio, otherwise prohibited, for weather reports or other fishing information. Taylor's new exclusivism established a set of rules clearly marking their membership off from other members of the community. For example:

1. Children were not permitted to take part in religious services in school.

2. Children were not permitted to take part in out-of-school sports or clubs.

3. Brethren were not permitted to eat with non-Brethren. This sometimes led to conflicts on boat where both Brethren and non-Brethren were crew members.

4. There were restrictions on university attendance. One had to avoid all student associations and unions.

5. Occupations involving Sunday work or those where membership in unions or professional associations were required could not be pursued.

6. Brethren could not live in flats where one shared bathrooms or even a front door with non-Exclusives.

7. Members could not move from one house to another without the permission of the assembly.

8. Entertainment was prohibited. No radios or television.

More specific rules pertained to dress, such as:

1. Females could not cut their hair.
2. Females could not wear undergarments--no bras or girdles.
3. Neither males nor females could wear hats.

In the exclusive household, the day began and ended with prayers and hymns. Usually all members of a household were members of the same meeting, although there were cases when some household members were not members. In such a case, the Exclusives were expected to avoid that member of the household, be it wife, husband, brother, sister, or even child. Children who did not become members of the fellowship by the age of 13 would be prohibited from eating with the rest of the family. When they were old enough, they were "abandoned" and made to leave home (Wilson, 1967:328).

This exclusiveness was not just applied to the living, but also to the dead. A widely known story in the village concerns a man whose father had died. By kinship rights he should have been given a cord at the burial. However, his father and his brothers were Exclusives and he was not. Therefore, he was not offered a cord because the Exclusives prohibited non-Exclusives from participating in burials. In spite of this, the non-Exclusive son went to the burial and demanded his cord. When he was refused, so the story goes, he took out his knife and threatened to cut the other cords if he did not get his. He was eventually given a cord.

Taylor's tight rein over exclusive doctrine and practice continued until 1970 when he was caught, "in flagrante delicto" with a woman during a personal foot-washing ceremony. Because of this, many assemblies withdrew support of him and became what is now known as Close Brethren. Taylor's death a few months after the "incident" ended a 70-year dominance of the Exclusives by the Taylors, and many of the rules imposed by Taylor were relaxed. Women are now permitted to cut their hair. Drinking, which was permitted under Taylor, was forbidden. Now, more Brethren exchange presents at Christmastime and have Christmas tree. There has also been a relaxation on the prohibition of radios, but there is still controversy about the ownership of and/or watching of television. During the 1982 field season it appeared that some of the controversy concerning television had been resolved. Apparently after the death of one of the Close Brethren leaders, some of the younger members of the meeting urged a relaxation of the television prohibition. The result was the reopening of the meeting hall in the Seatown by members who held to the prohibition, while the halls up the brae left ownership and watching to individual members. This change was reflected in the behavior of a young lad whose parents were very active members of the meeting, and who was also a friend of the children of one of my main informants. During the 1981 field season he would often visit the children of my informant while they were watching television. During these visits he would stand with his back toward the television set. In 1982, he not only watched television but his family had two sets of their own.

Religion: The Objectification of Village Organization

Religious beliefs and practices do not exist in a social vacuum. They are embedded into a larger social matrix. Symbolically, these beliefs and practices attempt to objectify those rules of social life that make it orderly and predictable. Organizationally, religions reflect the varieties of organizational forms that characterize a society. Thus, religious practices and organizations change as the economic, political, and other institutional arrangements of a society change. In this section, the question of changes in the religious affiliations of villagers is examined.

In the 1700s the village organization was characterized by a simple division of power. The laird owned and controlled all land. The fishermen paid rents and were subject to the authority of the crown's appointee. The church followed this same pattern. The minister was appointed by the crown, and authority over education and morality was controlled through the "kirk session." Appointment of the school teacher and punishment of immoral acts was determined by a select appointed council. The Free Church movement in the 1800s retained much of the power of the Established Church of the 1700s, but more control over the appointment of church leaders was vested in the village. In the late 1800s control over education was taken away from the church and assumed by the state, and the Free Church was built in the village. The Free kirk became the church in the village in 1930.

In comparing the Brethren with the kirk, one notes different organization structures. The kirk has a leader who is appointed by the elders. However, the minister is also a representative of the formal hierarchy of the Church of Scotland, and he is not a villager. The elders of the kirk are villagers who have been elected to their position by the parishioners. The Brethren have a communal structure. There is no official leadership and all males have the "right" to address the assembly. Members are all from the village. These two organizational types fall toward the same end of a continuum of religious organization. At one end is the ecclesiastical form of organization with a full-time professional priesthood organized bureaucratically into offices of specialists. Information and

158

doctrine in this type of organization moves down to the membership from persons who hold offices with progressively more power as one moves toward the top of the hierachy. At the other end of this continuum is the communal cult or sect where power is diffused throughout the membership and there is no specialization other than that which emerges because of individual expertise or predisposition. The Brethren fall closest to the communal cult or sect end of the continuum. The kirk has characteristics of both the communal cult and the ecclesiastical form.

Fishing as an economic activity has been characterized by cycles of prosperity and depression. The migration of fish, changing markets, and shifts in technology led to uncertainty in economic outcomes. This uncertainty resulted in a wide variety of magical practices by fishermen at sea. On land, these changes in economic cycles resulted in changes in village organization. When people were uniformly affected by poor economic conditions, cooperation between villagers was essential to maximize what few economic rewards were available. This was accomplished by "leveling," a social mechanism that acts to even out differences between community members (Foster, 1967). Under these conditions, fishermen shared information with each other, and any attempt to display success was met with social disapproval. The revivals of 1921 and the subsequent diffusion of Brethrenism to small communities such as Gamrie grew out of such conditions. The communalism of Brethren organization was compatible with the cooperative organization of fishing. Villagers left the kirk and joined the various meetings in the village.

Watt (1974) suggests that this shift in affiliation from kirk to Brethren was, in part, responsible for the prosperity of Gamrie fishermen. Because most secular activities were banned by the Brethren, monies made in fishing were reinvested in modern boats, which enabled Gamrie fishermen to compete successfully with fishermen from other ports. Another attribute of Brethrenism was the belief that each member was a saint who communicated directly with God. This belief corresponded nicely with the entrepreneural practices of fishermen. Each skipper was independent of organization control. They did not work for others.

As noted, there has been a growing realization among fishermen that being independent may not be the most efficient system for dealing with market and governmental forces. The increased frequency of collective activities among fishermen and the increased importance of the Scottish Fishermen's Federation certainly attest to this change in organization. The lone skipper protesting prices in the market place will not be heard. The skipper who represents two or three hundred others, willing to strike, does make an impression.

159

Elsewhere it has been shown how changes in fishing technology have resulted in greater differentiation in the boat's division of labor. And, with investment costs rising, there has been a greater dependency upon outside financial support. The skipper now stands at the top of the boat's hierarchy and it would be almost impossible for him to reject the secular world. Corresponding to these changes have been changes in religious affiliations.

The first change was from the kirk to the Brethren. Now there is a shift back to the kirk or to no participation at all. It has not been a dramatic change in participation, but rather a slow eroding of identification with the Close Brethren. For some individuals, the break has been identified with specific practices, such as television, radio, or participation in fishing associations. Some members of the Close Brethren have changed their religious affiliation to other churches in nearby towns. Often this change in affiliation is related to age. Younger members of the Brethren are more likely to leave than older members. And even for those who remain members, the Close Brethren has changed. More Brethren are attending weddings and funerals of non-Brethren, a practice previously prohibited. It is no longer considered improper to purchase luxuries such as large houses or new automobiles. It can be argued that these intra-organizational changes are a reflection of adaptations that the Brethren have had to make in order survive as a social grouping. The rules and beliefs that characterized the formation period of the movement, and were consistent with social conditions at that time, are incompatible with changes that have occurred since. To doggedly maintain the early practices and beliefs would eventually lead to the demise of Brethrenism.

The changes that have been noted in religious affiliations offer an interesting example of the relationships between social change and religion. The literature on religious movements is filled with examples of changes in religion following catastrophic economic and political changes. Indeed, the birth of Brethrenism in the village is associated with poor economic conditions. The situation today is quite different. If anything, there has been an outbreak of affluence. Watt (1974) estimates that the village had an annual collective income of between £ 2.5-3 million. This may make Gamrie the richest fishing village in Scotland. What this suggests is that any change in social or economic conditions, good or bad, if it is dramatic enough, will result in a reevaluation of belief systems. In this case, a new religion has not developed to correspond to changes in technology and the resultant affluence of villagers because an alternative structure already exists in the kirk.

On the uses of Religion

It has already been noted that not all villagers attend the kirk or one of the Brethren meetings. This does not mean, however, that they do not identify with one or the other. For official events, the Church of Scotland is the village's representative. For individuals rites of passage, it is one of the local religious groupings.

The kirk no longer has an official connection with local education, but its presence in local school affairs is noticeable. For example, I attended a year's-end ceremony at the local school. It was a cold, rainy day and about 120 mothers were gathered in the main room of the school. Three officials were in attendance--the school master, the country laird, and the minister of the kirk. After the opening remarks by the school master, the minister led those assembled in three hymns, followed by a prayer. After this, pupils from Primary I sang two songs, one secular, one sacred. They were followed by pupils from Primary II who followed the same secular-sacred sequence. Then began a series of events related to school activities. The kirk is also involved in the Christmas party that is given for village children in the Public Hall and any other events that are village based. The Brethren, because they have no identified leader, are not represented, although they clearly have the largest number of religious participants in the village. The Brethren are active, along with the kirk, in providing a structure within which individuals move through the life cycle--baptism, marriage, and death.

Though baptism may be thought of as a strictly religious event with varied theological interpretations, it is nevertheless a marker for membership into a religious grouping. There are variations in this ritual between the religious groupings in the village, but it serves the same function in each group. Baptism enables the recipient to use other ritual services of the religious group. Thus, almost all people in the village have been baptised and, when asked, they are able to identify their religious affiliation, whether they are active or not.

In the village, only one person is licensed to perform the marriage ceremony--the minister of the kirk. The Open Brethren do have weddings in their hall, but they must bring in an outside member to perform the ceremony. The Close and the Exclusives are married by the county clerk, but they sometimes have a small ceremony in the meeting room. This practice is becoming less frequent for the Close. It is now more common to go directly from the clerk's office to a hotel for a celebration of the marriage.

Protestant Reformers in Scotland forbade any sort of

161

religious service at the graveside because of their strong aversion to prayers for the dead (Anson, 1965:162). This is no longer true. Both the kirk and the Brethren participate in the funeral and burial. Here again, whether or not a villager was an active participant in the kirk or Brethren during his lifetime, one or the other of the religious groups in the village will have a representative at his death. Burials all take place in the graveyard. The location of the funeral varies according to the religious involvement of the deceased. Activists in kirk or meeting can request that their funeral be in the kirk or one of the halls. Those less active will have a funeral at home.

What one notes here is that the religious groups within the village perform social functions as individuals go through major transitions in the life cycle. Thus, while actual participation may vary, religious affiliation is a very necessary part of a villager's identity.

In this section, the history, functions and practices of religious groupings within the village have been reviewed. I began this section with the assumption that religious groupings are characterized by formal codified explanations of a moral order. But in any moral community there are other sets of practices and explanation that are just as imperative, but that have not been formally codified. This public morality is shared by members of the community and serves as a mechanism of social control. It is to these informal systems of morality that we turn next.

VII: SOCIAL CONTROL AND PUBLIC MORALITY: INTEGRATION AND BOUNDARY MAINTENANCE

Only a small proportion of everyday behaviors are governed by codified rules and formal laws. Within cultural contexts, behavior is predictable because, through the process of becoming a group member, one learns what behaviors are appropriate and inappropriate. To insure that people engage in the appropriate behaviors, all social groupings have sanctions--rewards and punishments--that manifest themselves at two levels, individual-internal and collective-external. At the individual-internal level one "feels" a set of emotions in response to violation of, or conformity to, expectations. Thus, the feelings of guilt, fear, embarrassment, and shame effectively block the display of prohibited behaviors. Conversely, feelings of joy, self-satisfaction, and contentment accompany conformity to expectations. The collective-external sanctions are applied by outsiders. Verbally, this may involve the use of gossip and scandal (Gluckman, 1963) as an active form of control or the use of their opposite, avoidance, as a passive form. If the infraction of a community expectation is severe enough, the sanctioning could be behavioral--people will do something. In human societies, an individual's behavior is not left to chance. People are not permitted to do whatever they wish. In this sense, communities are moral entities having both a set of expectations and appropriate measures to insure that those expectations are met.

The emotions people feel and the behaviors in which they engage are measured by what they say and do. The observation of behavior and the recording of statements made by informants constitute the data base from which the anthropologist carries out his analysis. Thus, analysis is always at least one step removed from actual observation and recording. Implicit in this process of going from observation to analysis is the assumption that those providing the data are often unaware of the significance of their behavior for anthropological interpretation.

In this chapter the concern is in constructing the cultural categories that order the lives of these villagers and the ways these categories are maintained. In previous chapters, possible cultural categories that are reflected in the behaviors and beliefs of villagers have been suggested. These categories include such distinctions as male:female, married:unmarried, and inside:outside. Associated with each of these distinctions is a different set of expectations. Thus, the expectations for a male are different from those for a female. Expectations of the category "married" are different from those for "unmarried.

163

Morality, the expression of what villagers consider right or wrong, is derived from these definitions. For a male to act like a female is wrong; for a married person to act unmarried is wrong. These moral judgements by villagers serve to make explicit the social categories by which village life is organized.

It would be naive to assume that in any community the boundaries between social categories are clearly defined. Nor can one assume that every person within a specific category behaves the same as another person within the same category. Under conditions of change, the expectations within a category may change, so that what was appropriate in the past may now be inappropriate. Also, under conditions of change, new categories may emerge. In addition, even if people within the categories recognize the expectations, contingencies may encourage them to become private deviants while at the same time they declare their public support for the expectations. As noted, culture is not neat. But it is the task of the researcher to generate models that give the appearance of neatness. So, in this chapter a number of cases that illustrate social categories within the village will be reviewed. At the same time, it should be acknowledged that the divisions suggested do not exist in a pure form, but rather are abstractions from complex sets of behaviors and expressed attitudes.

Inside:Outside

A basic boundary for villagers is insider:outsider. Corresponding to this distinction are different dispositions for transgressions from village expectations. Persons defined as insiders* will be sanctioned by others within the village. For example, acts of vandalism by local children are reported to their parents rather than the police. Drunkeness or disorderly conduct by "locals" is felt to be a private local matter that can best be corrected through local means and it is rare that outsiders, such as the police, are called in. When outsiders violate expectations, there may be an appeal to outside authorities. If an offender is an outsider, then he or she is outside the boundaries of local informal social control and villagers feel justified in using whatever formal means they can to correct the situation. In 1973 a group of "hippies" moved into one of the houses in the Seatown. Their behavior and dress were markedly different from other villagers. But being

---

*Insiders or locals are persons born in the village to parent(s) from the village. Usually, insiders can be recognized by their name. However, being an insider is not simply a matter of having been born to villagers. The status "insider" requires some achievement, the statement, "___ is from the village, but not of the village" refers to a person born to villagers, but whose behavior violates village expectations.

outsiders meant there was no way villagers could sanction that behavior internally. However, it was discovered that they were using marijuana, a misdemeanor offense in Britain. The police were informed. The house was raided. The occupants were arrested and they moved away from the village. Had marijuana been used by a local person, this would have been stopped locally.

The following case, involving the National Health Doctor in the village, illustrates the use of outside authorities when a village moral code has been broken by a non-villager. The physician was in his second year of service when he was accused of "taking advantage" of one of his female patients. The "event" was supposed to have taken place on a Friday evening. By the middle of the next week the story had spread through most of the village. Reactions were mixed. Some believed the allegations; others reacted in disbelief. Those who believed the charges cited instances when the behavior of the doctor seemed "strange." Those who disbelieved the charges cited instances of the woman's behavior being "strange." It was rumored that formal charges against the physician were to be made by a relative of the woman. I do not know whether such charges were made, but within two weeks of the "event" there was an advertisement in the regional paper for a physician to take over the practice and the accused physician had placed his house on the market.

This series of events illustrates how far individual locals will go in "doing" something when it is believed that an outsider has violated a moral expectation. Both the physician and the local woman were married. Therefore, if the charges were true, they had both committed adultery; however, no action was taken against the woman. One might suggest that the differences in sanctions were reflective of a violation of a "professional" expectation. Yet, another physician in the village had been criticized for his professional incompetency. Allegations, in the form of rumor, suggested that he had misdiagnosed cases and people had died as a result of his incompetency. Yet nothing was done by villagers to replace this physician.

Violations of sexual morality are sanctioned differently depending upon whether a person is local or non-local. In the previous discussion of illegitimacy, it was noted that women who had children out of wedlock, while they might have been mistreated by other villagers, were not driven from the village. In some of those cases, the alleged fathers of illegitimate children were married, and they were not driven from the village. Even the illegitimate children survived the stigma, and some became successful skippers. The point here is that in spite of a violation of a moral code, there is a sense of community that obligates villagers towards each other, and does not extend to outsiders. The effect of this is the establishment of boundaries that clearly mark the borders between inside and outside. Those inside the boundaries of this moral community may be sanctioned in a variety of ways but are never totally ostracized. Those in the village, but not of the village, do not enjoy this same protection.

Leveling: Differentiation

The use of sanctions to insure conformity to cultural expectations is often rather subtle. Adults are usually more sophisticated in their use of social sanctioning devices. A facial expression or a few words may be enough to correct a social wrong. Children, on the other hand, tend to be less skilled in the use of social devices and therefore more direct in their sanctioning behavior. The following case illustrates how non-conformity to a pervasive village norm was sanctioned.

The person who was sanctioned was a country female who had since moved into the village. She attended the local school where she was both a good student and very active in extra-curricular activities. As a result, she won many of the school prizes and awards at the end of the school year. On her last day at the local school, her fellow schoolmates threw sticks and stones at her. The following year she came back to the school to attend the awards meeting and was again stoned. Such behavior on the part of children seems to be a rather direct way of punishing any behavior that results in a person receiving recognition.

The leveling process begins at an early age. Villagers, including children, are not suppose to engage in behaviors that distinguish them from others. Further, females are suppose to be subordinate to males. For a female to display behaviors of leadership and scholarship is a violation of two norms. The way in which school children reacted to these normative violations was to take action in a way they knew best--the application of physical force. The adult responses to a situation when a village female showed signs of leadership are different. Earlier, reference was made to the difficulties associated with organizing a summer Playschema. Local women responded to this situation by not responding. They simply did not cooperate. The failure of the Playschema had the effect of leveling the organizers, of making them indistinguishable from other village women.

In spite of the leveling process, the recent history of the village has been marked by increased differentiation. With affluence, especially differential affluence, there has evolved a kind of incipient social class within the village. The boundaries between the emergent "over class" and the rest of the village fishing population is marked by symbols of new wealth--including

166

the new bungalows, automobiles, house furnishings, and holidays abroad. However, the more traditional leveling mechanisms still persist among those in the general population. The explanation for why some have prospered more than others is couched in terms of what might be called, "luck attribution"* or "deviance attribution." Skippers who have become wealthy by local standards and conspicuously display their wealth are thought to have acquired their wealth by forces not of their own making. They were simply in the right place at the right time, or they became wealthy through devious manipulations in the market place. In either attribution, the location of the newly rich--up the brae and away from the rest of the village--is viewed negatively. This is reflected in statements such as: "It must be terrible cold up there in the Winter; it's much better down here" or "I heard that _____ didn't like living up there; there's nobody to talk to; it's very lonely." In this manner, differences in wealth are acknowledged, but they are leveled, either by reference to the means by which the wealth was attained or the consequences of that wealth.

Male:Female--Clothing

When I first went to the village in 1974 I was told by numerous informants about appropriate attire for females when they appeared in public. Females, for instance, should not appear in public in "breeks."** And indeed, I noted that when women were in the village shopping, or hanging out the laundry, or washing windows and door sills outside they always wore a dress. Even younger females, when standing around at the Braeheed on a cool evening, wore dresses. However, this dress code was not always followed outside the village. I encountered village women wearing breeks while doing their shopping in Fraserburgh or Banff. Over the years I did note changes in the code. By 1981 more local women were appearing in public in breeks. However, this change in clothing, while not universal, is related to age and residency. The females who appear in public in breeks are more likely to be younger and living up the brae. In the Seatown, even younger females are more likely to conform to the code.

The code for males is somewhat less rigid. At formal occasions such as weddings, funerals, and church services males are expected to wear a coat and tie. There have been some changes in attire for males at funerals, where they traditionally

---

*For an analysis of luck attribution Swedish herring fishermen see: Löfgren, n.d.
**I use the term "breeks" here instead of pants. As pointed out to me, pants refer to underwear, not outerwear. Knowing whether a woman was wearing pants would have involved a more intimate relationship to village women than I enjoyed.

wore black or dark blue clothing. More recently, they have begun attending funerals wearing jackets and ties of muted colors. This trend away from black is most obvious among younger males. On Sundays, the presence of a coat and tie usually indicates that a person is a religious participant, although many male villagers who are not participants in kirk or hall will "dress up" for the day. Those without coats and ties are definitely not religious participants.

Clothing is a cultural universal. Some form of body decoration is found in all cultures. This may range from body mutilation such as scarification and tatooing to elaborate garments. The function of body decoration goes beyond simply body protection and often serves to illustrate social distinctions. Thus the range of clothing styles often reflects a society's division of labor. Within the village, with its relativity undifferentiated division of labor, such distinctions are subtle. For example, on a fishing boat there is little distinction between what the skipper wears and the clothing of crew members. For males in the village, the coat and tie simply indicate one's intention to participate in some formal social activity.

The distinction between men and women is acknowledged in clothing differences. Women wearing breeks*--men's clothing--is discouraged, but there are occasions when men wear women's clothing. This was noted earlier in reference to the wedding and the blackening. Another clothing inversion was related to me by an informant. At one of the village galas, some males dressed in women's clothing. The reaction of people was much the same as at the wedding and the blackening. People were amused by this display. This tells us much about the sexual hierarchy within the village. Males are permitted to represent women, but women are not permitted to represent men. A man wearing a dress is funny; a woman wearing breeks is not. To understand this, it is necessary to examine the function of humor**. One function of humor is to enable people to talk about otherwise tabooed topics. This is why there is difficulty in translating humor from one cultural setting to another. In the sexually dichotomized world view of the villagers, male and female differences are not simply gender distinctions but rather represent two distinct social worlds. Men are associated with boats and sea; women are associated with the land and the home. Women do not fish; men do not do housework. Males who stay at home or males who engage in women's work are those who receive the most ridicule and scorn. Males are economically more power- ful than females. They are expected to go to sea and to earn a living for their spouses and children who are dependent upon

---

*According to Chalmers, "breek-folk" is an alloynm for male.
**See Underwood (n.d.) for an analysis of three jokes in
  Whitehills.

them. Males who are physically able but do not go to sea challenge this system of dependency. They become "women." The humor associated with a male wearing female apparel is not a response to a specific male wearing a dress, rather it is a statement of public ridicule of males who act like females and thus threaten the male-female distinction. Thus, one notes an objectification of the rules of social organization in an inverted format. We often turn things upside-down in order to understand them rightside-up*.

Time--Workday:Sunday

Within the village, the week is unequally divided. From Monday through Saturday, fishermen work at sea or on the boat. Monday through Friday are market days for fish sales and on Saturday there is a morning market. This, insofar as fish sales are concerned, the week begins on Monday and ends Saturday at noon. However, it is sometimes necessary to carry out maintenance or other activities on the boat after the week's fishing is completed. This may require some crew members to work on Saturday afternoon. All of this is part of the work expectations for fishermen.

But on Sunday a number of activities that would be appropriate during the week are considered inappropriate. Work is one of those activities. Already noted is the prohibition against going to sea on Sunday. Behaviorally, this means not leaving the harbor until after midnight. Fishermen from the village often leave before midnight to go to their boats, harbored either on the east and west coast. But it is unusual for them to actually leave the harbor before midnight. In Fraserburgh, wives and relatives of fishermen will park their cars at the point of the harbor to watch the boats go to sea. At midnight sharp the first of the fleet leaves, accompanied by the blowing of car horns and the lights of automobiles. Within the village this rule is difficult to violate without being detected. There are enough fishermen from the village at ports from which local boats sail to guarantee conformity to the expectation. There are no specific sanctions associated with nonconformity to this rule, except perhaps at the individual level. A crew member may refuse to sail before midnight if he feels strongly about working on Sunday. Other than that, people in the village might talk about the violation.

Some women's work is also considered inappropriate on Sunday. For example, during the week one finds laundry hanging from clothes lines on almost any sunny day. Thus, one has visual evidence of work having been done. However, it is

*For a detailed analysis of cultural inversions, See: Babcock, 1978.

169

seldom that one sees clothes drying on Sunday. Unlike fishing, some women's work can be done on Sunday without detection by others. To avoid public violation of the Sunday no-work expectation, a woman can dry clothes in an electric dryer rather than hang them out to dry. But much of the work a woman does is not prohibited on Sundays. Women cook and wash dishes and carry out many daily household tasks. What is avoided on Sundays is the periodic rather than the daily work associated with the household. Thus, one notes that the prohibition of work on Sundays applies basically to what men do rather than to what women do, and this further illustrates male:female distinctions.

The idea that Sunday is a day of rest or a day set aside for participation in religious activities is reinforced by the official closing of all shops in the village. But in spite of this, some goods can be purchased on Sunday. If a villager needs something it is possible to call the store owner and ask him to open the shop for the purchase. Also, the grocers and the butcher deliver the boats' stores on Sunday so, strictly speaking, some shops engage in business transactions on Sunday. The only business open on Sunday is the hotel, where, beginning approximately at noon, one can purchase drinks and food.

Activities defined as nonessential or nonproductive are also to be avoided on Sundays. One of those activities is bicycle riding. Bicycles are defined as devices associated with children's "play" and hence are not ridden on Sunday.

The following incident illustrates how influential the Sunday prohibitions are in determining how people behave. I was sitting in the living room of an informant on a Sunday afternoon, discussing what kinds of behaviors are prohibited on Sundays. One of the prohibitions that particularly annoyed this informant was the ban on bicycle riding. He condemned the religiousness of the villagers, especially how religion prevented children from enjoying themselves on Sunday. In the middle of this condemnation, he looked out in the street to see his son riding his bicycle. Thereupon he leapt from his chair, ran out the door into the street, and, shouting angrily, told his son to stop riding his bike as one is not suppose to do that on Sunday. He reminded his son that he had been told about this in the past and that he should know better. After sending his son to his bedroom for punishment, he chastised his wife for not noticing what the boy was doing and stopping him.

In this case, there appears to be an inconsistency between attitudes and behavior. The father was opposed to the rule yet would not let his son violate it. The explanation for this personal inconsistency but public conformity comes through an understanding of surveillance. When personal attitudes are at variance with public expectations, the behavioral outcomes of the personal attitudes will vary according to the ability of the public to view those outcomes. In this instance, people could see someone riding a bicycle on Sunday so the child was told to cease that behavior. Had nobody been able to see the behavior suggested by the attitude, there would have been a consistency between the two.

Another activity not considered proper by many is the reading of newspapers on Sunday. During the week newspapers are delivered at the shop up the brae and one grocer in the village. But there are no deliveries of newspapers on Sunday. The closest place to buy the Sunday newspaper is either Macduff or at a country store about five miles from the village. Many of the villagers order papers through the country store, and they pick them up while the kirk and the Brethren are having their morning services. Reading the paper on Sunday is a private activity, but picking the papers up is not.

Alcohol and Tobacco

In general, people in the village are not supposed to drink or smoke. And these expectations are sex specific. It is a more serious breach of the rule if women smoke or drink. It is less serious if men use alcohol or tobacco. Seriousness also varies with religiosity. Kirk and Brethren are both formally opposed to drink and smoke. However, drinking and smoking does take place among villagers, but not always in the village. The only pub in the village is located in a place where ingress and egress is easily observed. Therefore, if a villager wishes to be undetected in his drinking, he must do it outside the village or in the privacy of his home.

On Friday and Saturday nights it is not uncommon to see couples from the village in pubs and lounges located outside the village. On Friday afternoons in Fraserburgh, when the boats have berthed, one notes village males in pubs whom one never sees in the Gamrie "local." Under these conditions, how do they "get away" with drinking when it is otherwise prohibited? Moore and Tumin (1949) suggest a social mechanism that enables violation of public morality while at the same time presenting a public image of conformity. This mechanism is "ignorance." The following incident illustrates the use of this mechanism.

On a weekend evening, while out driving in the company of a couple from the village, we had stopped in an out-of-the-way pub. Soon after sitting at our table, I noticed another couple from the village at a table some distance from us. The couple with whom I was seated noticed that I was trying to make eye contact with the other couple. The other couple did look in our direction but didn't seem to notice we were there. I was then told, in a firm but joking way, that I should not try to get their attention. After one round of drinks, we left without recognizing the presence of the other villagers. The woman in our party and the woman in the other party were not suppose to be drinking. To recognize the other couple was to admit that we were also there. The same was true for them. Thus, our "ignorance" of them and their behavior was reciprocated by their "ignorance" of us and our behavior. We had both acknowledged the non-drinking rule through our mutual silence.

As Moore and Tumin suggest:

> Another way in which ignorance serves to protect the traditional normative structure is through reinforcing the assumption that deviation from the rules is statistically insignificant. This is especially crucial in those situations where there is a strong tendency to deviate which is repressed but which would be expressed if it were known that deviation was statistically popular rather than limited. . . In a sense, therefore, the normative system may suffer more from knowledge of violations than from the violations themself (791).

The Pub: A Microcosm of Community Boundaries

In spite of the fact that many villagers are openly opposed to drinking, this activity does go on in the local pub. The behaviors of those in the pub, while in violation of public sentiment, nevertheless reflect not only the major boundaries within the community but also how those boundaries are maintained.

When I first went to the village in 1974, I was told that local women did not drink in the local pub. In fact, the only women I saw in the pub during the first two field seasons were tourists, country women, or women who lived in, but were not from the village. Since then the hotel has gained a reputation for serving good meals, and more and more local couples are going there on weekends or special occasions such as Christmas or New Year's. I also noted that younger unmarried local couples are more frequent patrons of the lounge and the restaurant.

Among the regulars at the pub there is a ritual performance one might be call "fighting with liquor." It involves an elaborate system of drink reciprocity between and within circles of drinkers that serves to validate one's position in fishing and in the community. To understand this ritual it is necessary to know about the ecology of the pub and the players involved.

A distinction between "bar" and "lounge" is made in pubs throughout Britain. The lounge, often associated with the restaurant, has furnishings that are usually better than those of a bar. It is in a lounge that one finds couples. The bar often opens directly onto the street, and it is there that one goes to drink. The furnishings are usually functional and one would expect to find a one-armed bandit, a dart board, or a cribbage board. The bar side is the male side.

In the Gamrie pub, the names "bar" and "lounge" are retained, but there is only a slight difference between the two. The lounge side gives the impression of being cleaner than the bar side, and there is a dart board on the bar side. While there are no restrictions prohibiting females from being on the bar side, it is rare that females venture into the men's area, except on the way to the toilets. Males, on the other hand, move freely between the lounge and the bar.

The patrons in the pub can be divided into three categories--the regulars, the occasionals, and the visitors. The regulars are those one expects to find in the pub on specific evenings throughout the year. Some are there only on Friday nights, others on both Friday and Saturday. The way one distiguishes regulars is by noting that when they are not in the pub on "their" night, others will ask their whereabouts. The occasionals are those who are known in the pub but do not have any regular pattern of attendance. Some weeks they may be there Friday and Saturday night. Then they might not be back for a while, and then only for one night. The visitors are those who rent houses in the village or Crovie for a few weeks in the Summer. They may be in the pub every night during their holiday and then be gone for another year.

In addition to the sex distinction between the lounge and bar, one also notes an age distinction. Younger males tend to congregate on the bar side, older males on the lounge side. This distinction is related to the playing of darts. It is usually the younger males of the village who play. Therefore they go to the side where the dart board is located. A further division between patrons that reflects social categories in the village is fisher:farmer. The patrons can be categorized as follows:

Figure 6
Patron Categories

BAR			LOUNGE		
Male		Male		Couples	
Younger		Older		Local	Visitors
Fisher	Farmer	Fisher	Farmer	Fisher	Farmer	

173

The divisions presented in Figure 6 form the basis of reciprocal drinking "circles". These "circles" are composed of four or five persons who buy drinks for each other. Reciprocity in drinking involves two commodities--spirits and beer. Spirits--whiskey, vodka, gin--are sold in 1/5 gill units* that are measured into a glass. Whiskey is usually mixed with water. Any mixers for the other spirits are purchased separately. Beer is sold in 1/2 or full pint draft units or by the bottle. While not all drinking preferences are the same, one does find that the more or less standard drink for males is whiskey and beer. The circle within which one drinks may be relatively permanent or just for a single evening, but the rules for participation in the circle are the same regardless of its permanence. In the circle, the circulation of the commodity can begin anywhere. Thus, one person, when ordering a drink will say, "Give _____ a nip", or "give _____ a dram" to whomever is behind the bar. The person behind the bar will usually ask _____ what he wants. Or the recipient may be asked directly what he wants to drink, and the person buying will tell the bartender. A third option is that nothing is said. A patron suddenly finds another 1/5 of a gill in his glass, and then he has to ask the bartender who bought the drink. Once a drink has been accepted, by whatever method, there is an obligation to "stand your hand"--to buy a drink for the giver sometime during the evening. Once the drink has been bought for the giver the exchange is over.

This simple exchange between two people is rather easy to understand. But it seldom works out in such a simple way during an evening of drinking. What is more likely to happen is that a person will buy drink for two or three others. When one of them reciprocates, he stands his hand for the others in the circle. Thus, not only is the receiver obligated to repay the giver, but the other receivers as well. The net result of this is that a quiet evening in the pub for a drink or two ends up being five or six drinks. And a patron may spend far more than he had budgeted. As one young lad told me, he has stopped going into the pub on weekends because he can't afford to stand his hand.

What has been described thus far about drinking circles can be understood according to social-psychological principles of exchange (Homans, 1961; Blau, 1964; Gouldner, 1960). But the interest here is in the organization of village.

It has already been noted that drinking circles reflect major divisions within the village. Drinking circles made up of country people or fisher folk or younger and older persons further reinforce the world outside the bar or lounge. Also, it

*Gill or jil is a liquid unit equal to 1/4 pint.

is the men who buy drinks for each other or for female companions of other males. I have never seen a female stand her hand, nor is there any expectation that she might. Thus, females are in a perpetual state of obligation toward males because they are not permitted to reciprocate. This is no longer balanced reciprocity, but power.

This drinking ritual therefore reflects one dimension of the power structure of the community. Males are superordinate to females. The same kind of superordinate-subordinate relationship may exist between males. It is possible to "outbuy" another male. In some cases, the ability is known beforehand. There are some males who would be classified as "regulars" but who do not have the economic resources to participate in drinking circles. As long as their demeanor exhibits subordination, they will have drinks bought for them. And many times when they offer to reciprocate they are refused, the recipient will ask for a half pint of beer rather than whiskey. Some persons are able to participate in more than one circle simultaneously, thus increasing their sphere of superordination.

There is a potential problem when a patron of the pub increases his drinking circle--loss of control. It has already been noted that interaction between persons in public places is characterized by self-control. People act in an oblique, distant, and non-committal way. The same kind of indirectness is found in the pub. A received drink is acknowledged by lifting one's glass and saying "cheers." The same is true for cigarettes. If a person takes a cigarette out of his pack, it is considered proper to offer them to others, even people outside of his drinking circle. This same expectation is also operative outside the pub. After the cigarette has been received and lit, "cheers" acknowledges the transaction.

In both drinking and smoking situations, eye contact between giver and receiver is brief. A loss of control, due to alcohol, either verbally or behaviorially, is not tolerated. Among the rules of the drinking game are that one obligates others, and does not lose control. Persons who act or talk drunk are ignored by others. A person exhibiting excessive behavior--talking in an abusive manner or fighting--is banned from the pub, and is therefore no longer able to participate in the game.

Toward the end of the evening's drinking there is often a frantic exchange of drink within and between circles. This sometimes pushes people beyond the limits of controlled sobriety. Winners in the game are those who retain their public non-drinking demeanor. Losers are those who do not. Thus, men "fight with drink" each weekend to establish controlled dominance over each other. For those who cannot afford it,

175

their subordination has been demonstrated. For those who can, their power has been proved.

An interesting footnote to this practice is the fact that the players understand this system of obligations. Over the field seasons I have heard them say that it is costly and results in drinking too much. They then agree to buy only for themselves. But these treaties are short lived. They seldom last an evening, and then it is back to the same set of reciprocal obligations and committments.

Village Organization: Social Categories, Not Social Groups

Throughout this volume it has been suggested that villagers have a difficult time getting organized on any but a temporary basis. Whether it is a children's Playschema or a representative political group, there seems to be little interest in establishing formal charters, electing officers, holding meetings, and issuing reports. This observation should not be interpreted to mean that the village is not organized. In this chapter I have noted that organization is not grounded in named groups, but rather in cognitive perceptions of divisions and boundaries, each one of which is maintained by a system of rewards and punishments. To look for village organization in a network of named groups is, in this case, fruitless.

Throughout the field seasons, my frustration was increased due to my inability to identify a network of groups that gave this village its distinctive character and that distinguished it from other communities. It is only now clear that the unit of analysis is the village; the village is the group; it is the smallest social entity. Once having recognized this, morality, village morality, can be viewed as a system of expectations for all who fall within the cognitive categories. These distinctions are not translated into specific named groups with either short- or long-term goals, but rather they exist in people's minds. The village division of labor is cerebral, not social.

The category system within the village is maintained through a system of surveillance made possible by two factors--the size of the village and the kinship network. The size of the village, coupled with the arrangement of houses, makes it difficult to avoid observation by others. A common complaint, especially among younger residents of the Seatown, is that everybody "knows your business." But even where houses are more separated, such as the council houses, traditional practices prevent villagers from leading private lives.

As mentioned earlier, a villager is expected to open the blinds and drapes upon rising in the morning and to leave them open until going to bed at night. As long as they are open,

176

other villagers feel free to come into the house. Doors are seldom locked. The typical pattern of visiting others is for a villager to first open the door and then to announce his arrival to the occupant. The only people who would first knock at the door and then wait for it to be opened are outsiders--insurance salesmen, milk men, peddlers, the police, or strangers. While this practice may have certain benefits, e.g., having parcels received by neighbors or knowing who came to your house when you were away, the net result is that people never know when they will be visited by others. It is suspected that the negative statements about people living "up the brae" are primarily a reflection of the fact that those living there are out of the surveillance range of other villagers.

House surveillance is further extended to what might be called "automobile surveillance." Villagers not only know who owns and drives which automobile, but they often even know the license number. Thus, when driving outside the village, it is possible to observe the presence of villagers. Seeing another automobile from the village is often cause for reconstructive behaviors. Depending upon the direction of the other automobile, the conversation will turn to attempts to reconstruct where that person has been and what they were doing, to where they are going and why.

The second factor, kinship, permits access to other relatives. While the household unit in the village is the nuclear family, it is rare that a villager does not have both consanguineal and affinal kin in both the generation above and below. Persons related through blood or marriage generally have the right to take each other for granted, and they feel free to drop in on relatives unannounced and at any time. While unannounced visiting by relatives may be considered a prerogative, unannounced visiting between friends is more likely to be negotiated. But whether visiting is a kinship or a negotiated right, the consequences are the same--reciprocal surveillance take place continuously and acts to suppress any tendency toward deviance from public morality.

In this chapter, the social categories that govern the organ-ization of the village have been explicated. Through the process of explication one can understand both the cognative categories of villagers and how these are ranked. The primary categorical distinction is inside:outside. Thereafter comes the categories male:female; married:unmarried. Knowing how others fit into these categories enables villagers to make judgements about the morality of others and the appropriate action one either takes or condones in sanctioning another person's actions. In an anthro-pological sense, what has been presented in this chapter is the culture of the village, the mental constructions by which these villagers make the world both orderly and understandable.

VIII: SUMMARY AND CONCLUSIONS

In this chapter I shall discuss two related issues. One is the degree to which the ecological model "explains" the behaviors and practices of people in Gamrie. The second is why Gamrie has survived as a village of fishermen. These issues are related because in ecological theory the ultimate test for success of any practice is whether it contributes to the survival of a social unit in competition with other social units. Thus, one notes that there are very few hunting and gathering peoples left in the world today in spite of the fact that it was the only subsistence strategy employed by humans up until about ten thousand years ago. The failure of hunters and gatherers to compete successfully with peoples who had domesticated plants and animals is testimony to the differential success of exploitative practices.

The success of competing exploitative strategies has been clearly noted for fishing along the Moray Firth in general, and the Gamrie fleet in particular. Long-line fishing was replaced by drift-netting and later trawling. Sail power was replaced by steam and later diesel power. And boats of wood are being replaced by steel-hulled craft. But unlike the hunter and gatherer being replaced by the domesticator because he was able to increase the amount of food he produced and therefore could support larger populations, the impetus for adoption of more productive technologies by fishermen was determined by the market and how well one could compete in the marketplace. With each adoption of a more efficient technology there was a reduction in the number of people who survived in fishing. Today, there are fewer boats and fewer fishermen producing more and more fish. But what can be said about community practices such as those observed in Gamrie? Has one practice replaced another because it is more productive? If so, then how does one measure such productivity? Or are practices in Gamrie what Steward refers to as "accidents"? In other words, how does ecological theory "explain" Gamrie?

One criteria for judging the value of a model or theory is inclusiveness, or how many of any given phenomena are explained by that theory or model. In general, the more inclusive the theory, the better it is. My interest here is in applying the inclusive criteria to what we know about changes in Gamrie over the past two centuries. Through such an examination it is possible to define, albeit in a rather crude way, the limits of the ecological model in understanding the nature of community. Given that the unit of analysis is the community, it is instructive to review how communities differ as systems and how those systems change over time.

179

The Community: Open and Closed Systems

Elizabeth Bott (1957) makes a very useful distinction between open and closed communities. In closed communities members share many reciprocal roles in kinship networks, in work groups, or in peer groups, and they have developed a distinctive culture or subculture. In open communities members have selective attachments to a variety of associations or secondary groups, interacting with individuals from other areas as well as from their own.

In the discussion of various cultural practices in Gamrie, it is possible to see both open and closed elements, as well as changes over time from relative closeness to relative openness. Historically, the village was closed. Fishing was local, markets were limited, and kinship was the primary model for organization. The village remained closed until the shift to herring fishing, when the movement into waters outside the traditional fishing grounds brought Gamrie fishermen into contact with fishermen from other coastal villages and towns. The seasonal migration of local women to work at the gutting further decreased the closeness of the villagers. Along with this change came a slow but pervasive decrease in the dependency upon kinship and a greater reliance upon "outside" experts.

The increased openness of Gamrie was further facilitated by mandatory education of secondary school villagers away from the village, as well as more formal requirements for fishermen if they wished to be certified as a mate or skipper. In addition, the presence of the media--radio and television--has brought the rest of Great Britain and the world into the homes of villagers.

At the same time, one also notes certain continuities with the past and a persistence of closeness. The maintenance of boundaries based upon occupation--fisher:farmer--still characterizes the village. To a great extent, religion is still largely controlled at the local level. The reluctance to form secondary voluntary interest groups within the village and the use of "leveling" are reminiscent of past closeness, as is some continued reliance upon kinship networks. None of this is surprising. One would not, or should not, expect all the parts of village organization to be consistent with each other. Communities, as cultural systems, are never in a state of perfect equilibrium. There are always practices that lag behind or are inconsistent with other practices. To the strict ecologist, these inconsistencies are simply ignored or are explained away as not being important--secondary. However, if one is to understand community as a mosaic of parts, it is necessary to include as many of the parts as possible, even if some of them do not fit the theory.

180

Change: Endogenous and Exogenous

Another useful distinction in understanding the evolution of community is whether changes observed over time are internal--endogenous--and hence adjustments to other parts of the community, or whether such changes are imposed from outside--exogenous. In the case of Gamrie, the overwhelming source of change has been exogenous. Changes in fishing technology all came from outside. The same exogenous influence is seen in social legislation affecting the income of those working on the boats. While economic insecurity characterized both skippers and deck hands prior to the changes in social legislation, the deck hand, at present, can receive some income even though the boat is no longer running. The demands of fishing technology upon the size of boats, and hence the size of the harbor, was a crucial factor in the depopulation of the village. In the area of health, the National Health Service delivered medicine to all citizens of Britain. A consequence of this, as earlier noted, was a decrease in death rates, especially infant mortality. The housing patterns of villagers was structurally restrained by the fact that the water system could not supply houses much above the Seatown area. When, after World War II, the council installed a new water system, the building of the council houses was made possible and housing density decreased. Changes in marriage patterns were certainly influenced by the political decision to consolidate the local secondary schools in the region. The shift from marriages between villagers to marriages between villagers and non-villagers was made possible when persons in the pre-marriage age group were brought together from different locations. This in turn reduced the reliance upon tee-names. With reference to religion, both the kirk and the Brethren have organizational structures developed outside the village, in spite of the fact that they are both locally controlled. On the other hand, the formation of an incipient social class structure I would classify as an endogenous change. While differences in income characterized the village from its beginnings, it is only recently that such differences have been translated into obvious and conspicuous differences in housing and consumption.

These examples illustrate the nature of community in industrial societies. Some characteristic of all communities in industrial societies, regardless of their technological base, will be the same. When such similarities are noted, they may be due to policies that have exogenous origins.* And it is this

---

*Arensberg and Kimball (1965) make a similar point in their distinction between community as object and sample. I would suggest that many characteristics that communities share in common are a sample of the whole society while those differences that are local form the basis of community as an object.

observation that makes the study of industrial communities different from the study of non-industrial communities. This same consideration has consequences that limit the application of a strict ecological model to such communities. It is to this issue that we turn now.

Gamrie: 250 Years of Change

What changes have been noted for Gamrie can be summarized using a limited set of variables. In the preceding chapters of this monograph, detailed information has been presented on various aspects of fishing and community life in Gamrie. I have summarized this information in a series of continuua organized by time and grouped into two broad categories--fishing and community. In this way one can visualize specific changes that have occurred in each variable, and can compare one continuum with another over time. This summary is presented in Figure 7.

It is noteworthy that in almost all the variables there has been change. Associated with change in technology has been an increase in the amount of energy under human control. The productivity of modern fishing boats far exceeds that of earlier sail craft. This has led to a decrease in the overall number of boats in the Gamrie fleet and a reduction in the amount of manpower necessary to crew those boats. But it has increased the reliance upon outside capital to underwrite the costs of replacing humans by machinery. This dependency upon outside capital has changed the relationship between the skipper/owner and his crew--from kinsmen pursuing communal rewards to sharp economic and social distinctions between skippers and crew members. The changes in technology have also resulted in fishing becoming a year-round activity, rather than an activity dependent upon weather conditions and the migratory behavior of fish.

The consequences of changes in fishing technology on the organization of the boat is rather straightforward since the activities of people on the boat are directly concerned with the implementation of a given technology. Tasks are added or deleted according to the necessities of a technology, and the sequence of tasks varies according to technological needs.

It is in the area of consequences for the organization of people directly involved in the technological process that ecological theory makes its most accurate predictions. However, the organization of the village is not immediately affected by changes in fishing technology. The consequences of changes in fishing technology have a secondary or tertiary impact on village life and organization. Whether such changes in technology

Figure 7
Summary of Technological and Community Changes
in Gamrie: 1720-1981

Variables	1700	Year 1800	1900
Fishing			
Fishing Technology	Hand line	Drifter	Seine Net/Trawl/Purser
Boats (material)	Wood		Steel
Boats (power)	Sail/Oar	Sail	Steam/Diesel
Boats (use)	Single Purpose		Dual Purpose
Type of Fish	White Fish	Herring	White Fish/Herring
Marketing	Local	Bounty	Auction
Capitalization	Partnership/Kinship	Laird/Curer	Fish Sales/Banks/Government
Energy	Labor Intensive		Machine Intensive
Division of Labor	Undifferentiated		Differentiated
Social Relations	Cooperation		Competition
Community			
Population	Small	Large	Small
Density	High		Low
Social Relations	Cooperation		Competition
Social Differentiation	Low		Incipient Social Class
Social Control	Leveling		Conspicuous Consumption
Organization	Kinship		Interest Groups
Residence	Local	Semi-Nomadic	Local
Marriage	Village Endogamy		Village Exogamy
Sexual Division of Labor	Egalitarian		Male Dominance
Religion	Established Church		Kirk/Brethren/Kirk

influence community organization will depend upon the openness or closeness of the community, as well as the relative influence of imposed or adopted exogenous changes. Thus, changes in fishing technology have little to do with increased infant survival, but the health care delivery services of the National Health Service did. In contrast, changes in fishing technology did influence the months of the year when people got married.

The question we have to ask is: Which of these changes is more important? A strict ecologist would maintain that any practice that is directly altered as a result of the relationship between technology and environment is more important than a practice that is not. However, to compare changes in infant mortality with changes in month of marriage and then to evaluate the impact of these on the organization of a village can only prove an embarrassment to the strict cultural ecologist. Of course, changes in infant mortality have a greater impact on the demographic structure of the village. And, the month in which one is married is only a convenient option made possible by changes in fishing technology. It really does not make any difference in which month one is married, no more than it makes any difference what one names a boat or what color it is. This example points out a problem in applying the ecological model to communities in industrial societies. In closed, endogenous communities the model works quite well because such communities are characterized by a limited number of exploitative technologies. In industrial communities, even relatively closed ones such as Gamrie, the technological influences are local and national and international. To deny these exogenous technological influences is to deny what makes industrial societies different from non-industrial societies.

In addition to the technological differences between industrial and non-industrial societies, there are organizational characteristics of industrial societies that can deliver the products of those technologies to small isolated places such as Gamrie. Thus, systems of medicine, communication, education, transportation and even religion are part of a wider network of technological/organizational relationships that distinguish one state level society from another. And while some local variations are found in communities depending upon localized technology, e.g., farming, mining, manufacturing, and so forth, they are only important when one is comparing one community with another within the same wider cultural context. Here Geertz' observation that factors other than local technologies must be used to understand even technologically simple communities makes a great deal of sense.

Why Gamrie?

It was clear from the beginning of this research that Gamrie

184

is perceived, both by villagers and non-villagers, to be a unique place. However, there was not always agreement why it is unique. To non-villagers, for example, it is perceived as "strange" or "different." The non-village wife of a villager told me that when she identified her husband as a Gamrie fisherman, the most common response by others was that he must be rich. Others see the village as an inbred population, which they believe accounts for their being strange. Another response is that it is the "holy city," or a very religious place. To the villagers it is simply "special," or "a good place to live," or "quiet." Whatever the response, both insiders and outsiders view Gamrie as set apart, unique, and in some way dissimilar from places around it.

What was most important from my interest was the question: Why Gamrie at all? Why does it still exist as a village of fishermen when villages around it all along the Moray Firth have long since ceased to be fishing villages? This question haunted me from the beginning of this research, not just as a question about the unique history and organization of the village, but as a test of ecological theory. I think I may have an answer to this question, an answer that both explains the existence of the village and suggests limitations of ecological theory when applied to industrial societies.

In reviewing the history of the village it appears that the decision to remain at the herring fishermen may be the single most important factor in Gamrie remaining a fishing village.* Following the herring on their yearly migration meant being away for a good part of the year. Under these circumstances, it makes little difference where one's residence is. Being from Gamrie simply meant having a home there where one lived part of the year. Transhumance populations may have settlements anywhere, so long as they are convenient to their migration routes.

By the time the herring populations had decreased, two changes had occurred. First, most of the fishing fleets along the Moray Firth had adopted multi-purpose boats that were used for white fishing but could also be employed for herring. Since this technology was firmly in place, it was no problem for Gamrie fishermen to adopt this method. One might even suggest that being a late adopter of this technology gave Gamrie fishermen an advantage. Whatever problems there were with multi-purpose fishing boats had already been worked out by the time Gamrie fishermen began using them. The adoption of these boats made it possible to carry out the traditional herring fishing when it was

_____
*There is no way to know whether the decision was to remain at the herring fishing or not to change to white fishing. In either case, the outcome would be the same.

permitted by government quotas or regulations, and to engage in white fish fishing at other times.

The other factor was transportation. I have already noted that steam power, and the larger boats associated with steam power, made it impossible to use the local Gamrie harbor. But by the time fishing had changed from predominantly herring to both herring and white fish, systems of transportation were available enabling fishermen from the village to commute to ports located on either the east or west coast. At first, busses, and later the boat's car or van, made it possible to continue living in the village and fishing out of other harbors.

Thus, we note that the continued existence of this village has been determined by both technological factors associated with fishing, and by exogenous factors such as transportation. Had not these technologies been available in the temporal sequence in which they occurred, we might speculate that Gamrie could have been another derelict village, or certainly something different than it is today. In a way, this series of particular events is unique to Gamrie. Some villages along this coast had neither the opportunity to shift fishing nor to avail themselves of transportation. They are now villages of summer homes for people on holiday or housing for non-fishing commuters to nearby towns or cities.

What will happen to Gamrie in the future? Here we can only speculate based upon present trends. Houses in the Seatown area are slowly being bought as holiday homes. Villagers in general have expressed a dislike for living in this section of the village. And younger couples live there either because the house has been given to them or council housing is not available in the village or in nearby villages and towns. Therefore, we would expect the village fishermen of the future to be living in council houses--either rented or owned--and in the bungalows.

What of future marriages? Here again one might predict that more and more marriages will be between villagers and non-villagers. Where the male is employed in the fishing, one would expect post-marital residency to continue to be in the community of the wife.

If present trends continue, the number of fishermen in the future will decrease. With larger, more productive boats there will be less need for fishermen. Where are the excess fishermen likely to be employed? This is a difficult question to answer, but one place they are not likely to be employed is the oil industry. The recent "oil boom" in the North Sea did attract many workers, but only a handful of villagers. With major construction of land facilities almost completed, the need for labor has been decreasing. Thus, we should not expect the oil industry to absorb the unemployed fisherman. Perhaps Gamrie, like Scotland in general, will lose its population to the industrial areas of Britain or to the Commonwealth countries such as Australia and Canada. What is clear is that unless alternative employment becomes available within the region, people will have to leave.

A Final Note on Cultural Ecology

Does the previous discussion of limits to the cultural ecological approach mean that it has no application to change in industrial societies? My answer would be a definite "no." This study clearly demonstrates its value. Changes in fishing technology in conjunction with changes in the environment have altered village life. Both the increases and decreases in village population are a result of technological change. The development of an incipient class structure within the village has its etiology in income differences brought about ultimately by fishing technology. The changes noted in the sexual division of labor are a direct result of both changes in fish populations and the availability of alternative fishing technologies. Decreased dependency upon kinship affiliations are manifestations of greater technical specialization brought about as a result of modernizing the Gamrie fleet. Even participation in religious organizations can be traced to what was and is happening to the organization of the boat as a result of technological changes. In fact, the ecological approach, in spite of its limitations, is still more inclusive than any other approach, especially if one wishes to understand change and the consequences of change. It sensitizes the researcher to a wider range of variables than any competing approach. And while it may produce a certain amount of frustration if one attempts to explain all the variables and their changes in communities such as Gamrie, it produces far fewer ambiguities than competing theories or models. What is called for is not the scrapping of the ecological approach because of its failure to explain everything, but an expansion of the model to include an even wider set of variables, both environmental and technological.

In modern industrial societies one must consider the influences of multiple environments and multiple technologies on the cultural practices of a specific population. The analysis of individual communities, towns and cities within industrial societies as though they were autonomous social units is not a shortcoming of cultural ecology. It is a shortcoming of the researcher, including this one. If anthropologists are to turn their skills and insights to modern societies it will be necessary to adjust and modify models that were constructed to understand society in its most elementary form. And cultural ecology is the only model available at the present to begin such a task.

187

REFERENCES CITED

Adams, Norman
1972   Goodbye, Beloved Brethren. Aberdeen: Impulse Books.

Anderson, James N.
1973   Ecological Anthropology and Anthropological Ecology. In
        Handbook of Social and Cultural Anthropology. John J.
        Honigmann (ed.). Chicago: Rand McNally. pp. 179-240.

Anderson, Raoul and Cato Wadel
1972   Comparative Problems in Fishing Adaptations. In North
        Atlantic Fishermen. Raoul Anderson and Cato Wadel (eds.)
        St. John's: Institute of Social and Economic Research,
        Memorial University of Newfoundland. pp. 141-165

Anson, Peter F.
1932   Fishermen and Fishing Ways. Yorkshire: EP Publishing.
1950   Scots Fisherfolk. Banff: The Saltire Society.
1965   Fisher Folk-Lore. London: The Faith Press.

Arensberg, Conrad M. and Solon T. Kimball
1965   Culture and Community. New York: Harcourt, Brace and
        World.

Babcock, Barbara A. (ed.)
1978   The Reversible World: Symbolic Inversion in Art and
        Society. Ithaca: Cornell University Press.

Blau, Peter M.
1964   Exchange and Power in Social Life. New York: John
        Wiley.

Blehr, O.
1963   Action Groups in a Society with Bilateral Kinship: A
        Case Study from the Faroe Islands. Ethnology 2:269-275.

Bott, Elizabeth
1957   Family and Social Network. London: Tavistock.

Brand, Aat and Jaap de Kort
1978   Boycott: An Analysis of the Fleet Shift of Inshore
        Fishing Vessels from Aberdeen to Peterhead. Leiden:
        Institute voor Culturele Anthropologie en Sociologie
        der Neit-Westerse Volken.

The British Association for the Advancement of Science
1963   The North-East of Scotland. Aberdeen: The Central Press.

189

The British Association for the Advancement of Science
1963   The North-East of Scotland. Aberdeen: The Central
        Press.

Brodman, Keeve, A.J. Erdman and H.G. Wolff
1949   Cornell Medical Index Health Questionnaire Manual. New
        York: Cornell University Medical College.

Buchan, Peter
1977   Mount Pleasant. Peterhead: Peterhead Offset Printers.

Cameron, Kenneth J.
1961   The Parish of Gamrie. Third Statistical Account of
        Scotland. Glasgow: Collins. pp. 204-216.

Cargill, Cavin
1976   Blockade '75: The Story of the Fishermen's Blockade of
        the Ports. Glasgow: The Molendinar Press.

Carter, Ian
1977   Illegitimate Births and Illegitimate References. The
        Scottish Journal of Sociology 1:125-136.

Chambers Scots Dictionary
1977   Compiled by Alexander Warrack, M.A.. Edinburgh: W & R
        Chambers, Ltd.

Cove, John J.
1978   Ecology, Structuralism, and Fishing Taboos. In Adapta-
        tion and Symbolism: Essays on Social Organization.
        Karen Ann Watson and S. Lee Seaton (eds.). Honolulu:
        The University Press of Hawaii. pp. 143-154.

Cramond, W.
1888   Illegitimacy in Banffshire: Facts, Figures and
        Opinions. Banff: The Banffshire Journal.

Deas, Barrie
1981   Relations of Production in the Scottish Inshore Fishing
        Industry. The International Journal of Sociology and
        Social Policy 1:59-71.

Dimen-Schein, Muriel
1977   The Anthropological Imagination. New York: McGraw-Hill.

Donaldson, Gordon
1980   Scotland: The Shaping of a Nation. London: David and
        Charles.

190

Dorian, Nancy
1970   A Substitute Name System in the Scottish Highlands. American Anthropologist. 72:303-320.

Douglas, Mary
1966   Purity and Danger. London: Routledge & Kegan Paul.

Faris, James C.
1966   Cat Harbour: A Newfoundland Fishing Settlement. St. John's: Memorial University of Newfoundland.

Firestone, Melvin
1967   Brothers and Rivals: Patrilocality in Savage Cove. St. John's: Memorial University of Newfoundland.

Foster, George
1965   Peasant Society and the Image of Limited Good. American Anthropologist 67:293-315.

Fox, Robin
1968   Encounters with Anthropology. New York: Harcourt, Brace and Javanivich.

Frankenberg, Ronald
1969   Communities in Britain: Social Life in Town and Country. Miodlesex: Penguin.

Fricke, P.H.
1974   The Social Structure of Crews of British Dry Cargo Merchant Ships. Cardiff, Wales: Department of Maritime Studies, University of Wales Institute of Science and Technology.

Friedl, Ernestine
1975   Women and Men: An Anthropologist's View. New York: Holt, Rinehart and Winston.

Geertz, Clifford
1963   Agricultural Involution: The Process of Ecological Change in Indonesia. Berkeley: University of California Press.

Gluckman, Max
1963   Gossip and Scandal. Current Anthropology 4:307-316.

Goodlad, C. Alexander
1972   Old and Trusted, New and Unknown: Technical Confrontation in the Shetland Herring Fishery. In North Atlantic Fishermen. Raoul Anderson and Cato Wadel (eds.). St. John's: Institute of Social and Economic Research, Memorial University of Newfoundland. pp.61-81.

Gray, Malcolm
1978   The Fishing Industries of Scotland 1790-1914: A Study
        of Regional Adaptation. Oxford: Oxford University
        Press.

Gregor, Walter
1888   Notes on the Folk-Lore of the North-East of Scotland.
        London: Elliot Stock.

Gmelch, George
1971   Baseball Magic. Trans-Action 8:39-41, 45.

Gouldner, Alvin W.
1960   The Norm of Reciprocity: A Preliminary Statement. Amer-
        ican Sociological Review 25:161-178.

Gunn, Neil M.
1941   The Silver Darlings. London: Faber and Faber.

Hamilton, Henry
1961   The Fishing Industry. In The Third Statistical Account
        of Scotland. Glasgow: Collins. pp. 77-104.

Harris, Marvin
1968   The Rise of Anthropological Theory. New York: Thomas Y.
        Crowell.
1979   Cultural Materialism: The Struggle for a Science of
        Culture. New York: Random House.

H.B., R.C. A.G., J.P., A.W.W., AND H.G.W.
1968   A'tween Troup Heid and Gamrie Mohr. Gardenstown: Mimeo.

Homans, George C.
1961   Social Behavior: Its Elementary Forms. New York:
        Harcourt, Brace and World.

Johnston, Thomas
1946   The History of the Working Classes in Scotland.
        Glasgow: Unity Publishing Company.

Kaut, Charles
1967   Bansag and Apelyido: Problems of Comparison in Changing
        Tagalog Social Organization. In Studies in Philippine
        Anthropology. Mario D. Zamora and Carolos P. Romulo
        (eds.). Quezon City: Phoenix Press. pp.397-418.

Lewis, Helen M. and Edward E. Knipe
1969   The Sociological Impact of Mechanization on Coal Miners
        and their Families. Proceedings of the Council of Eco-
        nomics, American Institute of Mining, Metallurgical,
        and Petroleum Engineers, Inc. pp.268-307.

192

Little, Michael A. and George E.B. Morren, Jr.
1976   Ecology, Energetics, and Human Variability. Dubuque,
        Iowa: Wm. C. Brown.

Löfgren, Orvar
n.d.   Fisherman's Luck: Magic and Social Tensions in Two Mar-
        itime Settings. mimeo.

MacIver, Robert M. and Charles H. Page
1950   Society, An Introductory Analysis. New York: Rinehart
        and Company.

Martin, Angus
1982   The Ring-Net Fishermen. Edinburgh: John Donald.

Moore, Wilbert E. and Melvin M. Tumin
1949   Some Social Functions of Ignorance. American Sociologi-
        cal Review 14: 787-795.

Murison, David D.
1963   Local Dialects. In The North-East of Scotland.
        Aberdeen: The Central Press. pp. 196-202.

Napier, B.W.
1976   Individual Employment Law Within the British Fishing
        Industry. Judicial Review 113:189-209.

Nemec, Thomas F.
1972   I Fish with my Brother: the Structuring and Behavior of
        Agnatic-Based Fishing Crews in a Newfoundland Irish
        Outport. In North Atlantic Fishermen. Raoul Anderson
        and Cato Wadel (eds.). St. John's: Institute of Social
        and Economic Research, Memorial University of Newfound-
        land. pp.9-34.

Paterson, Neil
1950   Behold Thy Daughter. London: Hodder and Stoughton.

Poggie, John J. and Carl Gersuny
1974   Fishermen of Galilee. Kingston: University of Rhode Is-
        land Marine Bulletin Series, Number 17.

Prattis, J.I.
1973   A Model of Shipboard Interaction on a Hebridean Fishing
        Vessel. Journal of Anthropological Research 29:210-219.

Simpson, Moreen
1980   Spark of Life in a Dying World. Evening Express. Novem-
        ber 3.
1980   Secret Language of the Hopeman Fishers. Evening Ex-
        press. November 5.

Smout, T.C.
1976   Aspects of Sexual Behaviour in Nineteenth Century Scot-
        land. In Social Class in Scotland: Past and Present. A.
        Allan MacLaren (ed.). Edinburgh: John Donald. pp.55-85.

Steward, Julian H.
1955   Theory of Cultural Change: The Methodology of Multi-
        lineal Evolution. Urbana: University of Illinois Press.

Synge, John M.
1910   The Works of John M. Synge: Volume Three, The Aran Is-
        lands. Dublin: Maunsel and Company.

Testart, Alan
1983   The Significance of Food Storage Among Hunters-
        Gatherers: Residence Patterns, Population Densities,
        and Social Inequalities. Current Anthropology
        23:523-537.

Underwood, Charles
n.d.   Three Scottish Jokes: Information and Structure in
        Whitehills. Mimeo.

Watt, Christine J.
1974   The Study of a Moray Firth Fishing Village: An Unpub-
        lished Honors Thesis. Aberdeen: Department of Sociolo-
        gy, Aberdeen University.

Williams, Rory, Michael Bloor, Gordon Horobin, and Rex Taylor
1980   Remotness and Disadvantage: Findings from a Survey of
        Access to Health Services in the Western Isles. The
        Scottish Journal of Sociology 4:105-124.

Wilson, Bryan
1967   The Exclusive Brethren: A Case Study in the Evolution
        of a Sectarian Ideology. In Patterns of Sectarianism:
        Organization and Ideology in Social and Religious Move-
        ments. Brian Wilson. London: Heinemann. pp.287-341.

Wilson, Gloria
1965   Scottish Fishing Craft. London: Fishing News (Books)
        Ltd.

Wilson, Thomas
1845   Parish of Gamrie. The New Statistical Account of
        Scotland. Edinburgh: William Blackwood and Sons. pp.
        271-296.

Wilson, The Rev. Mr.
1791   Parish of Gamrie: First Statistical Account of
        Scotland. Edinburgh: Creech. pp. 469-477.

194

INDEX

Aberdeen,9
  Blockade, 103-104; Boycott,
  99-100; Conflict with
  in-shore fleet, 100; Dock
  Workers(Lumpers), 100; Fish
  Market, 100; Medical
  Facilities, 50;Trawlers,
  100; Pay System, 76;
  Size of Vessels, 76
Adams, Norman, 152
Allonym (See: Tee Names)
Anderson, James N., 1
Anderson, Raoul and Cato
  Wadel, 104-105
Anson, Peter F., 36,37,87,94,
  95,100,116,117,123,130,139,
  152,154,162
Arensberg, Conrad M. and
  Solon T. Kimball, 111
Automobile
  And Courtship,116
Auction System, 68,75-76

Babcock, Barbara A.(ed.),169
Banff, 16,65,80
Bicycle Riding, 170-171
Birth Control, 119
Blackening, 20,124-125
Blau, Peter M.,174
Blehr, O., 66,87
Blockade of Scottish Harbors
  1975, 104-105; 1980, 105
Bott, Elizabeth, 180
Brand, Aat and Jaap de Kort,
  101
Boat Design, 59-65
Boat Ownership, 65
Boat Costs, 68-69
Boat Launching, 46
Bounty System, 67
Bracoden Public School, 41
Brethren,20
  Attendance,43; Care
  Meetings,153;
  Close,121,157-158;
  Exclusive,121,152,153,
  156-158; Excommunica-
  tion,153; James Taylor Sr.,

153; James, Taylor,Jr
  (Big Jim),153,156; History
  of,152-15; Open,121,153,
  154; Participation in
  Blockade,103; Weddings and,
  122,126
Brodman, Keeve, A.J. Erdman,
  and H.G. Wolff, 50
Brucellosis, 53
Buchan, Peter, 54
Buchan
  Dialect, 54,56
  District, 54
Buckie, 10,60,62,64,65
Bus Service, 26
By Names (See: Tee Name)

Cameron, Kenneth J., 27,41,42
Cargill, Cavin, 102
Carrying Capacity, 112
Chambers, 130
Church of Scotland (Kirk),151
  Anti-Burghers,150
  Burghers,151
  Disruptions,150,152
  Early History
  Evangelicals,150
  Free Church,150
  In Gamrie
    Attendance,43
    History,151-155
    Social Role of,161
  New Light,150
  Marriage,126
  Moderates,150
  Old Light,150
  United Free Church,150-151
  United Presbyterians,150
Coal Mining, 6
Coal Strike, 1921, 62
Common Market (E.E.C.), 69,102,
  105
Community
  Closed, 180
  Definition, 6-7
  Open, 180
Core Culture, 1,112
Cornell Medical Index, 50

195

Fishwives, Role of, 70
Fly Cup, 12
Foster, George, 159
Fox, Robin, 130
Fraserburgh,10,13,16,80,82,
    87,116,152,167
    Harbor, 112
French Fishermen, 104
Fricke, P.H., 77
Friedl, Ernestine, 141
Funeral,141-145
    Appropriate Clothing, 168
    Attendance, 144
    Kinship and, 142-143

Gala, 47-48
Geertz, Clifford, 1,3
General Reciprocity, 79
    And Drinking, 174
George I, 59
Gluckman, Max, 163
Gmelch, George, 95
Gray, Malcolm, 107,108
Gregor, Walter, 93,122,124
Goodlad, C. Alexander, 64,73
Gouldner, Alvin W., 174
Gunn, Neil M., 66
Gutting Lassies, 12

Hamilton, Henry, 62,63,68
Harbor, 59,60
Harbor Committee, 45
Harris, Marvin, 1,3-4
H.B., R.C., A.G., J.P., A.W.W.,
    AND H.G.W., 45,60,67
Herring Board, 69,81,99,101
Highlands and Islands Develop-
    ment Board, 9
Hippies, 164-165
Horseshoes, 38
Homans, George C., 174
Home Help, 138
House Names, 36
House Furnishings, 36-39

Ignornace
    Function of,171-172
Illegitimacy Ratio,118
Infrastructure, 3-4,112
    Determinism, 4

Instituut voor Culturele Anthro-
    pologie, 16
Isle of Man, 71,115
Israeli-Arab War, 101

Johnston, Thomas, 152

Kaut, Charles,130
Kirk (See: Church of Scotland)

Laird, 10,43,65,97,158
Leveling, 159,166,180
Lewis, Helen M. and
    Edward E. Knipe, 6
Little, Michael A. and
    George E.B.Morren Jr., 112
Lofgren, Orvar, 94,167
Lowestoft, 154
Luck Attribution, 167

Macduff, 10,16,59,62,64,82,87,
    152,167
MacIver, Robert and Charles
    Page, 6
Malinowski, B., 95
Market, 75-76
Marriage
    Age of, 117
    Pregnancy and, 118-120
    Village Endogamy, 116
Martin, Angus, 99
Meals on Wheels, 138
Migration
    Of Crews, 71,108;
    Of Fish,88,106,107
    Of Women, 108
Minch, 71
Moore, Wilbert E. and
    Melvin M. Tumin, 171
Morality, 164
Murison, David D., 54
Myxomatosis, 94

Napier, B.W., 78
National Health Service
    (NHS), 48,53,184
Nemec, Thomas F., 65,86
Net Magic, 96
North East Atlantic Fisheries,
    102